M000016981

FIVE YEARS
WITH
ORTHODOX
JEWS

HOW CONNECTING WITH GOD'S PEOPLE
UNLOCKS UNDERSTANDING OF GOD'S WORD

BOB O'DELL *with* GIDON ARIEL

Five Years with Orthodox Jews:
How Connecting with God's People Unlocks Understanding of God's Word

Copyright © 2020 by Root Source, Ltd.

Numerous English translations of the Bible were used in preparing this work. In some cases, the translation was modified by the authors to better reflect the meaning of the original text, the passage's readability, and/or its context in this work. Bold face type, when present, is added for emphasis only. We encourage readers to look up the verses quoted herein in their favorite translation and consider the differences to more deeply appreciate the Word of God.

Unless otherwise indicated, all scripture references are taken from the New American Standard Bible, designated NASB.

Scripture quotations taken from the New American Standard Bible® (NASB),
Copyright © 1960, 1962, 1963, 1968, 1971, 1972, 1973,
1975, 1977, 1995 by The Lockman Foundation
Used by permission. www.Lockman.org

Scripture quotations marked (NLT) are taken from the Holy Bible, New Living Translation, copyright © 1996, 2004, 2007 by Tyndale House Foundation.
Used by permission of Tyndale House Publishers, Inc., Carol Stream, IL 60188. All rights reserved.

Scripture quotations taken from The Holy Bible, New International Version® NIV®
Copyright © 1973, 1978, 1984, 2011 by Biblica, Inc.®
Used by permission. All rights reserved worldwide.

Scripture quotations are from the ESV® Bible (The Holy Bible, English Standard Version®), copyright © 2001 by Crossway Bibles, a publishing ministry of Good News Publishers.
Used by permission. All rights reserved.

Scripture quotations from The Authorized (King James) Version, marked (KJV). Rights in the Authorized Version in the United Kingdom are vested in the Crown. Reproduced by permission of the Crown's patentee, Cambridge University Press.

Scripture quotations marked (TIB) are from The Israel Bible, First Edition, 2018 by Israel365 and Menorah Books, an imprint of Koren Publishers Jerusalem Ltd.
Used by permission of Israel365. All rights reserved.

All rights reserved. No part of this publication may be reproduced, distributed, or transmitted in any form or by any means, without the prior written permission of the publisher, except in the case of brief quotations embodied in critical reviews and certain other noncommercial uses permitted by copyright law.

For permission requests, write to the publisher, with the subject
"Attention: Permissions Coordinator," and send to: rspress@root-source.com

Root Source Press
Love of the Land Street #1
Ma'ale Hever, DN Har Hebron 90420 ISRAEL
www.root-source.com

ROOT
SOURCE

PRESS

Special discounts are available for churches, book clubs, corporations, associations, resellers, trade bookstores, and wholesalers.
For details contact the publisher at the address above.
Bob O'Dell and Gidon Ariel are available to speak at your church, fundraiser or special event.

Printed in the United States of America
Cover design by Alexander von Ness, book layout by Arnulfo Aquino

ISBN Paperback: 978-965-7738-20-7

This publication is designed to provide accurate and authoritative information in regard to the subject matter covered. It is sold with the understanding that the authors or the publisher are not engaged in rendering any type of professional services. If assistance is required, the services of a competent professional should be sought. Effort has been made to verify accurate Internet addresses. The authors and the publisher assume no responsibility for Internet address errors.

1. Christianity 2. Israel 3. Bible Commentary 4. Judaism 5. Prophecy 6. Bible Study

I. O'Dell, Bob with Ariel, Gidon
II. Five Years with Orthodox Jews: How Connecting with God's People Unlocks Understanding of God's Word

DEDICATION

For Paul and Virginia O'Dell,
and their visit to Israel in 1977

ENDORSEMENTS

A page-turner. A must-read. You will laugh, cry and maybe even repent. Five Years with Orthodox Jews will take you on a riveting journey into a revolutionary new mindset: that building relationship is far more important than winning the argument. When I first went to Israel more than forty years ago to study the roots of our faith with Jewish scholars, I quickly learned that the Christian world was not yet ready for the piercing challenge to the heart that this book humbly speaks. But the time for this book's message has come. Hear, think, study, pray, and decide for yourself what you will do in response.

Brad H. Young, PhD

Professor Emeritus in Judaic Christian Studies in Biblical Literature at The Graduate School of Theology, Oral Roberts University, and Bible Translator, *Hebrew Heritage Bible Newer Testament*

If you are a Christian interested in learning more about Israel and the Jewish people, "Five Years with Orthodox Jews" is the most important book - besides the Bible - for you to read this year. I am so grateful that God would raise up such a faithful friend to Israel, in our generation. I pray that every Christian would read Bob's book to better understand the heart of a Jew, and in doing so, we could finally move past our bitter history and bring about our shared destiny articulated by the Prophet Zephaniah (3:9), "For then I will make the peoples pure of speech, so that they all invoke *Hashem* by name and serve Him with one accord."

Rabbi Naphtali "Tuly" Weisz

Founder of Israel365 and Publisher of *The Israel Bible*, Beit Shemesh, Israel

I couldn't put it down! Relevant and meaningful, this was one of the greatest literary experiences I have ever encountered in thirty-seven continuous years of pastoring a congregation. Every pastor needs to read it.

Rev. David Swaggerty

Senior Pastor, Charismalife Ministries, Columbus, Ohio

Grab a cup of Israeli coffee, pull up a chair in a Jerusalem café, and get to know these two fine men as I have known them both for years. Through Bob's expert guidance and Gidon's thoughtful framing of Jewish tradition, you will see Judaism through a Christian prism, yet without judgement or forced conclusions.

Jonathan Feldstein

President, Genesis123 Foundation and Columnist, Townhall.com and Charisma News, Efrat, Israel

This work is a strikingly original read that provides, without acrimony, fresh insights on what Christians can learn from Jews and Jews from Christians. Candid, honest and personal, this work reads like a gripping adventure story, not a tedious textbook. Moving from discovery to discovery in the Bible, archaeology, history, economics, and Jewish life in Israel, the reader listens in on an inspiring and informative dialogue between friends. Yet ultimately this book reveals in surprising ways, the greatness and awesomeness of God. I pray this book creates an insatiable hunger within all Christians to eagerly explore their Jewish roots and to visit the land of Israel, ASAP.

Marvin Wilson, Ph.D.

Professor Emeritus, Gordon College, Department of Biblical Studies, Author of *Our Father Abraham* and *Exploring Our Hebraic Heritage*

Not only does this book boost my faith for a promising future between The People of Israel and believers from the Nations, this book is a reflective mirror for us, allowing us to see ourselves as we are seen. Sincere yet modest, so many passages touched my heart. From this book we gain a deeper understanding of what Hashem expects from The People of Israel and His chosen Jerusalem as a light to the nations. I pray we are worthy of this assignment.

Rabbi Yehudah Glick

President, Shalom Jerusalem Foundation and former Member of Knesset

TABLE OF CONTENTS

PREFACE

"Would you be willing to travel to Israel?"

That's what they asked me. I was interviewing for a job at a high-tech company in Austin, Texas in 1988. The team I had just met at Motorola in Austin, Texas was working closely with another team in Tel Aviv, Israel. There, the Israelis were readying a new kind of microprocessor (which is a kind of "semiconductor chip" or "integrated circuit") for the communications market. I quickly realized that this new microprocessor could become the "next big thing," and I wanted to join! But they had one last question to ask me, which had been a sticking point for other applicants: would I be willing to travel to Israel?

That was not a trivial question in 1988. Those were the days of a new kind of Palestinian uprising — *The First Intifada* — and that turmoil in Israel was showing no signs of abating.

"Before I answer, I will need to speak with my wife," I said.

I'll never forget that uneasy feeling I had on the drive home while I pondered the conversation that I was about to have with Marisa. Since first meeting her two years earlier at our church, we had discussed every possible topic imaginable — or so I thought! As a Christian, the stories of Israel were planted deeply into my faith, and the unlikely success of that young country was intriguing. But on the drive home I realized that my wife and I *had never discussed the topic of Israel* even once!

After telling her about the exciting interview, I then asked, apprehensively, how she would feel about my working with Israeli Jews and taking business trips to Israel. Her response is one I still remember word for word:

"Oh, I've always loved Israel," she said.

Those five words changed the direction of my life. I took the job! And her next five words would change both of our lives:

"Can I go with you?"

That microprocessor would take the market by storm and become known as the very first "communications processor." Then our team would begin riding the wave of an even bigger storm, the Internet. In 2000, I left Motorola to start a new Israeli company, Wintegra, with an Israeli Jew named Kobi Ben-Zvi. He led Wintegra from Israel, while I led marketing and sales from Texas. Wintegra sold for a large profit in 2010. Then in 2013, after working with Israeli Jews daily for twenty-five years, I left high-tech to hear what God wanted me to do next.

God incredibly blessed me through my association with all those Israeli Jews. I was free — I would never need to work again. But wait, something felt incomplete! I hadn't lived the pattern about which Paul wrote:

> For if the Gentiles have shared in their [the Jews'] spiritual things, they are indebted to minister to them also in material things. ROMANS 15:27 (all references are NASB unless otherwise noted)

In fact Paul's statement was the *opposite* of my experience! I had received significant *material blessings* from my Jewish colleagues, rather than spiritual ones.

Therefore, in 2013 I decided to *attempt to give something back to Israel*, the country that had given me my economic freedom. However, instead of continuing my work with secular Jews, I decided to *try to make connections with the Orthodox Jews of Israel*. Why the Orthodox? Because while Christians and Jews have many differences, we have something critically important in common: we see the Old Testament (the Hebrew Bible) as God's word.

So in January 2014, I went to Jerusalem as a Christian business consultant to look for Orthodox Jews who might want advice about starting new companies. Once there, I found myself standing on top of the walls of the Old City of Jerusalem listening to Gidon Ariel, an Israeli Orthodox Jew share his idea to use the Internet

Bob and Gidon standing in front of the walls of the Old City where Bob heard God say, "That's your man!"

to teach Jewish insights about the Old Testament to Christians. When he shared this, it was as if God spoke to my inner ear and said clearly and powerfully, "*That's your man!*" A new organization, *Root Source,* would soon be born.

Over the next five years, Gidon would help me meet and befriend dozens of Orthodox Jews over the internet and during regular visits to Israel — more than fifty visits to Israel since 1990.

While my original motivation was to be a physical blessing to Israel by teaching Orthodox Jews *what I knew about starting businesses,* God had a surprise in store. As I opened my heart and allowed myself to truly connect with Orthodox Jews without any agenda towards resolving our differences, God began to unlock new understanding of the Bible for me. Yes, some of this understanding came from the direct teaching and insights of Gidon and many other Jews, as you will soon see! But that alone did not explain the unlocking. For God was adding an unexpected ingredient into the mix — He was adding Himself!

This book is not just my story, it is also an *invitation!* Allow your heart to open towards the Jews in unconditional love, and see what God unlocks for you!

About the Author

Bob O'Dell was raised in the evangelical and charismatic traditions, and has been an ardent follower of Jesus/Yeshua for more than fifty years. He believes Jesus is the Christ, the Messiah and Son of God, who is returning soon. He supports gospel sharing around the world, prays fervently for revival of nations, and has read widely in Christian and Hebraic Roots literature. Then he spent five years with Orthodox Jews.

INTRODUCTION

Contained herein are forty essays filled with surprises, new insights, new thoughts, or new spins on old ones written by me, but with a concluding twist! Each chapter is followed by my direct questions to **Gidon Ariel** to get his reactions to what I just wrote! In addition, many footnotes are added along the way to allow a reader to easily go deeper and wider on a multitude of topics.

Regarding my interaction with Gidon, one thing I have learned is that even though God said to me about Gidon, "That's your man!," Gidon is fully his own man. And he is not a broken record. No matter how many times I interact with him, I keep getting surprised. They say "you can't put God in a box," and neither have I seen anyone put Gidon in a box. Yes, I suppose I could have taken all my asked questions, and spread them around to a dozen Orthodox men and women to answer, and in each case picked the answers I liked the best. But then you would only read the information that I wanted you to read. Instead, by asking each question to *one person*, Gidon, you will receive a more authentic and nuanced look at a *real person*.

In the Prologue that follows you will meet Gidon for yourself. Gidon is a good baseline for our readers to gain understanding in Jewish thought, because he is at the same time both traditional (meaning that he does not walk outside the bounds of normative beliefs and behaviors within the Jewish community), but is, at the same time, his own person with his own ideas. I think you will see what I mean as the book progresses.

But what about the insights themselves? What is my goal?

Over the last five years of working with the Orthodox community, I began to keep notes of things that I had seen and learned through my interaction with the Jewish world, things that I had never read or seen anywhere before.

Therefore, my goal — I hope I can mostly achieve it — is to offer you a new insight in every single chapter, something you have never considered before, something you have never thought about before, even if you have spent many years studying the Hebraic/Jewish roots of your faith. That is my goal, but my **hope** is even bigger. My hope is that as you read this book, you whisper "ooh" or "ah" or "wow" from time to time, giggle occasionally, and every so often catch yourself with your mouth hanging open. My hope is to *deliver that feeling* to you, because that is the feeling I often had during my five years with the Orthodox Jews of Israel. Whenever it happened, I made note, and have now circled back to write on those very topics, visits and experiences.

Many of these thoughts were originally published as a set of Root Source columns, one every week for a year: insights from the intersection of the Jewish and Christian worlds. We have selected thirty-six of them to edit and enhance, written four brand new ones, added footnotes galore, and arranged them all in an order that makes for a very nice flow. We begin with some new takes on some very old topics. Some chapters interlaced between chapters 14 through 24 take on the great issues which divide us. And the last half of the book presses the boundaries in many different directions that I hope will inspire and increase your awe of God. The book ends with what the future may hold.

What you are about to read was not always easy to write, but I felt urged by the Lord not to hold anything back. You will hear some very personal stories. Also, what I have written is not always easy to read, whether it be my opinions, or that of Orthodox Jews. Sometimes I propose answers to tough questions. Other times I take ideas to a certain point, and then leave you with the questions I'm still pondering. Once in a while, an essay ends with a suggested prayer. But what I hope doesn't happen ever, is that you find any chapter boring.[1]

This book is primarily *for* Christians, believers, those who believe in and follow Jesus/Yeshua,[2] and it is intended to offer insights that can enrich Christians. It is not intended to convince Jews of these beliefs, although some Jews may find this book interesting from the standpoint of "how what they do" can positively impact us, as Christians. Yes, the topic of Yeshua/Jesus does arise in multiple chapters, but always as a Christian assumption, never as a topic of debate.

My email is bob@root-source.com. Be in touch by email or at bobodellauthor. com.

---

[1] One of my most treasured quotes was the first time my wife ever turned to some new friends over dinner and said without hesitation, "He doesn't like to bore people."

[2] While I grew up calling Him Jesus, my work with Messianic and Hebrew (or Hebraic) Roots Movement believers has caused me to very much enjoy saying and praying with the Hebrew name, Yeshua, depending on the situation. Since this book addresses all manner of Christ-followers, both terms are used in various ways throughout, but in this introduction I purposely used both.

PROLOGUE

Before we begin we have one final matter to accomplish. You need to meet someone. You need to meet my friend, partner, co-founder and CEO of Root Source, Gidon Ariel. I don't believe I have ever written such a long title of Gidon before this moment, and neither has he read one! He simply goes by "Gidon,"[1] which is the Hebrew form of "Gideon." The "Gi" rhymes with "key," and the "don" rhymes with "tone." Thus, "Gidon" rhymes with "keytone," and I usually put the accent on the "tone".

Gidon's story will help you understand who is answering the questions at the end of each chapter. Also, I hope you will notice that Gidon is a *very* open person. Later in the Prologue, and again in his very first answer to my first question, you will see his email address listed. I *assure* you that he would genuinely love to hear from you, and that he *will* answer your email personally.

The rest of what follows is Gidon's story told in his own words, as adapted from an earlier book. The footnotes you read below, and throughout the book are mine.

We Are Living In Momentous Times
by Gidon Ariel

I was born in Queens, New York to a traditional but not strictly observant Jewish family. In the 1960s and the 1970s, this was not out of the ordinary.[2]

I went to a private Orthodox Jewish day school (called a *yeshiva*) until fifth grade, when my parents decided to enroll me in a local public school. I assume this was for financial reasons. Even though the majority of kids in the public school were Jewish, I felt that the Jewish focus was missing. To paraphrase Joni Mitchell, I didn't know what I had 'til it was gone. During that year, I made a conscious decision to actively pursue and adopt my Jewish identity.

Sure enough, my parents saw how miserable I was out of the yeshiva, so they

---

[1] Israelis are very informal. First names are fine. Even the word Rabbi is often shortened to "Rav."
[2] If you want to see him tell this story, rather than just read it, here is a link to a 58-minute interview with Al McCarn which can be found on YouTube: https://youtu.be/2jQjJcEHoYE

put me back for sixth grade. Thank God a local youth group leader from Bnei Akiva, the world's largest religious Jewish Zionist[3] youth movement, introduced himself that year, and I was hooked. The idea of attaching myself to timeless values of Jewish identity — the religion of Israel, the Nation of Israel, the State of Israel, the Land of Israel, and above all the God of Israel — was so vitally attractive to me that, although I was barely twelve years old, I knew that I had found my life's calling.

For the next three or four years, I spent more time in the youth movement's club house than my own home. So much so that my parents invited me to discuss where I would attend tenth grade. The high school I was in was not a very good one; it closed soon thereafter. They surprised me and asked, "Gidon, have you ever considered going to Israel for high school?" Well, I jumped at the chance!

I landed in Israel a few days before the start of tenth grade. Luckily, as was traditional back then, Israel was having its annual teachers' strike to start off the school year.[4] This gave me an opportunity to hang out with my newfound friends and learn Hebrew.

But beyond Hebrew, I was overjoyed to learn something else: *Torah.*

This multifaceted word encompasses a number of things. It includes the Pentateuch (the Five Books of Moses), the entire Tanakh,[5] and the orally transmitted laws, stories and ideas given to the Jewish people at Mount Sinai together with the Written Torah. It also includes any idea that any student comes up with related to any of these, from the time of Moses some 3,400 years ago to this day.

After finishing yeshiva high school in Jerusalem, I continued on to an advanced Jewish Studies academy, also called a yeshiva. This program was unique: it was a combined study-military program for soldiers in the Israel Defense Forces. Instead of spending three years in the army, participants in this program spend five years in the army, but only eighteen months or so in active training and

---

[3] Zionism was a primarily secular movement begun by Theodor Herzl in the 1890s that ultimately led to the reestablishment of the Jewish State in 1948. Religious or biblical Zionism is the belief that God, through His biblical prophets, supports the return of the Jewish people to and the development of Israel, and Bnei Akiva is one of the leading organizations for Jewish youth. While not all Orthodox Jews in Israel are biblical Zionists, the majority of the Orthodox Jews with whom Bob O'Dell became friends are, and believe that their living in Israel is a fulfillment of biblical prophecy.

[4] In the early years of Israel's existence, strikes were very common.

[5] Tanakh is an acronym (TNK) that stands for Torah, Nevi'im (Prophets, including Joshua, Isaiah, and Zephaniah) and Ketuvim (Writings, including Psalms, Job, and Proverbs).

duty. The rest of the time we sit and study Torah. By the way, that is what yeshiva means — to sit and study.

My experience in the high school yeshiva was wonderful, but this advanced yeshiva was literally out of this world. From dawn to midnight on average, we would sit with a study partner, reading and explaining to each other a text, trying to understand it and, when appropriate, disagree with it. Respectful disagreement with sources and teachers is an inherent, substantial component of Torah study. As the Jewish Sages say in *Chapters of the Fathers:*[6] *"The timid cannot learn, and the strict cannot teach."*[7]

Each day I had a lineup of some dozen study partners, studying something different with each one. Over my six years at that yeshiva, I must have spent time studying with over a hundred different people! This experience of pitting my mind and personality against so many others' made for especially sharp wits and sensitive personalities. As taught in PROVERBS 27:17: *"As iron sharpens iron, so a friend sharpens a friend."* (NLT)

During a break one day from studying to run some errands in Jerusalem, I spotted a sign on an apartment building across the street. Now it was a hobby of mine to read the signs in Jerusalem. Did you know that you can get a degree in Jewish history just by reading Jerusalem's street signs?[8] In any case, upon crossing the street and looking closer at that sign, I saw that it said ICEJ — The International Christian Embassy Jerusalem.

Now THIS was a surprise. I mean, I am just a regular, garden-variety Jew. We are pretty keep-to-ourselves-in-a-friendly-to-others-sort-of-way kind of folks. I mean, over the past few thousand years, we've learned a lot, but mostly that everyone who isn't a Jew is an antisemite. Jewish history is pretty much a thread of horrors: prohibition of fundamental Jewish practices such as Shabbat, circumcision, kosher food, and learning Torah; blood libels; forced conversions; destruction of synagogues; burning of the Talmud;[9] the Crusades; the Inquisition; pogroms; and the horror of horrors — the Holocaust.[10]

---

[6] A classic compendium of Jewish teachings compiled around the third century.

[7] https://bit.ly/Avot2-5

[8] This is one of Gidon's favorite jokes. Jerusalem street signs cover a lot more than just Jewish history. For example, Jerusalem may be the only city outside of the United States that has a street named "Martin Luther King."

[9] The Talmud is the full body of Jewish literature that comprises clarifications of, discussions about and commentary on the written word of God. Much of what is in the Talmud today was passed down orally for centuries until it began to be written down after the destruction of the Second Temple. Most of the Talmud was written down between the second century and the eighth century, most in Babylonia but some within the Holy Land.

[10] This important topic will be covered in chapter 5.

Yet here I was, facing a sign testifying to another kind of Christian. I walked inside.

After collecting some of the fliers, I started looking into this phenomenon of pro-Israel, philo-semitic (Jew-loving) Christians. I walked around Jerusalem and surfed the Internet, and discovered other pro-Israel Christian organizations: Bridges for Peace; Christian Friends of Israel; Friends of Israel; Christians for Israel; Christians United For Israel; International Fellowship of Christians and Jews.

I dared to step out of my comfort zone and began attending events hosted by these organizations in Jerusalem, at first as a wallflower, but little by little introducing myself and finding my place as a speaker at their events. I have found that, while I am happy to offer to teach Christians about the Jewish roots of their faith (that is, Torah), more and more Christians are more interested in simply having a friendly relationship with me.

Soon enough I discovered the linchpin: the Knesset Christian Allies Caucus.[11] This official Knesset caucus assembled the most comprehensive list of Christian leaders with a heart for Israel. Little by little, I began to make friends with many of these leaders. The fact that I was a member of the central committee of the Likud political party didn't hurt.[12]

One of those leaders was Christine Darg. Christine is a mighty woman of God. She divides her time between the USA, England, Arab countries (where she evangelizes Muslims to Christianity), and Israel, where she shares her love for Israel with her Christian friends from all over the world, and her Jewish-Israeli friends, amongst whom I am humbled to be counted. I frequently address the groups she brings to Israel through her organization Exploits Ministries, sharing this story of my own new-and-growing relationships with pro-Israel Christians, and introducing Jewish concepts, to the delight of my Christian audience.

I started slowly, consulting with my rabbi if I ever felt I might be floating into unchartered waters, and cautiously sharing my hobby with only a few of my religious friends. I think there is no use in pursuing topics with friends who can be antagonistic to them. That being said, I think that more and more Jews in Israel are lowering their defenses like I did

---

[11] The Knesset is the legislative body of the Israeli government, analogous to the United States Congress.
[12] Likud is the large center-right political party led by Benjamin Netanyahu, who has been Prime Minister of Israel longer than anyone in Israeli history.

with regard to Christian Zionists, as they have proven their bona fides.

One brisk winter's day in January 2014, I decided to share with Christine's group an idea I had. Since I enjoyed teaching Christians so much, and so many of them enjoyed learning from me, what if I would do that, just on the Internet? A Christian online yeshiva, if you will. Well, there was a collective gasp that came up from the group, followed by one word: "Hallelujah!" Afterward, many people came up to me to encourage me in this new endeavor, including one, Bob O'Dell, who told me that he wanted to be the first sign-up in the venture.

Well, as they say, the rest is history. Bob, an unassuming, ever-smiling high-tech executive, had recently completed an "exit" (an Israeli word that means "a sale of a startup to a big company for a lot of money") and after a few initial meetings with me, we created Root Source, the first online platform of Israeli Jews teaching Christians about Israel, Jewish concepts, Torah, and the Jewish/Hebrew roots of their faith.

I had always believed that Jews teaching the world about the God of Israel is a prophetic commandment, as Isaiah spoke: For out of Zion shall come the Torah, and the word of God from Jerusalem.[13] The Jewish people had been mandated thus in the Sinai Covenant: You shall be for me a Nation of Priests.[14] Israel's priests, the sons of Aaron, are commanded to teach the rest of the Jewish people as it says in MALACHI 2:6-7: For the Torah of Truth was in the Priest's mouth... and the people will ask to learn Torah from his mouth.[15]

So the analogy is clear. If Aaron's sons are commanded as priests to teach their brothers, the Jews, Torah, and the Jews are the priests among the nations, then the Jews are commanded to teach Torah to the nations. This is not to mention the explicit mandate that Abraham was given by God to spread the knowledge of Him throughout the world.

But we Jews had a slight handicap in executing this requirement for 2,000 years or so. We were a bit preoccupied trying to survive. We must thank our friends, the Christians, for picking up our slack and spreading the good news of ethical monotheism throughout much of the pagan world in our absence. And now that we Jews have come back to our Homeland, thank God, we can and must once again pick up our job of teaching the world about the God of

---

[13] Isaiah 2:3, paraphrased for clarity.
[14] Exodus 19:6
[15] Paraphrased for clarity.

Abraham.

Since I knew that there were many Christians who would appreciate such teaching, I thought that I could do my little part with a few blog posts and online videos. But Bob saw things quite differently. "This is a tremendous way for Christians to bless Israel!" he exclaimed. And in fact, Christians, like all nations of the world, are promised a reward of being blessed if they bless Abraham and his people.[16] "By blessing the teachers of Root Source, prolific teachers who step out of their comfort zone to teach Christians, our students will be doubly blessed — empowered with new knowledge of God and His plans for the world, and biblically rewarded for this fundamental commandment!"[17]

I was a bit surprised by Bob's vision.[18] Surely, blessing Israel today can take many forms: advocating for the besieged State of Israel in op-ed pages, campuses, and parliaments; supporting poor Jews in Israel and worldwide; visiting Israel and strengthening the economy while enjoying the sights; and in general being a good person *vis-à-vis* the Jews. But Bob truly discovered a new facet to this Christian commandment as written in Romans 11:18: *"Do not be arrogant toward the branches. If you are, remember it is not you who support the root, but the root that supports you."* (ESV)

All of the blessings I listed above — and more — assume the Christian blesser has something that the Jewish blessee does not have. Think about that: there is a measure of arrogance in this position. When Christians take their spot at the feet of their teacher, much as Mary did in Luke 10:39, they are assuming a position of humble student. Now the last thing my fellow teachers and I want is to be venerated. We just want to teach what we like to teach, to people who want to learn what we want to teach them. But it is clear from the hundreds of unsolicited comments and accolades that we receive that we have clearly struck a nerve.

I do not suggest that Root Source students refrain from other methods of blessing Israel. If there is one thing I have learned from my interactions and relationships with Christians, it is that there is no limit to the human spirit, to the Christian spirit. I sincerely believe that following your *yetzer hatov* —

---

[16] Genesis 12:3
[17] A new model for blessing Israel is presented in chapter 10.
[18] Bob says, "Root Source was Gidon's vision not mine. And he had already come up with that name before I met him. I just suggested he extend the vision by bringing on multiple Jewish teachers at once. I also saw that "Christians learning from Jews" would be both a blessing to Jews, and an act of humility for Christians."

your good inclination, your conscience — is listening to the divine spark in you. And everyone's spark is different, suited uniquely to them. Some people contribute money to the poor, some volunteer to teach English, some battle on Facebook. But we challenge you to challenge yourself! And browse our offerings at root-source.com.

Today, we are witness to countless miracles: the Industrial Revolution; the information age; worldwide independence of nations; educational and political democracy. All these and more are signs of the maturing of the human race. Many of these can be traced back to the first revolutionary, our aforementioned father Abraham. And so his most important innovation — belief in the One True God — must also be included in this list, because more and more people are coming to a considered, deep understanding of the importance of that belief. And when people consider the greatest miracle of all — the return of the Jewish People from the depths of their exile to their Promised Land, as detailed in the Prophets[19] — it is no wonder that so many of these thoughtful believers in the God of Abraham are drawn to His miraculous nation, the Jews, and their miraculous country, the modern State of Israel.

But of course, this development was plainly prophesied in ZECHARIAH 8:23:

> *Thus proclaims the Lord of Hosts, in those days, it will happen that ten people from each of all of the languages and cultures of the nations will hold tightly and grab on to the tzitzit (the ritual cloak fringes) of a Jewish person and say we are going to go with you Jews, because we understand that God is with you!* (original translation)

I do not know what the future will look like, but for the foreseeable future I think we must all respect each other and allow each other's faith and life story. Just as each of us got to where we are at our own pace, I think that it is up to God to guide all people to where they belong, when they belong there.

Gidon Ariel, lives in Ma'ale Hever, Israel, a Jewish suburb of Hebron. Together with Bob O'Dell he founded Root Source (root-source.com), the Internet's first platform for Jews to teach Christians Torah and the Jewish roots of their faith. Gidon also is the director of Root Source Press, a publisher of books by and for pro-Israel Jews and Christians. Gidon served in the IDF reserves as a Captain in the Military Spokesperson's Office after spending over twenty years in the Armored (Tank) Corps. In Israeli politics, Gidon is a delegate to the

---

[19] Isaiah 11:11-12; Jeremiah 29:14; Ezekiel 20:41-42; and many more. See this short video clip: root-source.com/dry-bones-clip/

Likud Party Central Committee (the Merkaz) and once ran for the Ma'ale Adumim city council. Today, he is a member of the community council in Ma'ale Hever. Gidon is married to Devra, who was born in Kansas City, MO. They are the happy parents of Elisheva, Akiva & Rivka, Shira Rina & Ori, Chayim Zvi & Liel, and Moriyah. Gidon can be reached at gidon@root-source.com.

CHAPTER I

Turning and Returning

You couldn't write fiction better than this, but yet it wasn't fiction.

Do you remember how you felt in the spring and summer of 2015? It was a time when the Christian world was reaching levels of end-times hysteria unlike anything since the late 1980s. Two major predictions were being made in 2015 that connected end-times prophecy to the nation of Israel in specific ways: the Blood Moons theory,[1] and the *Shemitah* cycle.[2]

By 2015, we were right in the midst of the four Blood Moons cycle, two lunar eclipses having passed ominously in 2014 with two more coming in 2015, with all eyes pointing to that fourth and final eclipse in September 2015. John Hagee's book, *Four Blood Moons*, was a best-seller.

In addition, we were also about to conclude the Shemitah year, the seventh year when, according to the Jewish calendar, the land is supposed to rest. This year would also conclude in September 2015 heading towards its dramatic conclusion on the anniversary of 9/11. The writer of *The Harbinger*, Jonathan Cahn had put out a new book on the historical patterns of the Shemitah cycle, called *The Mystery of the Shemitah*.[3] His evidence was compelling: 9/11 had occurred at the conclusion of the Shemitah year in 2001, and the biggest stock market collapse in decades had occurred exactly seven years later in 2008, almost to the very day. He said that eighty percent of the historical stock market collapses had occurred during or *just after* a Shemitah cycle had ended. This latest seven-year cycle was about to conclude in September 2015!

---

[1] This will be explained more fully in chapter 21.
[2] The Sabbatical rest year of Israel's seven-year agriculture cycle, as described in Leviticus 25.
[3] https://amzn.to/2ZXwPEw

With the Shemitah and Blood Moons events underway, amid many economic concerns and moral matters, such as abortion and the redefining of marriage by the Supreme Court, it seemed as if all eyes were focused on the fall of 2015. Bank failures? War with Israel? Gog/Magog? Apocalypse? The Great Tribulation? And right into the center of this emotional vortex came the crescendo of a fourth and final Blood Moon on September 28th 2015, perfectly timed — and the only one of the four Blood Moons that was visible from Jerusalem.

The Fourth Blood Moon over the Jaffa Gate in the Old City of Jerusalem in the predawn western sky. September 2015.[4]

---

[4]   Image attributions for all photos and graphics may be found at the end of the book.

While not denying the moral concerns as legitimate, when it came to one particularly scary "sign," (the Blood Moons), Gidon and I saw them very differently from the popularly held view. In this chapter we will discuss his view, and return to mine much later.[5]

This Book just broke a Cardinal Rule

Any editor will tell you, if you want people to come along with you on a journey of thought, you don't begin the journey with a controversial topic on which many people are either angry, outraged, confused, mystified, or consider to be an invented hoax! I only remember one moment from a 1980s lecture by comedy science-fiction writer Douglas Adams, who wrote *Hitchhiker's Guide to the Galaxy*. A young woman asked him, "Do you have any advice for aspiring science-fiction writers?" He quickly replied, "Yeah. You might not want to blow up the Earth in the first chapter. You might need it later." It was by far the best laugh-line of the evening. And so editorial wisdom is you don't want to blow up your credibility with your readers in the first chapter — you might need it later. And in this book, given that we will shortly be talking about the long history of The Church, it is not just breaking an editorial rule, but a Cardinal Rule!

Here's my answer. In this book, you don't have to agree with what's being proposed. It's not the *destination* but the *journey* that's most important here. At every moment we find ourselves *somewhere*, specifically *here*! Whether we were right all along, or whether we "should have taken a left turn at Albuquerque," is not nearly as important as the love of God that accompanies the journey, and the hope and faith that God will "work all things together for good." That said, Gidon's opinion on the Blood Moons is amazing, and I will gladly expend every ounce of credibility I have on it, even in the first chapter of the journey! Now, back to the story.

Back to our Story

I have learned over the years that Gidon will actively listen to anything that someone has to say. Anyone! But when it comes to speaking, he is his own person. I often tell people that every time he speaks I learn something new — because there is just so much knowledge in him! He often smiles and admits that when he speaks, he's never quite sure what he is going to say. (I think that's exactly because of that knowledge!) So, when it comes to a topic like the Blood Moons, he listened carefully to what I believed about them — that the Blood Moons were *not* predicting any kind of war against Israel — but he didn't allow *that* to influence him.

---

[5] In chapter 22.

As our work at Root Source progressed, the time came in spring 2015 when we needed to take a stand on this topic that everyone was talking and asking us about. Ultimately we answered with a free online video series, and then followed it up with a book.[6] So when it came time, for Gidon to weigh in on the Blood Moons — to commit to *print* forever what he thought about them in the midst of all that end-times hysteria — here is the quote he sent me to include:

> "In Jewish tradition, the Jewish people are likened in many traditional parables to the Moon, and the nations of the world are likened to the Sun.[7] There are many ideas that branch out from this, but I think the tremendous interest in the current eclipses and Blood Moons emphasizes the relationship between these two celestial bodies and, in turn, the relationship between the Jewish people and the nations of the world. Throughout Jewish history, there is an almost uninterrupted tradition of fear and suspicion by Jews for the rest of the nations, with — I might add — good reason.

> "But in our generation, we are noticing a tremendous outpouring of *teshuva* (repentance) on the part of many righteous Christians: recognition of the historical wrongs perpetrated by Christians against Jews, remorse, and attempts to right these wrongs. This year's Blood Moon phenomenon is perhaps actually a message from God to the Jewish people, to recognize that this outreaching in friendship by Christians is a sign for us to recognize the sincerity of that overture, and to work together to bring about the expansion of the knowledge of God amongst Jews, Christians, and all the people worldwide."

His words rang true for me from the first moment I read them, but now, more than five years later, I would like to add two perspectives that benefit from the advantage of time.

First, I find it amazing that a Jew would speak before Jews and Christians, and say that sincere Christian repentance is a *message* from God that needs a *Jewish response*! We as Christians should be touched by such words of generosity and sincerity. Given the horrific history between Christians and Jews that Gidon fully understands, which had its roots in Replacement Theology, such a comment brings hope that the Jewish world and the Christian world might be at the cusp of a new stage of development, a new intersection. We need to let Gidon's statement sink in! That there are Jews like Gidon who would make a statement like that — read it again if you need to — is nothing less than a gift from heaven!

So beginning in the next chapter we will first define, and then offer some new

---

[6] *Israel FIRST!* It was written in spring/summer 2015 and was released just before the fourth Blood Moon.
[7] https://juchre.org/talmud/sukkah/sukkah2.htm#29a

takes on the Christian-era, 2,000-year-old topic: Replacement Theology, the cause of that horrific history.

Second, I find it amazing that Gidon stood against the prevailing end-times hysteria, and called forth a trend that began accelerating in the following five years. Indeed, Jews have responded to Christian repentance. Consider a few facts:

- Rabbi Yitzchak Ginsburgh said it is time for a Jewish revolution — the time to change Jewish history and to begin to teach Torah to non-Jews.[8]

- Israel broke records for tourism in 2017 by an unheard of 25 percent year-over-year increase.[9]

- Israeli Prime Minister Benjamin Netanyahu said that the tables are turned whereby the nations of the world now seek out Israel to strengthen relations and initiate trade rather than the other way around.[10]

- Since 2017, a new direct flight was established from a new country to Israel nearly every month.[11]

- Mixed Jewish/Christian Bible studies have begun in the Knesset.[12]

- The Iranian nuclear threat propelled Israel into new relationships with Saudi Arabia, the UAE and others.[13]

- Nations are beginning to move their embassies to Jerusalem.[14]

The list goes on. The turning and returning (*teshuva*) continues on both sides.

Seventy years is one of the biblical definitions of a generation, and Israel is now past the seventy-year point since its rebirth in 1948. Put aside the rumor of war for

---

[8] https://www.inner.org/chassidut/the-fourth-revolution-in-torah-learning
This is a first mention of an important topic that we will return to in later chapters.
[9] https://en.wikipedia.org/wiki/Tourism_in_Israel
[10] PM Netanyahu's Remarks at the Start of the Weekly Cabinet Meeting, December 3rd, 2017. One paragraph reads: "When I say again and again that Israel is a rising global power – I know what I am talking about. Today Israel is a sought-after country. One need only see the 12 hours I was in Africa, or in Latin America on my recent tour there, or on visits to Asia and everywhere else, to see this. Israel is a sought-after, developed and strong country that even the citizens of countries with which we do not have official relations understand the benefit of relations with Israel. We are going from strength to strength and developing even more links." Short link to Israel Ministry of Foreign Affairs: https://bit.ly/BibiRemarks
[11] In October 2017, Ryanair added fifteen new routes to Israel, as reported on this Tourist Israel short link: https://bit.ly/15newflights
In March 2018, Air India began with three flights to Israel. In January 2020, they doubled it, as reported on this LiveMint short link: https://bit.ly/flightsdoubled
More details for other countries in recent years on this Tourist Israel short link: https://www.touristisrael.com/flights-israel/
[12] Short link to article on CBN News: https://bit.ly/Knessetbiblestudies
[13] Short link to article on The Atlantic: https://bit.ly/IsraelSAnuclear
[14] Short link to article on JC Reporter: https://bit.ly/embassymoves

a moment and look at what has actually happened in the last few years! Something big is happening between Jews and Christians. What if Gidon was right? What if the **TURNING AND RETURNING** is a big thematic story behind the work that God is doing? What if this work was important enough, that God might have placed signs in the sky so that we might wonder what He is up to?

Thanks, Gidon.

Shalom.[15]

Asking Gidon

Gidon, what is your reaction to reading about yourself in a very positive light in this chapter? How is a Jew supposed to behave when one speaks kindly to him in print?

Aww shucks 😊 I try not to let compliments go to my head, but especially when Bob writes about me, I recognize the educational value that his comments might have. But readers should not mistake me for some sort of prophet. I am just a regular guy, who even likes to respond to emails. So try me! ☺ gidon@root-source.com

Gidon, what is it you wish Christians generally understood about the Jewish view of end-times events?

First of all, Christians who want to learn more about the Jewish view of the End Times should read articles written by my good friends Dr. Rivkah Adler[16] and Adam Eliyahu Berkowitz,[17] who write often about that topic in *Israel365 News* and elsewhere. That being said, I perceive that the Jewish view of the End Times is very different from the Christian view. An expanded explanation of that might be called for, but for this forum, let us just say that Jews focus more on what we are supposed to do, than on what God is "supposed" to do.[18]

---

[15] When this was a weekly article series, after several months I started to end each essay with "Shalom" which means peace, but even more so *completeness or wholeness*. It is both a closing, but also a prayer for you as a reader, and me as a writer. During the review phase of this book, both Jewish and non-Jewish readers suggested that I extend the closing to every chapter. May you partake in the ever increasing Shalom of the Lᴏʀᴅ in the reading of each and every chapter. Amen!

[16] https://www.breakingisraelnews.com/author/rivkahadler/page/7/

[17] https://www.breakingisraelnews.com/author/adam_berkowitz/page/26/

[18] Gidon will give more insight on the Jewish view of end-times events in chapter 33.

Gidon, is there anything you would like to add, some five or so years after you made this original prediction about what "message" God might be sending to the Jewish world?

I think you summed it up very well in your second point at the end of this chapter. I would like to add something about the way Israeli society works, in the context of the model for adopting new technology made famous in Geoffrey Moore's book, *Crossing the Chasm*.[19] That model has Innovators, Early Adopters, Early Majority, Late Majority, and Laggards. I have observed that Israelis have a very strong but fairly small group of Early Adopters of new technology; but the Late Majority and Laggards hardly exist, with most Israelis residing in the Early Majority group.

For instance, I remember seeing digital cameras in Israel about once a month, then all of a sudden *everyone* had one. Regarding the Jewish view of Christians, I think we are still very much in the Early Adopter stage regarding Jews' evolving opinion of Christians, if not still in the Innovator stage! But I feel very strongly that when Early Adopters do come on board in a strong way, then very soon after that it will be *the* trend for Israeli Jews to jump on the "befriend a Christian (or ten Christians)" bandwagon.[20]

---

[19] https://amzn.to/2XmtmNQ
[20] Gidon is paraphrasing Zechariah 8:23 here, which he discussed in the Prologue.

CHAPTER 2

Was Replacement Theology Invented in Heaven?

The most common definition of Replacement Theology is: *the belief that the Church has replaced Israel with respect to the promises and purposes of God.* A more complete definition is generally considered to be *any one or more* of the following ideas:

- While individual Jews may be saved through acceptance of Jesus as LORD and Savior, God has rejected the *Jewish people as an instrument of His purposes* because they rejected Jesus as their Messiah.

- Because the Jewish people have transgressed God's covenants, God has abolished those covenants with respect to them.

- The Church has taken Israel's place as the covenanted people of God, or has at least replaced them with respect to *the purposes of God.*

- Modern Israel is therefore an aberration of history or irrelevant.

- The biblical promises given to Israel are now subsumed by the Church.

Prior to reading this book, had you ever heard the words: "Replacement Theology"?

Those words escaped my hearing for more than fifty years. It's not like I had grown up specifically believing and intentionally believing those things. I didn't. But only when those words were first spoken to me by a Christian woman would my eyes begin to be opened to the impact of this particular set of beliefs.

The impact of Replacement Theology on the Church is immense, if not subtle. Just open any English-language Bible and read its partitions into "Old Testament" and "New Testament."

I quickly learned that, in the pro-Israel Christian lexicon, the words *Replacement Theology* are used for more than just theology; they are used to separate the Christian world into that which is pro-Israel, and that which is not. In the Jewish world I have seen "Replacement Theology" understandably equated with antisemitism. Within the pro-Israel community I would begin to hear questions like, "Does such-and-such pastor/leader *believe in* Replacement Theology?" Another person declares openly, "I *do not believe in* Replacement Theology."[1]

But over time, I began to wonder if the dividing of the Christian world into those who believe in Replacement Theology versus those who don't, might be dangerously superficial. Yeshua warned us in LUKE 18 about the dangers of creating distinctives in "relative righteousness".

> *The Pharisee stood and was praying this to himself: "God, I thank you that I am not like other people: swindlers, unjust, adulterers, or even like this tax collector."*
> LUKE 18:11 *(all references are NASB unless otherwise noted)*

Could it be that those who believe God's promises to the Jewish people are still intact, are falling into the trap of essentially praying, "Thank you God, that *we are not like those other* Christians who believe in Replacement Theology?" Yikes!

At some point in my work to help Gidon launch his idea for Root Source, I suddenly realized that the right question was not: "Do I believe in Replacement Theology?", but rather "Do I have *any* replacement in my heart towards Jews?" I began to wonder if I would not be better off praying along the lines of PSALM 139:23: *"Search me and know my heart, try me and know my thoughts,"* to see if there was any replacement *in me*?

And so, over the next several years, in a series of almost daily phone calls and email interactions with Gidon, the LORD would regularly place His finger on certain motivations in my heart and call them out as replacement. It was more like a tap on the shoulder rather than a stunning rebuke. What tasks was I offering to do, and why? What was I afraid might happen in a developing situation at Root Source, and why? Then, somewhere along the way, I happened onto an idea that Replacement Theology might be a bigger issue than I realized. Perhaps it was not unique to the relationship between Christians and Jews; perhaps it was endemic to *all humanity*.

I began to see Replacement Theology in play in many more situations. I saw it

---

[1] Those who do believe in Replacement Theology do not say so in those words. Instead they emphasize the importance of the New Covenant, which of course is extremely important. The term Covenant Theology is sometimes interchanged. While this book will not dwell on the problems of Replacement Theology *per se*, readers not familiar with the term will get a larger understanding of its implications in various chapters ahead, as we explore other insights.

present while siblings rival for the affection of their parents, or when a younger sibling wishes he/she were the firstborn.[2] I began to see it present as parents declare one of their children to be their favorite. We can see it in the workplace as employees look upon other employees (or management), and consider how much better they would handle certain situations if only they were put in charge.

I also began to see replacement as not necessarily about replacing someone in their *entirety*, but rather that replacement is a judgement made about another person. *"Judge not that you be not judged,"* warned Yeshua in MATTHEW 7:1. We can even see hints of replacement (judgment) curled up inside complaints directed towards all manner of people, especially all manner of leaders and politicians. All that the sin of replacement requires to develop in our hearts is that we *raise ourselves up* in our own minds as *compared with* someone else. In other words, Replacement Theology begins with pride!

Enter The Garden of Eden

I had grown up with the understanding that the root of all sin is pride. I had also been taught that the sin of Adam and Eve was more than that of simply eating from the Tree of Knowledge of Good and Evil; their sin was rooted in pride, of wanting to be *like God*. This is a general understanding among Christians around the world, and I don't disagree.

But after I learned what Replacement Theology was, I began to wonder if it is possible that this pride that was exhibited in the Garden of Eden by Adam and Eve might have been seasoned with a certain *flavor* of Replacement Theology. In short:

Is it possible that "Replacement" played a role in the "original sin" in the Garden of Eden?

We will look deeply into this question in the next chapter.

But before we leave this chapter, I would like to propose an idea for your consideration. Let us go back in time even *before* the Garden and its serpent, and consider that being which we in Christian teaching refer to as Satan, the Devil, or Lucifer. The question I would like to ask you is:

Was "Replacement" a factor in Satan's original rebellion, prior to him being cast down to earth?

---

[2] In his book, *Not in God's Name*, Rabbi Jonathan Sacks does a superb job in revealing God's purposes and heart in the sibling-rivalry confrontations of Genesis.

The answer I would like to propose to you is: *yes.*

As it was in Heaven

A large body of Christian teaching interprets ISAIAH 14 and EZEKIEL 28 as telling the story of Satan/Lucifer as being cast down to earth:

> *"How you have fallen from heaven, O star of the morning, son of the dawn! You have been cut down to earth, you who have weakened the nations! But you said in your heart, 'I will ascend to heaven, I will raise my throne above the stars of God, and I will sit on the mount of assembly, in the recesses of the north. I will ascend above the heights of the clouds; I will make myself like the Most High.' Nevertheless you will be thrust down to Sheol, to the recesses of the pit."* ISAIAH 14:12–15

Do you see the attempted replacement in the claim, "I will make myself like the Most High"? Christian theologians correctly point out the pride in this passage, and note how the serpent subsequently offered to Adam and Eve the very same temptation to which he himself succumbed: to be like God.

A passage in EZEKIEL 28 adds additional perspective, now specifically mentioning Eden:

> *You were the seal of perfection, full of wisdom and perfect in beauty. You were in Eden, the garden of God; every precious stone adorned you: carnelian, chrysolite and emerald, topaz, onyx and jasper, lapis lazuli, turquoise and beryl. Your settings and mountings were made of gold; on the day you were created they were prepared. You were anointed as a guardian cherub, for so I ordained you. You were on the holy mount of God; you walked among the fiery stones. You were blameless in your ways from the day you were created till wickedness was found in you. Through your widespread trade you were filled with violence, and you sinned."* EZEKIEL 28:12–16 (KJV)

While these passages are well studied, a question I have rarely heard discussed among Christians is what exactly *precipitated* the fall of Lucifer? These passages are silent on that. Did the desire to challenge God come upon Lucifer suddenly and out of the blue?

I propose that a specific realization precipitated his fall: I believe that he was jealous, not just of God, but of *mankind.* I believe that Lucifer, the most beautiful of all the angels, either heard from God directly about His plan to make the world and mankind, or else he watched on day six as God formed man, and became extremely jealous.[3]

Why should the creation of man precipitate Lucifer's fall from heaven? I believe it was the decision by God to create man *in His image*! I suggest that this radical new heavenly idea shook Lucifer to his core. He realized that given time, mankind would grow up and multiply, and begin to challenge and even replace his own glorious position in the heavenly hierarchy.[4] For as amazing as Lucifer was, he did not contain God's essence. That was the destiny and honor of mankind alone.

Lucifer sinned because of his own distorted Replacement Theology, a view that would NOT accept God's choice to reorder His creation according to His own great plans and purposes. Lucifer thought he was going to be replaced![5]
How then did Lucifer's distorted theology play a role in the original sin of mankind?

We will take up that topic in the next chapter.

Shalom.

Asking Gidon

In general, how do Jews react to the term Replacement Theology? Have they ever considered the Christian mentality that "the Church has replaced Israel" as an idea that seeded some, if not most of the persecution that has come towards Jews over the last 2,000 years?

In general, it is hard to talk about Jews in general ☺ I would say that most Jews in Israel don't know the difference between a Catholic, a Greek Orthodox Christian, or an evangelical Christian, much less ever hearing that "the Church has replaced Israel." If one of those Israelis was asked what they think of such an idea — that some Christians believe that Christians have replaced Jews as God's people — they would consider it bizarre,

---

[3] While this idea did not come from Jewish literature, I learned later that the idea that angels could be jealous of mankind is actually found there! See Shabbat 88b commentary by Rabbi Yehoshua ben Levi, concerning Moses' interaction with the angels on Mount Sinai. Gidon adds more to this idea in his answer to the last question at the end of this chapter. http://bit.ly/Shabbat88b7

[4] Psalm 8:4-6 speaks to the elevation of all humanity as compared to the other works of His hands.

[5] The view expressed in this chapter does not necessarily contradict the traditional view that Lucifer rebelled because of pride and his desire to be like God. It is possible that Lucifer had long wanted to be like God, but it was the decision by God to create man in His image that forced Lucifer into action, revealing his pride and giving him a sufficient cause around which he could recruit other angels to join him in a war of rebellion. Many wars have begun with "an offense."

as they feel very confident in being the same Jewish People that God entered into Covenant with through Abraham close to 4,000 years ago. Surely, the Jews of history who bore the brunt of Christian persecution, and to some extent Jews who live as minorities in Christian countries today, might have thought of this possibility.

I have heard from you that Jews, when it comes to evil, tend to spend most of their attention on controlling the nature of sin, referred to as "the evil inclination." While this concept exists in Christianity, many Christians, especially those of the Charismatic persuasion, put great attention on "the enemy" and other powers of darkness. I have even heard the claim made by Christians that "Jews don't believe in Satan." Is that true?

This probably deserves a long discussion, to discover if the difference between Satan and the evil inclination is merely semantic. Again, I'm hesitant to speak for all Jews, but my own understanding is that Jews amplify the authority of God on the one hand and each individual's autonomy on the other, and minimize any other Power in between, such as Satan. To try to put one of the most difficult ideas of Jewish philosophy into a tweet-sized sentence, Jews believe that Everything is in God's hand except for the fear of God (Brachot 33b).[6] In other words, God has absolute power over everything, except what each individual person decides for himself or herself.

I put forth the idea in this essay about Satan being jealous of mankind, as soon as he learned they were going to be "made in His image." Does this idea exist in any form in Jewish literature?

The Babylonian Talmud which I quoted above is a colossal collection of Jewish thought written down over hundreds of years, capturing Jewish thought that was passed down orally, in some cases all the way back to Mount Sinai. It is the most popular Jewish source of that period. While your idea is certainly not the mainstream one in Judaism, I would be surprised if it doesn't exist in one of those volumes. That being said, the idea of angels (not necessarily Satan) being jealous of man is well known in the Babylonian Talmud, specifically in Shabbat 88b,[7] but there it states the reason for that jealousy to be *the giving of the Torah*, not the creation of man.

---

6 http://bit.ly/freewill123
7 http://bit.ly/Shabbat88b7

CHAPTER 3

Was "Replacement" the Original Sin?

In the previous chapter we speculated that Lucifer's sin and subsequent fall from heaven may have been precipitated by a jealous belief that he was going to be subsumed and replaced by mankind, which was being created in the image of God.

Now we'll look to see how *replacement,* or even more specifically a variant of Replacement Theology, might have played a role in the original sin of Adam and Eve.

Only One Command

Our story begins in GENESIS 2 when God told the man:

> The LORD God commanded the man, saying, "From any tree of the garden you may eat freely; but from the tree of the knowledge of good and evil you shall not eat, for in the day that you eat from it you will surely die." GENESIS 2:16-17

After that God decided that it was not good for man to be alone and formed Eve from Adam.

Then in GENESIS 3, the serpent was introduced as posing a crafty question to Eve:

> Now the serpent was more crafty than any beast of the field which the LORD God had made. And he said to the woman, "Indeed, has God said, 'You shall not eat from any tree of the garden'?" The woman said to the serpent, "From the fruit of the trees of the garden we may eat; but from the fruit of the tree which is in the middle of the garden, God has said, 'You shall not eat from it or touch it, or you will die.'" GENESIS 3:1-3

Notice here that Eve, who was not even formed when Adam received the command from God, had wrong information about the tree. She told the serpent

Eve picks the apple from the tree as the serpent emerges. J.E. Ridinger Etching, c. 1750.

that touching it would kill them, and this incorrect understanding was exploited by the serpent to persuade her to believe that God was lying about the tree entirely.

Jewish practice today includes a beautiful safeguard concept referred to as "fencing the Torah." This means that they set the limit of their behavior a little bit back from the edge of right and wrong, giving themselves a safety margin. For example, Orthodox Jews see *buying and selling* on the Sabbath as a breaking of God's commandment to rest. Therefore, Orthodox Jews "fence the Torah" by making the decision *not to even touch money* on the Sabbath.

This is perhaps what Adam was doing when he relayed God's commandment to Eve. It would be quite reasonable that he should not want her to even touch the tree, as a matter of safety. However, in Jewish practice, the fencing of the Torah is never done in secret. Jews are taught God's commandment as *well* as the existence of the fence. If the Jews agree together that as a people they will practice a certain safeguard, they do not redefine the Torah as if God's original commandment was: "Stay behind the fence." But apparently, when Adam relayed the commandment to Eve, he did not distinguish the difference between God's commandment and the fence.

This might have been the **"original mistake."** And the responsibility for that mistake fell completely upon Adam. He stood in the position of God and enlarged one of God's commandments when he relayed it to Eve. Whether it was an unintentional mistake, a misunderstanding between them, or a deliberate concealment by Adam, we don't know, but this story strongly implies that the very first act of replacement on earth came from Adam himself: **he *replaced* one commandment with a more expansive version of it.** This is precisely where *replacement* first entered the Garden of Eden.

However, that original mistake is not the *original sin*. That only came upon the actual breaking of God's original command ***not to eat*** from that tree. And this sin fell first upon Eve. Having found replacement in the story of Adam, can we even go further and find *replacement* in the story of Eve?

Was "Replacement" the flavor of the Original Sin?

To see it, we must put ourselves in Eve's situation.

When Eve was formed by God, she quickly learned that Adam had been formed first. Certainly Adam told Eve about the one command he had received from God. There was absolutely nothing wrong with Adam taking on a certain positional authority, by relaying the commandment to Eve! If God did not want this to happen, then He would have waited to reveal His command to both of them at once. But, this positional authority that Adam had by being formed first was not lost upon Eve.[1]

Later, after being tempted by the serpent, when Eve took the fruit off the tree and did not die, she had a decision to make. Would she stop the conversation with the serpent, and go discuss this amazing situation "of touching the fruit and not dying" with Adam? Would she decide she wanted to eat, but suggest to Adam that they eat it together? Or would she make her decision and rush ahead to eat on her own?

She rushed ahead and ate. Why?

To see the *replacement* in this situation, we must ask ourselves: If Eve had gotten her desired result from eating this fruit, *how would her relationship with Adam have changed?*

---

[1] Both Orthodox Jews and many Christians hold the view that originally Adam was created both male and female (Genesis 1:27). But here, we are talking about the forming of Eve out of Adam's body, which came later.

The promise that the serpent made to Eve regarding the fruit was a *new kind of existence* — to live at a higher level than ever before. If the fruit would have done what the serpent said it would have done, by eating the fruit quickly, on her own, Eve would have obtained something very useful, something that could never be taken away from her. Can you guess what that was?

In Jewish learning styles, questions are often proposed and left for the students to wrestle with in pairs. You're probably alone right now, but even alone, here is your chance to try that learning style for yourself. I suggest you close this book, and think about this for at least one full minute before reading further. Wrestle with this question for yourself:

> **What would Eve have obtained by eating the fruit quickly and on her own, that she would have found very useful, and could never be taken away from her?**

If you read past this line you are going to read the answer.

Eve would have obtained, for the rest of eternity, the honor of being *first*. Yes, Adam might have been *formed first,* but she would be the *first* person to lead mankind into this new, higher level of existence. Eve, whether consciously or not, was making a play for a new kind of positional authority, a form of replacement over Adam. This was *replacement theology* in its most basic form.

Summary

Lucifer wanted, if it were possible, to be like God and even replace Him. Then when that failed, he offered Eve a similar proposition: the chance to replace Adam as the first one to move into a new kind of existence, one that Lucifer had secretly desired as well. Yes, the original sin initiated by Eve involved pride. But her pride was flavored by the chance to replace Adam and be the first human being to move into this new kind of existence. The decision, the honor, and the being *first,* would always be hers. This is why Lucifer deliberately approached *her.*

Replacement, as a sin, did not have its beginnings in the Christian attitude towards Jews. It did not begin with the Church! And neither is it sufficient to define Replacement Theology simply as the idea that *the Church has replaced Israel before God.*

It is a whole lot older, and much more *fundamental* to the human condition!

Replacement Theology is a sin of the heart, a flavor of pride, in which we justify to ourselves our hidden desire to elevate our status, or improve our position, at the expense of someone else. And it began in the Garden.

Shalom.

Asking Gidon

Gidon, what do you think of this idea I had regarding Eve?

Very interesting! I am not familiar with any earlier commentaries that give this perspective and lesson.

In the Root Source series, *Women in the Bible* by Rivkah Adler,[2] she relates Jewish commentaries as saying that the Tree of the Knowledge of Good and Evil was actually the fig tree. This makes a lot of sense to me, since Adam and Eve both covered themselves with its leaves. Do Jews spend much time studying the story of Adam and Eve, and the story of Noah, or does Jewish education put all its focus on that third great beginning: the call of Abraham?

That is a good question. In general, the Five Books of Moses, Genesis through Deuteronomy, referred to as the Torah, are divided up to approximately fifty-two portions, each studied one week out of the year. So Adam and Eve get their place in the sun for one week a year, as does Noah the week after. But yes, I think that Judaism emphasizes the Jewish People's connection to Abraham (and his son and grandson, Isaac and Jacob, the rest of our forefathers) more than to Adam or Noah.

In this chapter, I proposed the idea that the "original mistake," happened when Adam enlarged the command from "don't eat" to "don't touch." Because this shifting in the boundary of the command causes so much trouble, do Jews take lessons from this when they discuss how to "fence the Torah?"

There is definitely a commandment in Deuteronomy 12:32: *"Be careful to observe only that which I enjoin upon you: neither add to it nor take away from it."* I think this commandment is in response to the human nature of some people

---

[2] https://root-source.com/channels/

to want to add to rules (make a bigger fence) and some to take away from them (tear down that fence). The problem is, the people who lean towards the narrowing of rules, forget that doing so is also a sin when they chastise others who lean towards lenience; and vice versa.

Speaking of early commandments, in Jewish thought, is God's directive to mankind to "be fruitful and multiply" considered to be a commandment? If not, what is considered to be the earliest commandment?

Yes, "be fruitful and multiply" is the first of the 613 commandments listed in the Torah. That is a difficult issue though, because it is a commandment to humankind and not specifically to the People of Israel. The first commandment to them, via Moses, was about the calendar: *"this month shall be the first of the months for you"* (EXODUS 12:2). Another commandment that might vie for the title of first would be the first of the Ten Commandments. Although, believe it or not, *what commandment* is the first commandment in that list is not without its own controversy.[3]

---

3 https://en.wikipedia.org/wiki/Ten_Commandments#Numbering
The list of the ten commandments, from the Jewish perspective, is covered in detail in chapter 5.

CHAPTER 4

What is Women's Work?

I wrote this title knowing it would call to mind those very stereotypes that are probably coming to your mind right now! Even so, stay with me, because I hope to bring you to a new shoreline and land you there safely and peacefully.

When I first began to spend time with Gidon in 2014, I quickly began to observe how Jewish men such as him pray three times a day, and the content of those prayers. But Gidon did something extra: during the middle of his prayer time, I would see him pull a piece of paper from his pocket, and pray over a list of names. What fascinated me was that he had written not just the person's name, but the name of their mother. For instance, he wrote: "Paul O'Dell, son of Effie." Why had he included his mother?

This Jewish practice has partly spurred on an idea that I have been pondering relating to the work of Eve, and ultimately of all women. But first let us consider Adam and all men.

The Problem with Adam and All Men

Most Jewish commentaries place Adam outside of earshot of the conversation that occurred between Eve and the serpent that led her into sin. Adam was apparently doing something else at the time, and even if Adam *was* present, he simply looked upon the situation passively. What we *know for sure* is that by the time he was asked to eat, he passively agreed.

Many Christian leaders have noted that the number one problem *with men* in the Church today is passivity.[1] While a few men stand up front and lead, many

---

[1] Dr. Marvin Wilson talks about men's passivity in an even more focused way. He says the number one problem with men in the Church is the abdication of our responsibility to be spiritual leaders in our own

men often hold back and let the women do the majority of the real work of the Church: the prayer, the service, and engaging in community life. Then, when men *are* purposeful and active, they tend to work on their own projects: women are not often active partners in the work men do in the church.

It is in this context that I see two very strong and positive decisions made in Judaism that push back against the trend of passivity and separateness in men. First, men pray three times a day with other men, putting their focus on God and His overall purposes. This not only turns them towards God, but presses them into daily spiritual contact with other men. This repeated gathered prayer structure pushes back against the inclination for passivity. Most Christian men only experience this with other men in special events, such as a men's retreat. Second, on every Shabbat, a husband not only blesses his children, he declares PROVERBS 31:10–31 over his wife. He calls out and affirms her in her giftings, callings, motherhood, creativity, and initiative, as if she is already that amazing woman, and has been for years!

With this as background, I would like to share an idea regarding Eve and the work of all women.

Wartime Poster by J. Howard Miller from 1943.

---

home. This topic is taken up in his book: Wilson, Marvin R., *Our Father Abraham*, (Grand Rapids, MI; Dayton OH: Eerdmans Publishing Company, 1989), 213-217.

The Work of Eve and All Women

After Adam and Eve sinned, God speaks out His very first formal prophetic word in the Bible.

> The LORD God said to the serpent, "Because you have done this, cursed are you more than all cattle, and more than every beast of the field; on your belly you will go, and dust you will eat all the days of your life; and I will put enmity between you and the woman, and between your seed and her seed. He shall bruise you on the head, and you shall bruise him on the heel. To the woman He said, "I will greatly multiply your pain in childbirth; In pain you will bring forth children; Yet your desire will be for your husband, And he will rule over you." GENESIS 3:14-16

This passage is famous for its phrase: *"I will put enmity between you and the woman, and between your seed and her seed, He shall bruise you on the head, and you shall bruise him on the heel."* This phrase has long been taken within Christian circles as foretelling the work of the Messiah in the coming of Jesus/Yeshua through Mary/Miriam.

I would like to propose the idea that such an interpretation is too narrow and the passage actually applies to the work of *all women*, not just Eve. Take the woman in PROVERBS 31, for instance. Is her work not redemptive in nature? If so, then might she not have a role in fulfilling this prophecy by God?

I believe we have the clues right in front of us, in God's foundational prophecy in GENESIS 3 that helps establish the right relationships between men, women and the work of God. Here are four principles I see.

Principle 1: **The work of redemption *begins* with *women*, not men!**

God validates and affirms all women by referring to *her* seed, not his seed, or their seed. When new life is brought forth onto earth, it is the hidden work inside the woman's body for the first two weeks before conception that begins that process. Could it not be that this same idea extends to spiritual birthing as well? We often think about famous men who launch the new works of God, but as I have studied famous moves of God, the real and full story always seems to include a key role for women. For instance, read the stories of revivals in the Church, and you will commonly find they are preceded by praying women.

Could it be even larger? Could it be that every good thing that advances the work of God's redemption on earth has its seed inside a woman (or women)? Ultimately I can persuade you the answer is yes, because even if you were to show me a work that was fully conceived solely by a *man*, I will simply point you to his *mother*. The great work of Moses, for instance, began with his mother and sister, and even required an Egyptian princess.

I think it is *just like God* to take Eve's interest in going ahead, going first, eating first, and to use that same characteristic to defeat the serpent in the end! Wow! Yes she ate first and sinned, but she also gives birth to all the great works of redemption! God (and women) get the last laugh! We also see this birthing on a massive scale in the birthing of Israel in ISAIAH 66:8 and again in REVELATION 12. And even that ultimate redemption of New Jerusalem coming down, the city is a *she*, not a *he*![2]

Principle 2: **The work of redemption involves *partnership* between men and women!**

Eve's seed, her children, will deliver a blow to the head of the serpent. That seed, that "new birth" that delivers the blow. And how does "new birth" happen? Through relationship![3]

I have begun looking back at every good work in my life and have started noticing the role of my wife, mother, sister, my sisters-in-the-LORD, and others in surprising ways! I just needed to start opening my eyes to see it!

With my eyes now open, I ran across a quote from David Ben-Gurion, regarding Golda Meir in 1948. Then the Political Secretary of the Jewish Agency, she convinced him to stay in Israel, and instead let *her* travel to America and raise the five million dollars he desperately needed to buy arms to defend the yet-to-be born Jewish state. Golda arrived in New York with ten dollars in her purse, and left a month later with fifty million. He would say upon her return:

> *"The day when history is written it will be recorded that it was thanks to a Jewish woman that the Jewish state was born."*[4]

Principle 3: **God was *not punishing* women when He increased their pain in childbirth!**

Have you ever considered the possibility that by increasing the pain in childbirth,

---

[2] In Hebrew, all cities are treated as feminine gender.
[3] Woman and Man must interact, at least briefly. Imagine how the attitude of men would change if they realized that God's plan for their work did not just involve "them and God?" If all men knew that new moves of God on the Earth were not possible without women being involved in the gestation and birthing, perhaps we would be less arrogant and less prone to dismiss the role of women in God's world!
[4] Collins, Larry & Lapierre, Dominique, *Oh Jerusalem!*, (New York, NY: Simon and Schuster, 1972), 353.

God was doing something wonderful and redemptive, rather than simply placing upon women the sign of the curse of the fall of mankind?

We all agree that birthing is hard. Whether physical or spiritual birthing, the entire process is complex, more than just the labor pains at the end. Was God, the author of all compassion, simply being mean when He greatly increased the pain of childbirth? Many men have said that this is an ever-present sign of women's sin in the garden.

Dear women, have you ever considered another possibility as to why physical and spiritual birthing has been made so hard and painful? Could it be that by *greatly multiplying* the pain of birthing, God increases the **amount of effort and work** required to bring it about, so that He can also **greatly multiply** the glory and honor He bestows on all women for that great work?

Principle 4: **God has left a clue to His heart in "labor" pains!**

It is interesting that the word we use for the struggle to birth a child, the *labor*, is the same one we use for all kinds of physically demanding work, such as *manual labor*. And we often use the word *labor* when speaking of a kind of work which is not at all fulfilling; for instance when we use the terms *hard labor* and *slave labor*. Indeed, women are not only saddled with the labor of bringing forth children, but usually take on most of the child rearing as well — a laborious task which for many women feels ever-present, almost without relief or escape.

But God has left a clue to His heart in that word "labor." The Hebrew word that is most often translated as *hard labor* in this context, like forced service, bondage, or the laborious work that the Hebrew slaves did for the Pharaoh in Egypt, is the word: *abodah.*

But wait! This is the same word used by God in describing the work to *construct* the Tabernacle![5] But we're not done! It is also the word used to describe the Levites who dedicate themselves to the *service* of God.[6] The point? If your labor is in service to other people, know that your labor is in service to God Himself. Orthodox Jews are taught not to see any distinction between secular work and sacred work, and I don't believe God does either.[7] A woman's ongoing, daily work is nothing less than worship and service of the almighty God!

---

[5] Exodus 39:32
[6] Numbers 3:8
[7] The fact that after the amazing story of the giving of the Ten Commandments, the very next chapter, Exodus 21, which begins with commands about Hebrew slaves, is inferred by Jews as evidence that there is no separation between the sacred Ten Commandments and the secular world.

Plus you get to birth new things too!

So then, what shall we make of GENESIS 3:16, *"I will greatly multiply your **pain** in childbirth"*? Why must it be painful? I believe that God, in order to *greatly* honor women for birthing the new works of redemption on earth, chose to *greatly* increase their pain in that work.

As a man, I would like to be one of those who try to learn how to honor and affirm you for facing the greatly-increased pain of birthing *whatever* God calls you to birth!

Personal Wrap-up

The original column series that became this book, was an idea I came up with myself. Or so I thought. Once that series started on Root Source, my arrogance came crashing down to earth when I was reminded by a dear woman, Becky Lyttle, one of the first ten subscribers at Root Source, that this column I was starting was *exactly* what she had asked me to do from the first days of Root Source, an idea I had initially rejected. Yes, this book was birthed from her idea, as well as the re-orienting idea from Jews that no human being is an island to him- or herself, but is connected to his or her mother.

Jews are today honoring the connected flow of life that flows down from Sarah, Rebecca, Leah and Rachel, but ultimately all the way back to Eve, who was called "Eve" (in Hebrew, *chavvah*) by Adam because he knew "she was the mother of all living."[8]

Thank you Jewish forefathers for honoring the role of women in your perspective of life on earth. Thank you Becky Lyttle for suggesting this idea and praying for it over the years until your "child" — this book — was born.

And finally, and most importantly, we shall end with a heavenward blessing of God:

> *Blessed be the LORD God, King of the Universe, who commanded that women shall greatly increase their pain in childbirth, and receive their due reward for that birthing.*

Shalom.

---

[8] *Eve* is *chavvah* in Hebrew, and *living* is *chai*. In other words, her name means "life's mother".

Asking Gidon

In this chapter, Gidon, I spoke about the list you pulled out of your pocket. Tell us more about that list, where it came from, and how often you pray for the names on that list.

It is a pretty widespread tradition that Jews pray for people in need of something, usually health, success, help in finding a mate or raising children, and much more. Prior to starting Root Source, I offered people the opportunity to have a prayer said for them in the Holy Land. I continue to pray for some of the people I met back then, and it makes me feel good to be connected to them in that way. I usually recite those prayers at the end of my formal thrice-daily prayer of the Amidah, the "Standing prayer," also called the *Shemonah Esreh*, the Eighteen, alluding to the eighteen blessings it was originally constructed from.[9]

How does your wife react to the weekly blessing you speak over her from Proverbs 31? Does she enjoy it? Can it become a perfunctory tradition after many years of doing it?

I think you touched on a very important point without necessarily even noticing it. I am speaking of impromptu prayer vs. formalized prayer. Traditional Judaism is heavy on formal prayer, while most of the Christian prayer that I have been witness to is impromptu. And what you hint at is true and natural; by repeating the same thing for many years, it can become perfunctory, or rote. But, if we discard that formalized prayer because of the danger that it will become rote, then we lose the chance that it will not become rote, but will remain or return to being tremendously spiritual. And if we depend on ourselves to always be spiritually fresh and able to create a new prayer at every given moment, then if we ever fall into a funk, we will not read prayers by rote, but cease praying completely.

Regarding my wife Devra's feelings about this specific recital of the excellent wife of Proverbs 31, we both love singing it together, even with our children in multiple part harmonies. So some weeks we might be tired, but those weeks are few and far between, and usually we all appreciate this time to connect to King Solomon (the passage's author), God and each other.

What is the Shabbat blessing you speak over your daughters at Shabbat?

---

[9] For more on the Amidah, see: https://en.wikipedia.org/wiki/Amidah

Traditionally, fathers and often mothers bless their sons and daughters with the Aaronic blessing, *"May God bless you and keep you, may God light up His face upon you and give you grace, may God turn His face towards you and give you peace."* (NUMBERS 6:24-26). This is preceded for a boy, with "may God bless you as He blessed Ephraim and Menashe" (GENESIS 48:20) and traditionally for a girl, with "may God bless you like Sarah, Rebecca, Rachel and Leah." I add the "boy's" blessing for my girls also as I think Jacob had girls in mind when he blessed Joseph's children, and I also add another blessing from GENESIS 24:60: *"…Our sister, may you become (mother to) thousands of thousands…"* (paraphrased).

Does the blessing for daughters stop at any certain age, and if they are celebrating Shabbat in another location that particular week, do you simply skip the blessing?

Oh no! It is so beautiful to see a great-grandfather blessing a grandfather! What a marvelous example of keeping the chain of tradition going. After a while, most children move out and do not spend every Friday night Shabbat meal with their parents. I cannot speak for all Jews, but in our family we make an effort to talk to each other every Friday if we will not be together on Shabbat, and speak these blessings to each of our children by phone. Shabbat Shalom!

Does the idea I proposed in this chapter appear in Jewish literature?

Yes, in the following sense: the thought in your essay that the pain in childbirth is to increase the honor of women, this is exactly the teaching of Ben He He in Pirkei Avot, chapter 5, Mishnah 23. In fact this early teaching may be the origin of the common phrase we use today: "No pain, no gain." See:

> https://bit.ly/Avot523
>
> https://en.wikipedia.org/wiki/No_pain,_no_gain#Origin

Pirkei Avot is taught on Root Source by Rabbi Elan Adler.[10]

We Broke All Ten

I still shake my head sometimes about the fact that I spent twenty-five years working daily with Israeli Jews in high-tech, and visited Israel thirty-three times, without ever knowing the massive extent of Jewish persecution by Christians. All I really knew was the Crusades. I had no idea about Martin Luther's role in the Holocaust, for instance, and I certainly didn't know about the deplorable history of the Church since the time of Constantine.

Not only was this history shameful, but the Church had fallen prey to the conspiracy of silence, whereby uncomfortable facts were left unstated. We are all prone to that tendency, but I had to ask myself: how had I lived fifty years of life, partaking in perhaps a dozen streams of the Christian faith, without knowing the extent of the truth?

Once I discovered some of this truth for myself in 2013, I began to ponder which of the Ten Commandments were most closely associated with antisemitism, and which of them were broken in the historical persecution of Jews by the Church. But as my knowledge of the tragedy increased, I kept increasing the number, until finally I threw in the towel and had to admit that we had broken everything. *We had broken all Ten Commandments.*

We or They?

Many Christians have questioned whether *true Christians* could be responsible for the kind of Jewish persecution that happened. I understand the claim that "real Christians would have never done those things." But I beg to differ. We must include ourselves in the "we." Why?

First, we cannot emphatically say that "we" who are alive today would have acted differently. We cannot go back and live their lives, steeped in their environment, commanded by their priests, pastors and family members to join them in persecuting Jews, *or else.* We cannot know that we would have been willing to disobey orders, stand up against the tide of hate, put our children in peril, risk our own lives, and been willing to lose our livelihoods and risk excommunication from our own Christian community for the sake of the Jews. We simply cannot know that.

Second, we cannot emphatically say that the mercy of God, or the forgiveness of God, is unable to reach and forgive those who do terrible things, and we can't possibly know who cried out for forgiveness later in life.

And third, while we soundly condemn their actions, when it comes to them as persons we need to heed the words of Yeshua and Paul who warned us to *"judge not that we be not judged,"* (MATTHEW 7:1-3; ROMANS 2:1).

Therefore, I say we must not separate ourselves from the countless Christians involved. We need to own the idea that *we Christians,* did these things — *we and our forefathers.* This is the same decision that Nehemiah took, when in Susa he heard about the problems in Jerusalem, both past and present, and prayed: *"I and my*

The Ten Commandments as displayed in Corpus Christi, Texas.

father's house have sinned." (NEHEMIAH 1:6). It is the same decision Daniel took in DANIEL 9:5-6, where he prayed to God with the word "we" even though he had not sinned those sins personally.

If so, of what sins are we culpable? Since the list of the Ten Commandments vary slightly, I have chosen to use the Jewish titles and English translation of the Hebrew as printed in the *ArtScroll Chumash* for EXODUS 20.[1]

---

[1] Using the Jewish list makes sense here, because we are discussing how we transgressed these commandments towards Jews.

We Broke All Ten

One. To have faith in God's existence, that He is eternal, and has complete and unfettered power: "I am Hashem, your God, who has taken you out of the land of Egypt, from the house of slavery."

The fundamental basis of persecution over the centuries, in my opinion, results from *unbelief in God's unfettered power to complete the process He started in Egypt* when He promised to bring them out, deliver them, redeem them and take them for His people, and to be their God (EXODUS 6:6-7). As Christians, especially after the fall of the Second Temple, we believed God's plan for the Jews was over. We limited His ability to write a story that brings the Jewish people out of slavery (again) after that destruction in 70 CE. We saw His promises as temporary rather than eternal, which set the door wide open to step into Replacement Theology: that the Church has replaced Israel in the plans or purposes of God.

Two. Prohibition of Idolatry: "You shall not recognize the gods of others in My presence. You shall not make for yourself a carved image..."

The good news of the Christian faith is not the death of the Messiah, but the Resurrection of the Messiah. However, the attacks against the Jews centered around the death of Jesus, with Christians often holding up the Cross during such attacks. Those crosses were made of wood, carved by men, and were never used in the early days of Christianity. Constantine, who legitimized and promulgated his version of Christianity across the Roman Empire that stressed separation from Jews, was obsessed with the "death of Christ," and began to focus much of his attention on the physical Cross, rather than on Christ's Resurrection. What resulted from his obsession? Death. In the last two years of his life, Constantine killed his own son to prevent him from succeeding him as Emperor, and then he murdered his wife. Historically it was Constantine's focus on "death" and "the Cross" that sparked Christian interest in the physical symbol of the Cross that is still present today.[2]

Has our historical use of carved images of crosses transgressed this very commandment? I say yes. We have historically exalted that symbol, focusing on Yeshua's *death* over His *death-and-Resurrection*.[3] One may contend that the Cross, although it is a carved image, could never be considered by God to be idolatry, but

---

[2] Carroll, James, *Constantine's Sword*, (New York, NY: First Mariner Books, 2002), 199-203.
[3] Please note that if you wear a cross, I am not accusing you of idolatry — that is between you and God. I'm just asking that you be aware that the symbol you wear carries for Jews a different message than what you intend: not of Jesus' death, but theirs.

one cannot disagree with the historical result: our Christian focus with the Cross has resulted in the massive death of Jews. Idolatry and death are not strangers, but bedfellows, and one always leads to the other. For as Yeshua said: *"Wisdom is vindicated by her deeds."* (MATTHEW 11:19).

Three. Prohibition of vain oaths: "You shall not take the Name of Hashem, your God, in vain."

While people differ on what it means to transgress this commandment, I believe the shouting of "Christ killers," or any kind of assertion that the Jews "killed God," crosses the line. Yeshua said about His life and upcoming death: *"No one has taken it away from Me, but I lay it down on My own initiative."* (JOHN 10:18).

Four. The Sabbath: "Remember the Sabbath day to sanctify it."

Historically, Christians have harmed the Jewish people on the seventh day of the week, that being the day that Israel was commanded to rest. The first harm was economic. Jews were forced by law to close their shops on another day of the week, like Sunday, so that if they closed on Saturday also, they suffered an economic disadvantage.[4] Second, during the Inquisitions, it became illegal to keep the Sabbath in the manner that Jews keep it. For instance, having lit candles in the home on Friday evening just before sundown, or the absence of smoke from a home's smokestack on Saturday, was seen as proof of being Jewish, and punishable by torture or death.[5] In this way Jews were forced to violate God's Sabbath command, *"You shall not kindle a fire in any of your dwellings on the sabbath*

---

[4] In 321, Emperor Constantine I decreed Sunday as a day of rest: *"On the venerable Day of the Sun let the magistrates and people residing in cities rest, and let all workshops be closed."*
Montgomery, Ray & O'Dell, Bob, *The LIST: Persecution of Jews by Christians Throughout History*, (Jerusalem, Israel: Root Source Press, 2019), 54.
In 1092, the Council of Szabolcs, Hungary, stated that Jews who *"did work on Sundays were to be punished by having their tools confiscated."* Ibid, 129.
In 1227 at the Council of Narbonne, France, Canon 3 states in part: *"We forbid them moreover, to work publicly on Sundays and on festivals."* Ibid, 163.
In 1434, the Council of Basel, Switzerland issued the Decree on Jews and neophytes, which includes the statement: *"On Sundays and other solemn festivals they should not dare to have their shops open or to work in public."* Ibid, 242.
[5] The Spanish Inquisition (1478-1834) was *"established by King Ferdinand and Queen Isabella, ostensibly to root out heresy, but serving to consolidate power in the monarchy of the newly unified Spanish kingdom. The King and Queen believed that corruption in the Catholic Church was caused by Jews who, to survive centuries of antisemitism, had converted to Christianity. Known as Conversos ("New Christians"), they were viewed with suspicion by old powerful Christian families, and blamed for a plague, accused of poisoning peoples' water, and abducting Christian boys. Some were also suspected of secretly practising Judaism, known as Marranos, and were perceived to be an even greater threat to the social order than those who had rejected forced conversion. Specific signs, such as no fires on the Sabbath, no eating of pork, washing hands before eating, turning the face towards the wall when dying, etc. were given to root them out. According to modern estimates, around 150,000 were prosecuted for various offenses during the three centuries of duration of the Spanish Inquisition, out of which between 3,000 and 5,000 were executed."* Ibid, 251.

day." (EXODUS 35:3).

Five. Honoring parents: "Honor your father and your mother."

In LUKE 16, Yeshua spoke of Abraham as an active participant in heaven, holding and comforting those Jews who have died. We Christians are taught that we have been grafted into Abraham's family through God's great mercy and grace, and that we are considered by God to be "sons of Abraham" and "daughters of Sarah" along with the Jews. When a man dishonors his brother, he dishonors his parents as well. Thus, by persecuting Abraham's children, we dishonor our father Abraham, and our mother Sarah.

Six. Prohibition against murder. "You shall not kill".

We Christians murdered Jews.[6]

Seven. Prohibition against adultery: "You shall not commit adultery."

We Christians raped Jews.[7]

Eight. Prohibition against kidnapping: "You shall not steal."

We Christians have stolen from Jews. We have stolen massive amounts of property from Jews, but in the larger sense we held their lives hostage to a series of restrictions on how they can make a living, and on their personal freedom.[8] Jewish

---

[6] *The LIST* (Ibid.) is replete with references to Christians murdering Jews, but special attention is drawn to the following in which there is direct involvement with the Church:
1096: The Rhineland Massacres. Ibid, 131.
1298: The Rintfleisch Massacres. Ibid, 195.
1348-49: The Black Death. Ibid, 205-214.
1370: Brussels massacre. Ibid, 217.
1389: Massacre at Prague (Bohemia), Easter. Ibid, 221.
1506: Lisbon massacre. Ibid, 268.
1939: Jozef Tito. Ibid, 415-16.
October 27, 2018: Pittsburgh massacre. Ibid, 495.
[7] April 1903: Kishinev, Moldova, Russia. Ibid, 387.
1917-21: Kiev pogroms, Ukraine. Ibid, 394.
[8] 414-15: Jews expelled from Alexandria, Egypt. Ibid, 88.
694: 17th Church Council of Toledo, Spain. Ibid, 110-11.
1188: Saladin tithe, England. Ibid, 148.
August 1349: Black Death riots in Germany: Cologne, Mainz. Ibid, 213-14.
1391: Anti-Jewish riots Seville, Spain. Ibid, 221-22.
1500: Pope Alexander VI. Ibid, 265-66.
1567: Pope Pius V. Ibid, 296-97.
1569: Jews expelled from Papal States. Ibid, 297-98.
1736: Peruvian Inquisition: Last person to be executed for practising Judaism. Ibid, 332.

commentary tells us the worst kind of stealing is to kidnap another human being, because it literally steals a life. We have even kidnapped Jews in this literal sense as well.[9]

Nine. Prohibition against bearing false witness: "You shall not bear false witness against your fellow."

We Christians made up evil stories about how Jews were stealing Christian children and engaging in ritual killings of them.[10] Then we charged that Jews were using the blood of these innocent children in their own Passover meal preparations.[11] We even blamed tragedies like the Black Death on the Jews.[12] Not one of those Christian claims was validated with factual evidence. The sin of bearing false witness continues today. Today for instance, many Christians characterize Christ as one who sides with Palestinians, because they, like Christ, were mistreated at the hands of the Jews.[13]

Ten. Prohibition against coveting: "You shall not covet your fellow's house, etc."

This may be the most common sin of all, because it is a sin of the heart. We who are not Jews have coveted to be "God's chosen people," coveting the "Jewish blessing" if you will, and have formulated theological ideas, like Replacement Theology, to try to obtain that which we covet.

Wrap-up

In 2013 when I discovered that we had broken all Ten Commandments, I honestly did not know what to do.

What will you do?

---

9   1508: Ulrich Zasius. Ibid, 268-70.
    Aug 26, 1827: Jews in the Russian military. Ibid, 352.
    1858: The Mortara case. Ibid, 360.
10 1144: First ritual murder libel: St. William in Norwich, England. Ibid, 140.
    Dec 28, 1235: Ritual murder (Blood Libel) charge in Fulda, Germany. Ibid, 167-68.
    1255: Little St. Hugh of Lincoln, England. Ibid, 178.
    1490-91: Blood Libel: The Holy Child of La Guardia, Spain. Ibid, 256-57.
11 1247: Blood libel in Valréas, France. Ibid, 173.
    1287: Werner of Oberwessel, Germany. Ibid, 191.
    1407: Cracow Accusations, Poland. Ibid, 232-33.
    1475: Simon of Trent, Italy. Ibid, 250.
12 1348-49: The Black Death. Ibid, 205-14.
13 https://www.tabletmag.com/jewish-news-and-politics/97155/christians-for-palestine

My repentance for our collective past sins, and the refusal of the Church to publicly discuss and own our past, came in several forms.

In 2018, Ray Montgomery and I combined our personal research on this topic and began to work on a volume, released in 2019, that we believe is the most thorough compilation of the persecution of Jews by Christians ever published. It is called *The LIST: Persecution of Jews by Christians Throughout History*,[14] (hereafter referred to as *The LIST*).

In 2019, we founded the Nations' 9th of Av[15] together with Christians:

> Martin and Nathalie Blackham of Israel First,
> Christine and Peter Darg of The Jerusalem Channel,
> Laura Densmore of Bridge Connector Ministries,
> Donna Jollay of Israel 365,
> The Evangelical Sisterhood of Mary,
> Ray Mongomery, co-author of *The LIST*,
> Bob O'Dell of Root Source,
> Sharon Sanders of Christian Friends of Israel,
> Tommy and Sherri Waller, of HaYovel,
> Zac Waller, of HaYovel,
> Steve and Doris Wearp and their family,

and many more, along with Jewish advisors including:

> Gidon Ariel of Root Source,
> AnaRina Heymann of Align with Zion,
> Aaron Lipkin of Lipkin Tours,
> Abe Truitt of International Fellowship of Christians and Jews,
> and Rabbi Tuly Weisz of Israel 365.

The Nations' 9th of Av held its first events in summer 2019 in both Jerusalem and around the world. We owned up to the historical record of the past, and asked for God's forgiveness of the impact this past sin is still having on the Church today. We then looked forward in prayer and asked that God would soon fulfill His promise to turn the day of the 9th of Av from fasting to feasting, as stated in ZECHARIAH 8:19.[16]

---

[14] https://9-av.com/marketplace/
[15] https://9-av.com/
[16] *"Thus says the LORD of hosts, 'The fast of the fourth, the fast of the fifth, the fast of the seventh and the fast of the tenth months will become joy, gladness, and cheerful feasts for the house of Judah; so love truth and peace.'* Zechariah 8:19

Finally, as part of this effort, and so that *The LIST* would not stand solely as an indictment but as a call to repentance, Laura Densmore initiated and led the effort to publish a companion book to *The LIST* called *40 Days of Repentance, A Companion Guide to The LIST*,[17] which contains forty devotionals, each one referencing a topic or an event in *The LIST*, explaining it, and suggesting how Christians might process the implications of those events and pray into that history.

Shalom.

Closing Prayer

NOTE: Due to the somber nature of the content of this chapter, and upon consultation with Gidon, I will not be asking him any questions relating to these Ten Commandments. Instead, he will be happy to answer any questions you might have via email.[18] We will instead conclude with a prayer.

Would you pray this prayer with me?

Father in Heaven,

As we contemplate the litany of sins against the Jewish People in this chapter, it stretches our hearts and minds to even know how to respond.

Would You please use the difficult historical facts covered in this chapter to prepare our hearts for Your purposes? Would You prepare opportunities for us to make different choices from the many wrong choices of the past? Would You, by Your Holy Spirit, bring us into a valued relationship with Your Jewish people, and give us insight on how to show kindness to them when opportunities permit?

Would You take out the heart of stone in Your worldwide Church, as exhibited in Replacement Theology, and replace it with a heart of flesh?[19] Would You providentially allow the worldwide Church, the body of Messiah, in the days ahead to stand in friendship with the Jewish people in ways and manners that go far beyond the historical records of the past? Bring us into a place where it might one day be said collectively to us regarding our treatment of the Jews,

---

[17] https://9-av.com/marketplace/
[18] gidon@root-source.com
[19] Paraphrase of Ezekiel 36:26.

"Well done, my Church, my good and faithful servants."

In Jesus'/Yeshua's name we pray.

Amen.

CHAPTER 6

The Next Revival?

In 2018, we made a preliminary spreadsheet of *The LIST* available online for free,[1] for anyone who would sign a declaration of repentance.[2] Almost 2,000 people downloaded the document and over 200 people took the time to write back to us and share their reactions. From that feedback I saw that the vast majority had been awakened to the full extent of the tragedy committed against Jews in the name of Christ. While we only asked people to *read* the document, many went beyond that. Many felt and acted on the need to *repent* for the actions of their Christian forefathers.

This chapter dips its toe into the larger question: whether repenting for the sins committed against the Jews might play a role in preparing for the next revival among Christians. This connection wasn't our idea, it was something readers have suggested to us after they heard about some of the work we were doing to document the historical record of Jewish persecution by Christians. Rather than writing about this personally, we are going to let two of them speak their minds publicly in this chapter.

But before that, let us set up some background on the meaning of revival.

What is Revival?

The term "revival" is the most common term that Christians use to refer to an extraordinary move of God in a region. Other words used in this way are "awakening," "outpouring," "outbreak," "renewal," or "movement."

Perhaps the largest such event in recent memory, is the house church movement

---

[1] https://root-source.com/blog/9av-resources-post/
[2] In 2019, when the Nations' 9th of Av was formed, the declaration to sign was moved to this website: https://9-av.com/sign-the-declaration-of-repentance/

in mainland China. Others might argue for parts of Africa, or Iran.[3] But the rest of this chapter will focus on the USA and the UK, because that is the focus of the writings of two women whose comments will be presented below.

In the USA, the largest revival that happened in our lifetimes was the Charismatic Renewal of the 1970s, related to and sometimes called the Jesus Movement. Interestingly, its beginnings can be traced to the period of 1967. The year 1967 also marked the year which began a renewal of interest in the Jewish roots of Christianity, which found its expression most visibly in what has been termed the Messianic Movement, or more recently the Hebrew Roots Movement.

Prior to 1967, the great revivals in the United States were called the Great Awakenings. The first Great Awakening came in the 1730s and 1740s, which corresponded with the Methodist Revival in England. The second came in the 1790s, and the third in the 1850s. More recently, the Welsh Revival in 1905 was followed by the Azusa Street Revival in California in 1906, which launched a wave of interest in the presence, manifestation and empowerment of the Holy Spirit. The Charismatic Renewal that blossomed in the 1970s renewed many features of the Azusa Street Revival, bringing many young people to faith (or back to faith) in Jesus, thus the term *the Jesus Movement.*

Azusa Street Revival Building.

---

[3] Short link to article on Christian Headlines: https://bit.ly/Iran-church

No revival in Christian history has ever occurred without transformation: of people "returning" to godly living, of people confessing and letting go of sinful and damaging habits, and of renewed interest in God and the study of the Bible. Out of revival, Christians read the Bible in fresh new ways and "suddenly saw" verses as applicable to them that past generations had ignored.

Azusa Street group photo with William Seymour at center right.

But how does revival begin? Historians all agree that revival, when it happens, is always preceded by small groups of people who pray and repent. One of the most often-quoted scriptures, and the one that has provided guidance for "how to pray in" a revival, is a verse Christians borrow from the nation of Israel when they pray:

> *When My people, who bear My name, humble themselves, pray, and seek My favor and turn from their evil ways, I will hear in My heavenly abode and forgive their sins and heal their land.* 2 CHRONICLES 7:14 (TIB)

But "repent" is a general word. Are there not many things of which we could repent? The central idea being proposed by two women below is that perhaps God is saying the time has now come for the entire Christian world to begin to repent *of our negative treatment of Jews* in the last 2,000 years.

These women, and others who have written to us, consider the possibility that God might want to use *The LIST* to reveal the depths of past sins, and to reveal underlying heart issues which are still present in the larger church today.

Listen first to what Vicki Stewart wrote after reading a blog post from Ray Montgomery published on Root Source in August 2018.[4] Vicki writes:

> Great article Ray, and so moving. Your story and Bob's ring true and it is no coincidence that the LORD has placed this issue of repentance for past sins committed by Christians against the Jewish people on both your hearts for such a time as this. He raises up those that He wishes to use for His purposes (EXODUS 9:16).
>
> One thing that has been on my mind since this whole issue of Christian persecution of the Jews and repentance has been the need for revival. Could our heartfelt and sorrowful repentance for these acts, bring about the revival that the Church so desperately needs? In reading about past revivals, you often read of how they involved deep levels of repentance.
>
> Richard Bewes wrote the following in an article titled, *It Begins with Repentance*, for the Billy Graham Association in October 2015, "In the great East African Revival — within which I was born and raised as a child of missionaries — widespread conviction of sin was followed by heartfelt and practical acts of repentance, as men and women turned to the cross of Christ by the thousands. Government officials were dumbfounded at the volume of stolen axes, hoes and other agricultural implements that were handed in by the repentant. Many convicted of their sins would, if necessary, walk 20 miles to right certain wrongs."[5]
>
> Frank Bartleman's statement from the 'Azusa Street' Revival: "I received from God early in 1905 the following keynote to revival: 'The DEPTH of revival will be determined exactly by the DEPTH of the spirit of REPENTANCE.' And this will obtain for all people, at all times."[6]
>
> Here is one last quote on this subject from Evan Roberts of the Welsh Revival: "First, is there any sin in your past with which you have not honestly dealt, not confessed to God? On your knees at once. Your past must be put away and cleansed. Second, is there anything in your life that is doubtful, anything you cannot decide whether it is good or evil? Away with it. There must not be a trace of a cloud between you and God. Have you forgiven everybody — EVERYBODY? If not, don't expect forgiveness for your sins..."[7]

These quotes show how important repentance is to revival. The fact that there

---

4   https://root-source.com/blog/studio-see-013-ray-completes-his-story/
5   https://decisionmagazine.com/it-begins-with-repentance/
6   "I received from God early in 1905 the following keynote to revival: 'The depth of revival will be determined exactly by the depth of the spirit of repentance.' And this will hold true for all people, at all times." Bartleman, Frank, *Azusa Street: An Eyewitness Account to the Birth of the Pentecostal Revival,* (New Kensington, PA: Whitaker House, 1982), 19.
7   Matthews, David, *I Saw the Welsh Revival,* (Pensacola, Florida: Christian Life Books, 2016), 126.

has not been more repentance for the atrocities committed by the Christians against Jews is due in part to lack of knowledge (Hosea 4:6) but also to hard-heartedness (Romans 2:5), both of which we are warned against in the Scriptures. I, too, love Corrie ten Boom and I end with this quote from her, "Four marks of true repentance are: acknowledgement of wrong, willingness to confess it, willingness to abandon it, and willingness to make restitution."[8]

Laura Densmore, who also believes that revival could be coming soon, writes from the vantage point of repentance as a "return to Torah." In 2018, Laura wrote:

> We are in a season of repentance. We are seeking for a great outpouring of the Holy Spirit. How might the God of Israel accomplish this with us today? Here is a key principle: the deeper the level of repentance, the higher, the wider and the greater will the outpouring of the Holy Spirit be.
>
> What keeps us from repenting? It is a wall we build of pride and self righteousness. If we have been in church for many years, we can develop the mindset, "Well, I am all right." This is pride. It can be very subtle. It likes to be cloaked, to be hidden, it is not overt. We must begin by repenting of pride. And then we can get to the rest of the sin behind that wall.
>
> What motivated Daniel to pray the prayer of repentance for himself and his people in Daniel 9:1-19? He had been studying the book of Jeremiah, and found that the time of the exile in Babylon for Judah would last for seventy years (see Jeremiah 25:11-12; 29:10). And then he understood that the seventy years were nearly up. He also knew that if he and his people were going to come out of exile and be allowed to return to the Land of Israel, they needed to repent and return to the Torah. He was following the pattern of repentance found in Leviticus 26:40-42. Daniel confessed the iniquity of his people and of his forefathers. He was very specific to say that they had departed from following the Torah. This is what got them kicked out and evicted from the land:
>
>> *We have sinned, and have committed iniquity, and have done wickedly, and have rebelled, even by departing from your precepts and from your judgments: Neither have we obeyed the voice of the Lord our God, to walk in his laws, which he set before us by his servants the prophets. Yea, all Israel have transgressed your Torah, even by departing, that they might not obey your voice; therefore the curse is poured upon us, and the oath that is written in the Torah of Moses the servant of God, because we have sinned against him.*
>> Daniel 9:5, 10-11 (KJV)

---

[8] https://www.azquotes.com/quote/862475

What *The LIST*[9] does is expose and reveal the sins of our Church forefathers in a way I have never seen before. We in the Church have been so blind for such a long time, spanning the centuries. What *The LIST* does is it shows us the big picture, the sweeping panorama of sin that our Church forefathers have committed against the Jewish people over the centuries.

What *The LIST* does is expose two very important things for which we can repent:

1. the specific events of sin done to the Jewish people; and

2. the mindset, the doctrine and the thinking that permeated the church culture at the time that permitted these atrocities to happen.

What was that mindset/doctrine? It is the notion of "Replacement Theology," that the "church" has replaced Israel and the Jewish people, and that all the covenants and promises made to Israel and the Jewish people are null and void, that those covenants and promises are now for "the Church." It is the notion of Age of Law/Age of Grace, that the Torah has been done away with, and we are now living in the "Age of Grace." It was a TURNING AWAY from the whole counsel of the Word of God.

It was this evil root of Replacement Theology thinking that gave us the heinous fruit of the Inquisition, the Crusades, the Pogroms, and ultimately, the Holocaust of Nazi Germany. This kind of thinking is still prevalent in much of the church today. The BDS movement,[10] the ever-rising antisemitism, the persecutions and unceasing terror attacks against our Jewish brothers and sisters, all have their roots in Replacement Theology.

As these "sins of our Church forefathers" are exposed in *The LIST*, my prayer is *The LIST* would be used by the hand of God to be as a "jackhammer" to break up the cement-like places found in our hearts and that it be used as an instrument to bring about deep, heartfelt repentance.

May we weep over the things that cause God to weep, and may it be His tears that slide down our cheeks.

Revival begins with repentance, one prayer at a time, one heart at a time, one

---

[9] https://9-av.com/marketplace/

[10] *The Boycott, Divestment and Sanctions movement (also known as BDS) is a global campaign promoting various forms of boycott against Israel until it meets what the campaign describes as Israel's "obligations under international law", defined as withdrawal from the "occupied territories" (Israeli governments prefer the term "disputed territories"), removal of the separation barrier in the West Bank, full equality for Arab-Palestinian citizens of Israel, and "respecting, protecting, and promoting the rights of Palestinian refugees to return to their homes and properties". The campaign is organized and coordinated by the Palestinian BDS National Committee.*
Montgomery, Ray & O'Dell, Bob, *The LIST: Persecution of Jews by Christians Throughout History*, (Jerusalem, Israel: Root Source Press, 2019), 485.

person at a time, in our prayer closet. From there, it spreads and grows. May it begin with you and with me…[11]

Laura would later propose that a series of devotionals be written to take lessons from what happened in *The LIST*, and propose prayers that can turn the difficult "truth" of *The LIST* into "peace" in keeping with ZECHARIAH 8:19b: "So love truth and peace." Written as a forty-day prayer guide by fifteen different Christian ministries, that book, *40 Days of Repentance, A Companion Guide to The LIST* is also available in book form.[12]

What Happened Before 2018

Several years before *The LIST* was published, back in 2016, I was able to speak at Christ Church in the Old City of Jerusalem on Saturday night, following the first full day of Passover. The event in Jerusalem was a conference held by Christine Darg, during what we suspected was the Jewish Jubilee Year of 2015-2016. We cried out for revival from Jerusalem.[13] It was a special time, and I wonder if that call from Jerusalem had something to do with the women who wrote what you just read in this chapter.

What Happened After 2018

In 2019, one year after the initial event in 2018, about a dozen Christian ministries gathered to form an organization called The Nations' 9th of Av.[14] For the first time in history, as far as we are aware, a group of Christians came to Jerusalem specifically to observe the 9th of Av alongside the Jewish People in Israel.[15] We sat on the ground and read Lamentations on Saturday evening August 10, 2019. The next day just over seventy Christians convened at the southern steps of the Temple Mount, in the Old City of Jerusalem, near the place where Peter preached his first sermon, and where 3,000 people repented and were baptised on Pentecost.[16] There we repented for 2,000 years of persecution of the Jews by Christians throughout history.[17]

---

[11] Short link to the full article on Bridge Connector Ministries: https://bit.ly/Laura-repentance
[12] https://9-av.com/marketplace/
[13] https://youtu.be/CFxFsktOZwo
[14] https://9-av.com/
[15] Rabbi Tuly Weisz explains that one additional reason the Nations' 9th of Av observance is meaningful to Jews is that Jews know their persecution history, and assume that most Christians know it too. Yet, the attendees expressed not only sorrow for the past, but sorrow that "we didn't know our own history."
[16] Acts 2:38
[17] Short link to article on Jerusalem Post: https://bit.ly/Christian-9av
Short link to article on Israel365 News: https://bit.ly/9av2019
Short link to article on Nations' 9th of Av events: https://bit.ly/9av2019events

What is specifically going to happen regarding revival in the months and years ahead? Besides the indication we received from God to continue the Nations' 9th of Av project, we don't precisely know. As a reader we would joyously receive your participation in future Nations' 9th of Av events. Or, God may call you to work in a different direction. But what we do know is that every one of us has a job to do, not just independently, but a job that involves connecting with others. Every one of us needs to do that which God puts in front of us to do. When enough people do their part, revival will come, redemption will come, and ultimately Messiah will come without any unnecessary delay.

Shalom.

Asking Gidon

Gidon, you were present in 2019 when seventy Christians gathered near the Temple Mount on the 9th of Av to repent for Christians' sins of the past. How did that make you feel personally to see that happening?

I did not participate in that entire repentance service; I was jumping between there and another historical gathering a few yards away. That morning, numerous records were broken regarding the number and nature of Jews visiting the Temple Mount, and I was one of those visitors.[18] For me, this was a juxtaposition that very few Jews appreciated, seeing Jews visiting the Temple Mount and Christians praying adjacent to it. I pray that both phenomena will grow.

While our 2019 event in Jerusalem was not publicized extensively, a few articles were posted in places like the Jerusalem Post,[19] Breaking Israel News,[20] and at least one large Jewish newspaper in New York.[21] What is your assessment of the impact of this event, if any, on the Jews of Israel?

I think that the 2019 event was a precursor to the bigger and more impactful events that must happen in the years ahead. I don't know what will tip the

---

[18] The current situation at the Temple Mount, referred to as the *status quo*, is difficult for most people to understand, including me. What helped me finally "get it," was a great interview of Orthodox Jew Yisrael Medad who tells the story of the modern-day Temple Mount and explains the viewpoints of those involved. We posted it on Root Source at this short link: https://bit.ly/TM-statusquo

[19] Short link to article on the Jerusalem Post: https://bit.ly/Christian-9av

[20] Short links to two articles on Israel365 News: https://bit.ly/9av-initiative https://bit.ly/9av2019

[21] Adler, Rivkah Lambert. "Christians Come To Terms With Ancestors' Anti-Semitism." *The Jewish Press*, July 12, 2019.

scales, but I believe that Jews will recognize that Christians who love them and repent for the horrific acts of Christians in the past, are not the same as those Christians of the past.

Gidon, so if something "tips the scales" regarding Orthodox Jewish opinion of Christians, would it be attributed to (a) the Providential work of God, (b) the fulfillment of biblical prophecy, (c) the recognition of the modern state of Israel as "opening the eyes of Christians," (d) the bringing in of the Messianic redemption, or what?

Frankly, I think all four of the options you gave me are all sides of the same coin (if a coin would have four sides ☺). Certainly such a sea change could only happen if God would want it to happen. I would say that the means that God would use would be more activities with Jews and Christians participating in together, and those activities getting significant publicity.

CHAPTER 7

The Face of God and Man

I once wrote the following sentence from that greatest of all cities — Jerusalem:

"One of my favorite places in the world is a place I have never visited."

That sentence above was written on location within the boundaries of that greatest of all cities — Jerusalem — the city of peace.[1] Jerusalem is not only a place on earth that God said He would dwell, but a place above this earth in heaven in which He dwells. Yes, of all places in the world, despite its narrow streets and traffic, despite the words spoken there that are anything but peaceful (try riding in a few taxi cabs!), despite great spiritual battles waged there in the unseen world, Jerusalem is my *favorite* place in the world.

But *one* of my favorite places in the world is in Jordan, just across the Jordan River from Israel. It is a white mound or rock, near where the Jabbok River (now called the Zarqa River) runs down from the heartland of Jordan and meets the Jordan River. Any guess as to what place I am thinking of?

It is the place where Jacob wrestled with the angel, and after doing so he called it Pni'el,[2] *the face of God*.

So Jacob named the place Pni'el, for he said, *"I have seen God face to face, yet my life has been preserved."* (GENESIS 32:30).

The Face of God

I have never personally seen the face of God. Have you?

---

[1] Chapter 19 discusses the name *Jerusalem* in greater detail.
[2] https://en.wikipedia.org/wiki/Penuel

The disciple John, tells us that no man has seen God at any time (1 JOHN 4:12). Yet we, who see Yeshua as Son of God and Son of Man simultaneously, would say that seeing the face of Yeshua would "check the box" for having seen God face to face. While Jesus never denied His own divinity, I cannot recall that He ever "led with that thought" in a public setting, but only when challenged, or in private conversation with His disciples (MATTHEW 16:13).

I have never seen the face of Yeshua in my years following Him. I saw Him in a dream once, but I did not recognize Him by sight in the dream, I only "knew" that this man who spoke with authority to me was Him. I was also approached by Jesus once many years ago while fully awake — I knew that the presence of God was right in front of my face — but only later did I realize from the context that it must have been Jesus.

The point of all this is to say that I cannot claim to have ever seen anything with my own two natural eyes, something that would cause me to exclaim like Jacob: "I have seen the face of God, and lived." This exclamation from Jacob, this place, this name, is why Gidon pronounces this word in two syllables "pnee-el" where the "el" of course means "God."[3] "The face of God" — Pni'el — is one of my favorite places on earth, even though I have never visited it.

Possible site of Pni'el surrounded by the ancient Jabbok River in Jordan. Today it is called the Zarqa River. (Google Maps).

---

[3] English Bibles usually write Peniel.

Maybe you, as a reader, are also able to say right along with me:

> "I too have never visited Pni'el, and I too have never seen the face of God."

While I would love to have seen God, and while I know it is right and good that David encourages every one of us to come along with him to "seek Your face" (PSALM 24:6), my educated guess is that I will *never* have that experience until I pass on from this body to be with the LORD. Why not? My guess is that I won't see Him because, while there is a blessing that comes in seeing Him, ultimately the blessing of doing God's will *without seeing* Him is even greater.[4] Said more simply, God withholds Himself because He wants us to have the best possible reward for our labors on earth.

And yet, having just said that, I must quickly add that if God actually *wanted* to appear to me and a few of my closest friends, I would be so thrilled!

But the "face of God" is not where my love ends for that place I have never visited: Pni'el. Because there is another face that I love to look upon: It is the face of man.

The Face of Man

Pni'el was not just about God appearing; it was about a man — Jacob — being changed in the process. His name was changed. His thigh was touched. He was never the same again.

It is my hunch, even though I don't see it in the text of that passage, that Jacob's own face was also changed in the process of this encounter with God.

And now we finally reach the central point I've been driving towards:

> **While I have not seen God's face, I have seen the faces of those who love Him, and those faces are beautiful.** *Their countenances are radiating the light of God on them.*

Why This Chapter, and Why Now?

This entire chapter was originally written during a visit to Israel, Jerusalem in particular. On this particular trip, I had the privilege of meeting people, putting a camera in front of them, and asking them questions about their lives — their stories — as they relate to Israel. In the hours and days that followed, the faces of

---

[4] John 20:29

those people kept passing in front of me.

Then I recalled some of my experiences meeting Jews and Christians in Dallas two weeks prior to Jerusalem. There I saw the same thing. The faces of some of *those* people were now passing in front of me, in my mind's eye.

I have seen thousands and thousands of faces of people who love God, but it just occurred to me that in my work surrounding Israel, Israel is getting "**the best faces**" of the Christian world coming to it.

I wonder if this is not, for the Jews, the best possible reaping for righteous sowing in centuries past? Jews have had to look at some of the angriest faces in the world in the last 2,000 years. It would be "just like God" to send them the best faces today — the due reward for all that their forefathers endured.

So, which is it: the chicken or the egg? Are the people who naturally have the light and love of God upon them hearing the call to come to this land, and look for ways to be a blessing to the Jewish people? Or are the people who take up the calling to come to this land, having their faces being changed in the process?[5] If the latter, is part of that change coming from their own encounter with the faces of the Jewish people, and their encounter with the God of Abraham, Isaac and Jacob?

I have no answer to this question, but what I do know is that I like being in Israel. I feel privileged to go there and relate the stories of these wonderful people, and show you their faces on video. But only a fraction of the faces passing before me are appearing on *any* video! It would be wrong to begin naming them, but if I did, I know that my list would be very, very long.

A Decision

Imagine you were offered the following choice from God Almighty: to see Him in His glory right now while you are still living, or to see the faces of the people that you have met, both Jew and Christian, in the Land of Israel and in the nations. What would you choose?

If He offered me this choice — to either see His face, or to see theirs (i.e. Jew and Christian) — I would have to say:

"I will wait to see You oh LORD, but do not take away from me the

---

[5] Or is it both!

memory of all the beautiful, smiling, light-filled faces I have seen in this land."

And speaking of Jewish faces, I never thought about it before, but I guess I saw in Israel, by extension, the faces of Abraham, Isaac and Jacob, who all walked with God, and whose faces must have had the light and life of God upon them as well.

In Closing

Pni'el is the face of God. It is the birthplace of Isra-El. How natural and normal that God's plan for this place would be that the people showcase, in their own countenance, the "face of God."

I wonder if God looks down upon Israel and sees the smiling, beautiful faces of the people who live within its borders, or who visit within its borders, and says to Himself:

"Of all the beautiful creation I have placed here, of all the agriculture and of all the fruit of My Land, those faces are my favorite *fruit* of all."

May the faces of the people of Israel increase your Shalom.

Shalom.

Asking Gidon

Gidon, this chapter talks about Pni'el. The name of your community in Judea has a similar name: Pnei-Hever. What does that mean?

Pni'el means the face of God. Pnei-Hever means facing Hever. Hever is the name of the ravine that runs near our community.

However, on the topic of names, the name we actually prefer in our community is *Ma'ale Hever*, as it was chosen by some of the very first residents. Ma'ale Hever means "the ascent to Hever." But the national naming committee objected to this name, because the road to our community goes downhill, rather than up, as it does for other communities like *Ma'ale Adumim*, the largest of all Jewish communities just east of Jerusalem, a community in which I used to live. Today, the road sign to our community turnoff reads "Pnei Hever" while the residents fiercely hold on to the original name, Ma'ale Hever, forcing the postal service to recognize both.

And what does Hever mean? Is the meaning related to the nearby city of Hebron (pronounced in Hebrew as Hevron)?

Yes, according to Wikipedia, it is named from Hevron.[6] It is related to the word Haver, which means friend. Pnei-Hever, which means "facing the (valley of) Hever," can also sort of mean "friendly face" which is one of the reasons I like the place ☺

I would say that you smile a lot yourself. What do you say about the Christian faces that come to Israel? Do you like what you see?

Oh yes! Everyone who comes to Israel is blessed and is a tremendous blessing for Israel.

---

[6] https://en.wikipedia.org/wiki/Ma%27ale_Hever

CHAPTER 8

House of God, Feet of Man

B esides Jerusalem and Peni-El discussed previously, I would have to say one of my other favorite places in Israel is Beth-El, the House of God. Few places in Israel are so well preserved as this one.

Like Peni-El, Beth-El is also famous for a visit by Jacob when he slept and dreamed of a ladder with angels ascending and descending on it. The historical site is just outside the Jewish community of Beit-El, which is about ten miles north of Jerusalem.

Mosque on the left and Crusader period Church on the Right.

The church and mosque nearby are proof that the site has been understood as a key location for centuries, as is the nearby *mikvah*[1] from Jewish antiquity.

---

[1] A mikvah is a Jewish ritual bath, and is used to perform the requirements for washing according to Mosaic law. Some of the largest mikvahs in the Second Temple period were at the bottom of the southern steps of the Temple Mount, where Peter preached his first sermon in Acts 2. There is little doubt that the baptisms in Acts 2:38 were carried out in those mikvahs, which were only a few steps away. The mikvah at Bethel is quite small in comparison.

But the main feature of this site is the flat circle of stone, which would be the absolutely perfect place to sleep if you were traveling by that way.

Place where Jacob probably slept.

Here is where the stories slightly diverge between the Christian version and the Jewish version. You may be surprised to learn that in Jewish tradition, Jacob has his dream on the Temple Mount in Jerusalem, rather than at Bethel more than ten miles to the north. The reason Jews favor the Temple Mount for his dream is clear from the description of angels ascending and descending, and Jacob's exclamation:

> "Surely the LORD is in this place, and I did not know it." He was afraid and said, "How awesome is this place! This is none other than the house of God, and this is the gate of heaven." GENESIS 28:16-17

These sound like remarks that can be made about the Temple itself as well. While I can understand the traditional Jewish view, the site itself meets every requirement of the place where Jacob slept. It was with this difference of opinion in mind that I viewed the site once again on a visit to Israel in late 2018.

At the time I was travelling with Gidon near Bethel. Gidon needed to stop and pray his afternoon and evening prayers. While I might normally have joined him, since we were also traveling with my friend Trey Graham, who had never seen Bethel, I took leave of Gidon to show Trey this site. While there, having just taken the picture shown above, I asked him,

"If you were sleeping here, which direction would you lie down?"

He responded, "Head on the rocks, and feet to the right."

"I agree," I said.

And indeed that is the only direction where your feet would be lower than your head, because while the rock was flat, it was ever-so-slightly tilted to the right, which was south.

And then it hit me that if Jacob was lying in that most natural of positions, his feet would be lined up exactly towards Jerusalem ten miles away. Therefore it would be as if his feet were "on the Temple Mount" while he was dreaming his dream! If angels were ascending from the Temple Mount, that ladder would eventually reach the zenith as viewed from Bethel as well, just as if a rocket shot straight up from the Temple Mount would eventually appear overhead at Bethel, once it got high enough.

If you stand in that stone circle and look south towards Jerusalem, you cannot see the city. Jerusalem is hidden by a nearby hill, meaning that if the ladder were descending to Jerusalem, it would not be so obvious to Jacob exactly where the angels were touching down on the Earth.

Looking south from Bethel. Jerusalem is hidden behind the nearby hills.

Another key event in the history of this site was the decision by the Northern Kingdom, and King Jeroboam in particular, to put one of the two golden calves here (1 KINGS 12:28-29). The raised mound on which that giant calf likely stood is clearly seen in the following photo.

I found this to be an eerie feature of the site: the defilement by idol worship of such an important place in the history and formation of Israel and God's promises to His people. And yet we do the same thing today in the United States. We idolize wealth and power in the midst of a nation that declares that it is one nation under

Raised Mound used for the Golden Calf.

God. We try to "build on" the righteous foundation of great men of the past, such as George Washington — a devout Christian — yet we also attempt to build "mounds" on that foundation for ourselves, mounds on which to place our wealth and our materialism.

While the site of Bethel was on the southern border of the tribal allotment of Ephraim (just before you cross southward into the territory of Benjamin), the site of the other Golden Calf was as far to the North as you could get within the Northern Kingdom: the city of Dan.

It was in the city of Dan that a variety of idol and cultic worship was practiced. This was a place where lawlessness was considered the norm, a place where anything goes, a place of sexual experimentation.

In modern day terms, Bethel was the place you would go to if you were naturally biased towards conservative values, at least the conservative values of the Northern Kingdom. You would visit that site on the highest ridge of hills in the Land of Israel, a place with views all around. Perhaps it would be like a visit to Mount Vernon, the home of George Washington. But Dan would be the place to go if you were naturally biased towards liberal values. It is a place that valued freedom of expression, freedom to define one's morality, and offered multiple choices of how to fulfill one's own natural desire for pleasure and comfort. Some of those choices are fine. Some of those choices were not right. So perhaps visiting Dan would be like a visit to New Orleans or San Francisco. But let us be clear, *both* liberal and conservative values have the potential to be defiled by idolatry.

It hurts to see Bethel, the beautiful site of Jacob's dream, marred by a mound on which a Golden Calf stood. But the good news is that such activities will never again occur on this site – the current and future residents of Beit-El will make sure of that.

Moreover, the site of Bethel has an amazing property, which shows that "God was here first." Indeed, Jacob exclaimed "Surely the LORD (YHVH) is in this place." When I first came to this site in 2015, I remember the tour guide asking us to take out our cell phones and google "Bethel name of God" and then click on images. When we did that, there was a satellite image that popped up on our phones. The image showed the valleys near Bethel as making a pattern similar to "YHVH" the four letter name of God.[2]

The tetragrammaton name of God is embedded in the pattern of the valleys in the hill country north of Jerusalem!

*Then Jacob awoke from his sleep and said, "**Surely the LORD [YHVH] is in this place, and I did not know it.**"* GENESIS 28:16 (emphasis mine)

Talk about a literal fulfillment of scripture!

I find this fascinating because we as Christians are historically quite skilled at looking for spiritual fulfillment of various verses of scripture in the Old Testament, while Jews are historically skilled at looking for literal fulfillment. The example above should be a lesson to all of us, never to discount the power of God to fulfill His word literally.

Here is a link to one-minute long 360-degree video I made on the hilltop of Bethel that day, starting and ending to the West: https://youtu.be/tXdATnSv8RM

God has placed His house among men, and has even written His name in the valleys where the feet of man tread. And years later, a man who grasped his brother's foot from the womb would himself be given a new name — Israel — that would be a name taken by God as His own.

The House of God and the feet of man are very much connected in this amazing Land of Israel.

Shalom.

---

2 That image was posted publicly at this short link to City-Data Forum: https://bit.ly/Bethel-YHVH

Asking Gidon

Gidon, how do the Jewish people generally perceive Jacob, as compared to Abraham or Isaac? For instance, does he get the respect of Orthodox Jews at the same level that respect is offered to Abraham and Isaac?

This is too deep a question to be dealt with in a short paragraph. Each patriarch embodies an important characteristic that we aim to model. There are probably hundreds of short and long teachings about Jacob alone! What comes to my mind is the value of truth that is linked to Jacob (Abraham is linked to compassion [in Hebrew: *hesed* or *chesed*] and Isaac to *gevurah* — strength or heroism) and the concept that Jacob is *b'hir ha-Avot*, the select of the patriarchs. I understand this to mean that he is a synthesis of the characteristics of Abraham and Isaac. So if your question hints that he might be less deserving of respect than his father and grandfather, there is weight to the tradition that he is even *more* respected.

I mentioned early on in this chapter that there is a difference of opinion between Christians and Jews about the site of Jacob's dream: Christians favor Bethel, and Jews favor Jerusalem. But for Jews is the matter fully concluded, or do some Jews also favor Bethel? Do you have a position on this question?

Jews actually have a tradition of being able to live with perceived contradictions. Obviously the tourism department of modern Bethel prefers what you call the Christian opinion ☺ which shows that it is also a Jewish opinion. I actually like the way you settled the contradiction, positing that Jacob slept here but his feet and thoughts were pointing towards the Temple Mount.

Regardless of where Jacob dreamed his dream, I completely agree that the place where God ultimately decided to "put His name," is Jerusalem.[3] The Bible also records the manifest presence of God being seen and experienced in mighty ways in Jerusalem in the past, especially when the Temple stood atop Mount Moriah, the Temple Mount. So how is Jerusalem perceived today? Do Jews sense or experience the presence of God (or the acts of God) today in Jerusalem at a higher level than in other places in Israel?

Jewish speakers and politicians would be forgiven if they declared that

---

[3] Deuteronomy 12:21

Jerusalem is a place where God can be perceived more than anywhere else. In fact, the Mishna in the tractate of Keilim, chapter 1, mishnayot 6-9 declares this clearly, that *"the Land of Israel is more holy than all other lands… and [Jerusalem] is holier yet…"*[4]

---

4   https://www.sefaria.org/Mishnah_Kelim.1.6-9?lang=bi

CHAPTER 9

A Reluctant Personal Story

B y reading this far, you have proven your interest level in some of the thoughts and perspectives that have dawned on me during my time spent with Orthodox Jews in Israel. Perhaps you would be interested to hear a story from this author's childhood?

The chapters you are reading were originally published in a less polished form, as a series of articles and blog posts on Root-Source.com. The title of the series was *Studio See*, a name that I promised to explain over time. I knew then that explaining the story behind that name, would be a story that would be told reluctantly. If you keep reading this chapter, you will understand why.

The Young Generation group photo.

The Young Generation

In 1976 at the age of fifteen, I was privileged to become part of a talent group that would go around and perform at various venues in Clearwater, Florida. It was an amazingly good concept with strong execution and organization driven by my friend Joanie Burton's mom Joan, who had herself been in show business. The group, the Young Generation, would open with a Vaudeville routine with all of us singing, and then we would each get a 5-minute solo act for the total 45-minute show.

Lori did jazz dance, Hunt did magic, Joanie did tap, I played piano, Greg was the MC and worked in some comedy, Kimberly did ballet, Chuck did impersonations including W.C. Fields, and Kim did gymnastics. As far as I know, only two took their performances to the next level: Joanie went on to Hollywood as an aspiring actress and ended up in production, while Greg, if I recall, became an excellent guitarist, and played and sang in a rock band.

While an excellent (adult) pianist played during our singing and dance performance, my act was to come out dressed as that great showman Liberace,[1] candelabra in hand, pompous in all my mannerisms, and then to play. We must have performed at least fifty times at various nursing homes, retirement centers, and community centers on weekends, sometimes three shows in a day. It was all done as an act of charity and the older people absolutely loved our performances. Three of the more unusual performances, however, stand out to me all these years later.

First, I remember playing at an outdoor neighborhood gathering in St. Petersburg, Florida on July 4, 1976, on the 200th anniversary of the USA. I was part of something much bigger than "our performance" that day. The stage floor was way too small and way too high in the air — with a big metal railing on all sides to keep us from falling off. It felt like we were performing on a raised postage stamp. Other than the gymnastics routine — which was smartly and quickly relocated down to ground level — I think everyone else managed to get through their acts OK on that tiny up-in-the-air stage.

I also recall the day we performed at Disney World in Orlando. Disney didn't *really* book us — I think our director must have pleaded until they finally gave us free admission to the park in exchange for a couple of shows on a big raised platform, completely exposed, with no seating anywhere. Had there been folding chairs, it would have made no difference, because nobody would have been foolish

---

[1] https://en.wikipedia.org/wiki/Liberace

enough to sit in metal chairs, in the sweltering heat with the direct overhead sun of a midsummer July day in Florida. They told me not to light the sixteen-inch-tall white candles, but it didn't matter. They had already begun to melt in the hot Florida sun, even as I walked towards the waiting upright piano, and they began to melt even more quickly once the whole candelabra now rested on the black piano's blazing, baking-hot surface.

The guests walking between park attractions, usually ignoring little performances such as ours, now stopped in their tracks, not for any interest in what I was playing, but to stare at the sight of a fifteen-year-old boy playing the piano in the hot summer sun while his two giant white candles began to slump over, each leaning in a different direction, before their very eyes. The growing audience was now fixated on my act, standing motionless, waiting to see if the little "Liberace boy" on stage would finish his piece before the first of his drooping candles would break free, falling off the candelabra onto the even hotter surface of that piano, or falling down onto the piano keys and the boy's lap. While sweat poured down my face and all inside my costume, I was playing against the clock, trying to play my piece ever faster, hoping to finish before my serious musical selection devolved into utter comedy.

Later on that day, when we were regrettably required to perform a second time, the little "Liberace boy" managed to play his piece in much more relaxed fashion, without any candelabra or candles present. Nearby, a waste bin had been fed two miserable, melted candles.

The third memorable performance was memorable because it wasn't supposed to be a performance at all, but rather a practice. A little non-profit PBS show had been funded in those years to try to keep kids watching PBS[2] after they became too old for PBS children's shows like Sesame Street. The new show was called *Studio See*. One of our group managers had written to them to propose that they do a story on our *Young Generation* group for one of their shows. They agreed and traveled down to Florida for filming. I was told that they would film us at a nursing home on Sunday (which they did), but that on the prior Saturday they wanted to see us practice. What was not clear to me was that the goal on Saturday was not to talk to them about the event on Sunday, but to *film our practice on Saturday*.

While the other kids wore nice, smart clothes, I wore a sloppy T-shirt of the lowly Tampa Bay Bucs, a team that was in the process of setting an NFL record for most consecutive losses. I was aghast when I walked in and saw all the cameras and

---

[2] https://en.wikipedia.org/wiki/PBS

Bob gets ready to play for the camera.

realized my misunderstanding. But I quickly got over it and was soon cheered up.

More than cheering me up, the story would turn for me that day in a good way, when they heard what I played. For rather than play a piece from Liberace, the 'wow-factor' of all my performances in the *Young Generation,* my feature piece was *self-composed.* It was called *Illusive Flight,* a name that my mother of blessed memory came up with as she heard it being created, and often practiced, at home. The producers really liked my little piece, liked me and my story within the group, and when our episode was eventually released, they gave me more than my fair share of coverage.

My Greatest Regret

And now I will tell you my greatest regret and the reason for naming the original article series *Studio See,* the series that eventually became this book you are holding.

One of the producers of the show called me a few weeks after filming and asked me if I would be interested in allowing them to use my piece as background music on another episode. She explained that they were working on a show where they filmed a girl taking her first parachute jump, and they needed a minute-and-a-half of music to accompany footage of the jump. She said she thought my *Illusive Flight* would be perfect for that. They would pay me $50 to sign a release form to allow them to use the music. That was a lot of money in 1977, and a lot for a kid. But I must have surprised her in my response.

My greatest regret was how I handled myself in the ensuing days, in front of them and my parents. I suppose that I thought I was "somebody now," and that this was a sign of my potential as a musician. (It really wasn't a sign, it was just a gift). Rather than be grateful for a bit of exposure for my music, I kept stalling and trying to figure out a way to negotiate a price that would be "more in line with the music's true value" and a price that would "not be taking advantage of me." Eventually, after they flatly said "take it or leave it," I signed, and they used it as promised. Studio See was cancelled after two seasons of twenty-six episodes each. But over the years, I have remembered, and been reminded again and again, how I treated those kind people who were trying to bless me, and fill a small need of their own. I took their interest in me, and used it against them, thinking that their interest proved my work was worth more than they were willing — or able — to offer.

Why Did I Name This Original Article Series "Studio See?"

Here was the thing. I had no idea about their world. I had no understanding of what it is like to pull together a show in the world of non-profit television. Because TV cameras were present I assumed about them what I did not know. I needed a different perspective.

And so, when I asked Gidon what he thought of my writing a column for about a year, I decided to name it Studio See in memory of that show.

When it comes to Jewish-Christian relations, I think we all need to have an enlarged perspective. Nobody can say they see everything at once. Even while I was compiling these essays, I was continually learning as well.

The topic of Jewish-Christian relations is big and expansive enough that it deserves many different perspectives, *more than just my own*. I have liberally borrowed from the words of others in the chapters you have already read.

We all need to come into a place, an attitude of being willing to "receive the bigger story" — the *Studio* — and then being willing to look at big topics from multiple vantage points — the *See*.

But the name *Studio See* did something else for me personally. Every time I wrote a new column, it was *a big fat reminder* for me *"not to think of myself more highly than I ought to."* (ROMANS 12:3, paraphrased). That painful memory serves as a shepherd's rod keeping me in continual check.

Today, my embarrassment, and the name, *Studio See*, are no longer sad, but redemptive.

Shalom.

Comments from Gidon

Very enjoyable story Bob! I was laughing out loud at the candles melting ☺ And your negotiation story is a teaching moment for every budding entrepreneur!

Chapter 10

Cornelius: Go and Do Likewise

Cornelius was a Roman Centurion who became the first Gentile "Christian," the first non-Jewish man to become a follower/disciple/believer in Jesus/ Yeshua the Messiah. The principle of first mention says that one should pay special attention to the first occurrence of a concept in the Bible.

Therefore, as per that first mention principle, what can we non-Jewish believers learn from this first Gentile disciple? I believe we can learn a great deal, if we see him as a foundational example for all of us, and do not fall into the trap of viewing him as a "special case."

Will you allow me to provide some verse-by-verse commentary about how I read and understand what that story can enlighten at the intersection of the Jewish and Christian worlds?

Let us begin in ACTS 10:1.

Now there was a man at Caesarea

This story does not begin in Rome, nor in any of the "nations," but right in Israel, on the coastline. Yes, Caesarea was a Roman city, with all the pagan trappings of such a city, but yet it *was* in Israel, just a stone's throw from the Mediterranean. Just barely in Israel, *but that was enough.* The lesson I take from this is that God's blessing is available for those who visit *the land* of Israel, who are willing to spend any amount of time there.

named Cornelius, a centurion of what was called the Italian cohort,

Cornelius' job required him to give his loyalty to Caesar, and he came from Rome of all places, the center of antagonism towards the Jews. Have you ever noticed how God loves to use someone from the most unlikely place? Do you feel like your own history makes you unlikely to be used by God? Think again! It is in

God's nature to use the unlikely.

a devout man and one who feared God with all his household,

Clearly God had been at work in this man for some time. We who are Christians are often taught that our journey with God begins after we "accept Jesus into our heart." Yet, this phrase shows God was at work well before then in the case of Cornelius, and that God had also been at work in his entire household, and in many under his influence.

and gave many alms to the Jewish people

This sentence strongly implies that Cornelius had friendly relations with the Jewish people in Caesarea. When one gives money — even more, when one gives a lot of money — it reveals a strong attachment. It also implies RELATIONSHIP with the Jewish people. They go together.

and prayed to God continually.

Besides giving, Cornelius spent his other most precious commodity — TIME — in pursuit of a relationship with God. What is God telling us? Is He not giving us hints about what has prepared Cornelius for the amazing favor of God that would soon be coming his way?

About the ninth hour of the day he clearly saw in a vision an angel of God who had just come in and said to him, "Cornelius!"

The favor of God begins from RELATIONSHIP as well. Cornelius was known to God, and God sent an angel to call him by name! God honors the relationships that Cornelius was willing to build with His Jewish people, and then surprises Cornelius with an invitation to hear directly from His messenger.

And fixing his gaze on him and being much alarmed, he said, "What is it, LORD?" And he said to him, "Your prayers and alms have ascended as a memorial before God."

God informs Cornelius that the key reason he is being favored by a visit from the angel, was that he had turned to God in prayer, and had given alms to the Jewish people! Do you want to be overwhelmed by the favor of God, and to have supernatural visions and visitations from God? There are many Christian books that tell stories and give advice about how a person can position themselves to experience the presence of God in a stronger way. But in this case God clearly tells Cornelius that God has been touched *by his prayer and his alms to the Jewish people.* Why is this other facet generally ignored in prophetic circles?

And now jumping to verse 22, Cornelius dispatches his servants to the town of

Joppa, where Peter was staying. Their description of Cornelius to Peter is:

Cornelius, a centurion, a righteous and God-fearing man well spoken of by the entire nation of the Jews...

How in the world would Cornelius have come to be known by the entire nation of Jews? I spent some time researching the topic, and ended up writing a *fictional monologue* of Cornelius coming to our day and time and telling us his personal story.[1] The monologue envisions Cornelius trying to walk the fine line between his allegiance to Rome demanded by his career, and his inner sense that the Jewish people were "on to something" with their worship of the One Almighty God. It envisions an event that forced his respect of the Jews to become known far and wide.

Jumping to verse 24:

Now Cornelius was waiting for them

Maybe in the movies you can have non-stop action, but in real life with God, there are *always* periods of waiting: periods that test our faith! Cornelius may have calculated how long it would have taken for Peter to jump onto one of the horses his servants took to Joppa (modern-day Yafo) and ride back to Caesarea. But Peter decided to walk! Cornelius had no option but to wait, and neither do we!

and had called together his relatives and close friends.

Cornelius was willing to put his reputation with his own family on the line. He believed in the goodness of God and wanted that goodness to be extended to those within his circle of influence.

When Peter entered, Cornelius met him, and fell at his feet and worshiped him. But Peter raised him up, saying, "Stand up; I too am just a man." As he talked with him, he entered and found many people assembled.

Whenever a shift occurs in history, there is always a period of confusion, and a propensity for error. This devout man Cornelius got so focused on the human messenger that God had promised to send, that he worshipped another man![2] We should acknowledge this as a problem that can happen even to the very devout: the mistake of viewing any person we respect, and turning them into an idol within our hearts. This embarrassing part of the story could have been so easily edited out of Acts by the writer Luke, but it was not. We need to know not only

---

to be careful, but that good leadership must always guide us to GOD, not to the LEADER.

Next, Peter explains "who is Jesus" to Cornelius and his household beginning in verse 44.

> *While Peter was still speaking these words, the Holy Spirit fell upon all those who were listening to the message. All the circumcised believers who came with Peter were amazed, because the gift of the Holy Spirit had been poured out on the Gentiles also. For they were hearing them speaking with tongues and exalting God.*

While many points could be made here, I want to concentrate on the main one. Jesus had promised His disciples that the Holy Spirit would be poured out upon Peter and the other disciples, and now that very same gift was being offered to the Gentiles. We Gentiles should therefore honor and not disdain that precious gift today.

> *Then they asked him [Peter] to stay on for a few days.* ACTS 10:48

Cornelius did not run away from instruction, having received the gift of the Holy Spirit. In fact the first instruction he received was from the Jew, Peter. And yet Peter stayed ONLY a few days. Why? Wouldn't God want to give the very first Christian a full education to get Christianity moving in the right direction? But the record is silent from here on about what happened to Cornelius, and how he moved forward in his life! What we do know is that he was surrounded by a number of Jews. By implication and context, only a very few *if any* of those Jews in the community of Caesarea had decided to follow Yeshua as the Messiah. From this we can infer an extremely important point: Cornelius continued to have a relationship with the Jews around him, even Jews who were not followers of Yeshua.

Can you even imagine a scenario, where God came to someone and said *"your alms to the Jewish people were extremely pleasing to God,"* and then that person walks away from those relationships? Wouldn't such a person be even *more* interested in pursuing and growing those relationships with Jews now more than ever? Wouldn't he want to continue learning all he can from them about the ways of God?

We must learn the lesson of Cornelius. Cornelius was not just the first Gentile Christian, he was the prototype pro-Israel Christian! When it comes to Cornelius, how can we not but be admonished by this story to *go and do likewise.*

Cornelius must have continued to learn from the Jews. This foundational passage does not spell out exactly what that learning looked like, leaving it not at all formulaic, but very open and flexible. This seems quite right to me.

An Example of Learning from Jews

I once asked Orthodox Jew and Bible teacher, Rabbi Chaim Eisen,[3] what topic he would be teaching if we extended him an invitation to speak in my hometown of Austin. The phone conversation went something like this:

"If you visit our city, what topic would you be teaching?"

His response was, "What would you like to learn?"

I said, "Why are you asking me this? Don't you have a topic already prepared for your speaking tour?"

"No, I customize it for each audience."

"Oh, in other words you mean that you have a set of prepared topics and you can teach from that list?"

"No, I teach whatever topic you request, as long as it's a topic based in the Tanakh."

Astounded, I said, "Are you telling me that I can pick any passage or topic in the Tanakh and you can teach it without preparation?"

"Well, if it's not a famous passage, I will certainly refresh my memory and gather my thoughts before I arrive. As far as topics go, I'm very flexible as well."

"So you are saying I can pick any passage or topical issue in the Tanakh and you would teach it?"

"Basically, yes."[4]

Finally convinced I said, "Alright. We will talk together as a team and come up with a topic.[5] But I have a question: *why*? Why do you make each audience pick

---

[3] Rabbi Chaim Eisen is one of the best Bible teachers I've ever met: Christian or Jewish. His organization is https://zionbiblestudies.org/. He also is a passionate singer, and sang Lamentations to Christians on a hillside in sight of the Old City of Jerusalem on the evening of the 9th of Av, 2019.

[4] In the full conversation, I could not resist taking the next half hour to test him on about twenty different topics and verses all over the Tanakh. I could not raise any topic or passage that he had not somehow covered in his forty-year experience studying and teaching at yeshivas.

[5] We eventually chose *The Life of King David*. It took ten hours over five sessions, and we asked him to teach us in true yeshiva style. He did that too! The after-class survey of the sixteen Christians who attended was remarkably high.

the topic of study?

He responded, "That is a very important question you have just asked! We teach this way because of PSALM 1:2, 'But his delight is in the Torah of the LORD.' From this verse we understand that a student learns best when he chooses his topic of interest. It is the very best way for the Torah to become a delight to him. My goal in teaching is to awaken the strongest possible hunger in every person, for learning and instruction from the Word of God, so I teach the topic of greatest interest."[6]

Wrap up.

So while we do not know exactly what Cornelius did after this story ends, what is absolutely clear is that Cornelius did what he did in relationship and friendship with the Jews!

Let us go and do likewise.

Shalom.

Asking Gidon

Gidon, had you ever heard of the story of Cornelius before talking about it with me? How do you react to this story?

I don't think I'd ever heard of this biblical story. If someone had mentioned the word "Cornelius" to me, I would have thought they were talking about the name of a movie character.[7] When you first introduced me to the story, I was taken by how much Cornelius' relationship with God, and even with Jesus, was through the Jewish People. In fact, I still think that the message of this story is not that Gentiles can become followers of Yeshua, but that they can and should be supporters and friends of Jews.

---

[6] Orthodox Jews have widely diverse opinions on many things, but one thing they all agree upon: the Hebrew word torah does not mean law, it means instruction. For example, the stories of Abraham predated the "giving of the Torah" on Mount Sinai, but since they are included for our instruction, they are torah, not just the commandments of Moses. When Paul translates torah as nomos in the Greek, he was following in the tradition of the Jewish scholars who wrote the Septuagint around 200 BCE. The word nomos had a larger definition then. English Bible translators who translate nomos as law in the New Testament, have chosen the narrowest of all possible definitions of the word torah.

[7] I think he may be remembering the main character Cornelius, from The Planet of the Apes! Yes, Orthodox Jews, at least those of the national religious Zionist persuasion, can watch movies!

What are some of the topics that Christians ask you about, when you interact with them?

Um, everything? I think that a good and strong relationship must be based on openness. I cannot promise that I will give an answer that my inquirer was expecting, but I will do my best to provide a sincere answer.

Cornelius gave alms to the Jewish people in his day. What do you think "giving alms" could or should look like today?

I expect that in Cornelius' time, there were plenty of residents of the province where he was stationed (Judea) who were underemployed and therefore poor. I assume Cornelius gave gifts to the most needy. Such people still exist, and there are numerous nonprofit organizations that focus on alleviating their hunger.

CHAPTER II

Do You Know THIS About Romans?

P aul's letter to the church in Rome, more formally entitled: *Epistle to the Romans*, is his longest letter. *Romans* contains many passages that help shed light on (a) how Christians of both Jewish and non-Jewish ethnicity should relate to each other within the Church, and (b) how the Church should relate to Jewish people overall.

However, the book of Romans is also considered to be a great foundational work in the topic of *salvation*. That is how I first came to understand the purpose of *Romans*. Actually reading the book, though, was another story. It is generally considered one of the toughest books in the Bible to understand. I remember sitting in Wednesday night Bible study, ignoring the discussion, while simply staring at the text trying to understand how and why Paul writes the way he does. "Does Christianity have to be so complex?" I wondered.

Concerning its complexity, I remember reading a comment by the late author Watchman Nee from China, that I will paraphrase as this:

*"Romans is not what you read to be saved, it is what you read **after** you're saved to explain what just happened."*

I carried that synopsis of the book in my mind for the next thirty years.

So which is it? Is Romans a book about the relationship between Christians and Jews? Or is Romans a book about salvation? Both? Neither?

Saint Paul in Prison, by Rembrandt.

Enter Pawson

In 2013, my perspective began to change about the book of Romans through a teaching I heard on ROMANS 9, 10, and 11, given by a Gentile Christian teacher named David Pawson. Pawson had his own ministry out of the UK, and was a regular invited speaker over the years to one of the largest Christian ministries in Israel, the International Christian Embassy of Jerusalem (ICEJ).[1] In a sense, Pawson's teaching opened up a door that allowed me to begin to see Romans differently, preparing me for a work in Israel even before I was sent in 2014 to connect with Orthodox Jews.

Before I continue, I'd like to set some boundaries. I do not mention Pawson because I agree completely with his 2008 teaching that I heard in 2013. I do not. Rather, I cite him because *God used him* to open up a door for me to begin to look at Romans in a *new way.* Those shared points of agreement *are the topic of this chapter*, and I don't want anyone to infer that I came to these insights on Romans simply from personal study. What I share below is that which I had to be *taught*, and that which I believe every Christian needs to know.[2]

Paul wrote Romans to prevent a church split!

Here is the *new* news, the understanding I never had about Romans growing up. **Romans was written to avert a crisis!**

I wonder if even 1 percent of Christians realize that *Romans* was not written to the church in Rome simply to explain their salvation in Christ! It was written to try to rescue them from a situation that was about to devolve into **the first denominational split in the Church!**

To prove this we need not rely on any extra-biblical sources for proof, although they also exist. We can find everything we need in the New Testament. What we will see in the New Testament is that the church in Rome had gone through four phases of development at the time that Paul wrote his letter to them.

The Four Phases of the Church in Rome

The church in Rome, comprised of people who were believers in Yeshua, went

---

[1] David passed away on May 21, 2020, age 90. May his memory be blessed.
[2] It is extremely important that we not discard all teaching from a teacher with whom we may disagree in part. I often remind myself that if God can use a donkey, and if God can use Balaam, an enemy of Israel, to speak words that find their way into the canon of Scripture, that God can enlighten me even through those with whom I *completely* disagree, although I can't recall ever *completely* disagreeing with anyone!

through four phases concerning its ethnicity:

1. Jews only
2. Jews and Gentiles
3. Gentiles only
4. Gentiles and Jews

In phase one, the church in Rome was founded by those who were ethnically Jewish. We know this because Rome is specifically listed among the locations of Jews who had travelled to Jerusalem to be present during Shavuot/Pentecost (ACTS 2:10). On that day, when a large group was gathered, including those from Rome, the Holy Spirit fell upon them. The verse states that some of those Jews from Rome were not actually born Jewish, but were proselytes; nevertheless, all had converted to Judaism.

As soon as those Roman Jews returned to Rome, the church in Rome began to form. It would not be until later, in ACTS 10, that the first true Gentile (also from Rome!) would be brought into the church. The story of Cornelius is widely believed to have occurred about seven years after Christ. So the Jewish-only church in Rome remained "just Jewish" for at least seven years, possibly twelve years or more.

In phase two, Gentiles began to become part of the church. This began when news circulated that Gentiles could be brought into the church *without* conversion to Judaism. The ranks of Gentile believers in the Roman church began to grow rapidly. Perhaps many of these Gentiles were already "God-fearers" who, like Cornelius, were respectful of Jewish teaching and traditions, but others would certainly have arrived into the assembly without such background.[3] It would be in this period of change that the events of the Jerusalem Council in ACTS 15 were written — that would rule on matters of how Gentiles could and should be brought into the faith.

And then a surprise happened!

In phase three, the Emperor Claudius expelled the Jews from the city of Rome. This was not the first ever expulsion of Jews from a city, but it was *one* of the first expulsions, and it is the *only* expulsion mentioned in the New Testament:

And he found a Jew named Aquila, a native of Pontus, having recently come from

---

[3] The Greek word translated "church" is *ekklesia*, which means "assembly." It is first used in Matthew 16:18, and parallels the Hebrew word for assembly, *qahal*, which is first used in Genesis 28:3.

Italy with his wife Priscilla, because Claudius had commanded all the Jews to leave Rome... ACTS 18:2

This event, around 50 CE, included *all Jews*, making no distinction about whether they believed in Yeshua as Messiah or not. Thus, all Jews had to quickly leave the city and find new residences and livelihoods. We see this mentioned in the New Testament with respect to one key couple, Aquila and Priscilla, who became friends with Paul because of the expulsion.

Historically we know that the expulsion edict lasted about five years, after which time Claudius changed his ruling, apparently realizing the impact of his mistake.

In phase four, many of those same Jews returned to Rome to re-engage in daily life together in the church in Rome. We see this return documented in the book of Romans, wherein Paul closes his letter by greeting a number of the believers there, beginning with Priscilla and Aquila, who had also returned.

Greet Priscilla and Aquila, my fellow workers in Christ Jesus, who for my life risked their own necks, to whom not only do I give thanks, but also all the churches of the Gentiles. ROMANS 16:3

The church in Rome now had a problem, a very big problem. **In those five years of absence, the Gentile believers in Yeshua had taken over the leadership and administration of the church in Rome.** But when Jews such as Priscilla and Aquila returned — Jews who had previously demonstrated great leadership, courage, and the ability to effectively teach at a high level (see ACTS 18:26) — they were simply not allowed to resume their prior levels of leadership! We can detect this in the book of Romans itself through the very points Paul was making.

Paul realized that the root issue underlying the trouble was an *attitude* that had taken hold within the Gentile-believing community toward the Jews *at large* — it was a bigger issue than simply a disagreement about who was capable to lead. Antisemitism seems to be present!

Paul responds not only with correction, but in the pouring out of his very heart. It would be in this book, *Romans,* where Paul would reveal much of what he carried inside his own heart and mind, revealing his own perspective towards his Jewish brethren. Paul's message in that letter, and his life overall, has confused Jew and Gentile alike. In the centuries that would follow, readers would begin to presume Paul was writing this letter as a Jew who had departed from Jewish practice, and living as the Gentiles did, even though a thorough reading of Scripture does not support this departure.[4]

So What's the Point?

The main point is this: the fact that many church Bible studies on Romans today focus primarily on chapters 1 through 8, and then breeze through chapters 9 through 11, is not only wrong, it is an assassination of the epistle!

Not only are Romans chapters 9 through 11 worth reading, but I have to agree with David Pawson that those three chapters *are the primary focus* of the book! They are the intended destination; the summit Paul has been striving to reach throughout the entire epistle.

That three-chapter summit itself builds to a crescendo, the peak of the peak, in ROMANS 11, from which Christians who love the Jewish people draw their words so often. Here are a few of my favorites.

In the very first verse of ROMANS 11, we see that God has not rejected the Jewish people!

> *I say then, God has not rejected His people, has He? May it never be!...* ROMANS 11:1a

We see that the Jewish people are holy to the LORD, and the holiness we have as Gentiles springs from theirs:

> *...If the root is holy [the Jews], the branches are too.* ROMANS 11:16b

We see in this chapter also, the introduction of that foundational concept: being "grafted in" to Israel:

> *...and you, being a wild olive [branch], were grafted in among them and became a partaker with them of the rich root of the olive tree,* ROMANS 11:17b

We see the stern warning that we must in no way be arrogant toward the Jews:

> *do not be arrogant [Gentiles] toward the branches; but if you are arrogant, remember that it is not you who support the root, but the root supports you.* ROMANS 11:18

We see that despite the disagreements we might have about who the Messiah is, and many other verses in the New Testament, none of those differences prevent

---

[4] Concerning Paul and his relationship with Jews and Gentiles, I recommend *Paul the Jewish Theologian*, by Dr. Brad Young: https://amzn.to/2ADoL0X

all of Israel from being saved:

> *and so all Israel will be saved...* ROMANS 11:26

And as we put that brief phrase into its larger context, we can also see Paul informing us that *what is happening* is part of a bigger plan than we might realize. He informs his brethren who follow Jesus to be *respectful* of the fact that most Jews do not "see Jesus" as their LORD and Savior; to treat it with the respect deserving of a biblical mystery, with the same respect given to other *biblical mysteries*:

> *For I do not want you, brethren, to be uninformed of this mystery—so that you will not be wise in your own estimation—that a partial hardening has happened to Israel until the fullness of the Gentiles has come in; and so all Israel will be saved...* ROMANS 11:25-26

We see that God's overwhelming purpose of this *biblical mystery* is to have *mercy* on all.

> *For God has shut up all in disobedience so that He may show mercy to all.* ROMANS 11:32

And finally, upon arriving at this summit of the summit in ROMANS 11, we find there, at the end of the chapter, a full orchestra in place, ready to break forth in a concluding crescendo, as if the book of Romans was not like the climbing of a mountain, but had been a symphony all along. Paul, the conductor, leaves no ounce of energy unspent, as he draws out the final power of the symphony like a conductor lost in the most climactic moment of a performance he has worked towards his entire life, drawing it forth in four final finishing measures:

> *Oh, the depth of the riches both of the wisdom and knowledge of God!*
>
> *How unsearchable are His judgments and unfathomable His ways!*
>
> *For who has known the mind of the LORD, or who became His counselor?*
>
> *Or who has first given to Him that it might be paid back to Him again?*
>
> *For from Him and through Him and to Him are all things.*
> *To Him be the glory forever.*
>
> *Amen.* ROMANS 11:33-36[5]

If you already knew these things, then I celebrate with you, and encourage you

---

[5] Three of the four closing lines of Paul's crescendo are drawn directly from the Hebrew Scriptures:
verse 33 quotes Job 5:9,
verse 34 quotes Isaiah 40:13,
verse 35 quotes Job 35:7.

to tell others. And if you, like me, had not heard these things before, then enjoy reading Romans in a whole new light.

Shalom.

How long have you been interacting with Christians? Did ROMANS 11 come up early in those conversations? What did you think when you first heard some of the key verses mentioned above?

I think my first interactions with Christians were of a "fly on the wall" variety, with me attending a Christian event in Jerusalem and sitting in the back row in the early 2000s. To my recollection, ROMANS 11 was mentioned quite a bit in those first few interactions with Christians. I believe that one of the first Christian books I ever read, Pastor John Hagee's book *Jerusalem Countdown*,[6] focuses a lot on those verses in chapters 14-20.[7]

How do Jews today see Paul?

Virtually all Jews, excluding perhaps those pursuing an advanced degree in New Testament studies, are clueless about Paul and his central place in the New Testament and the Church in general.[8]

---

[6] https://amzn.to/2XlDJBM

[7] Within one month of meeting Gidon I sent him a document that shared some of my thoughts about Romans 11. He replied, "It is refreshing to hear your perspective and that your perspective is as it is."

[8] Rabbi Berel Wein in his *5000 Years, The Crash Course on Jewish History*, said "Paul was the greatest marketer of all time." Given his impact on world history it would be hard to disagree, but I feel certain that Paul would have preferred to give the credit to God.

CHAPTER 12

The Largest, Longest-Running Bible Study

The eighth day of the Feast of Sukkot, also known as the Feast of Tabernacles, marks the joyous celebration of the turning over of the Torah (*Simchat Torah*)[1] — where the study of Deuteronomy has been completed and the study of Genesis begins anew.

The Jews read the Torah every year in a reading plan that begins in the fall at the closing of the Feast of Sukkot. The reading plan partitions the first five books (Torah) into sections (or *parashot*) that are read over the course of a single year. An individual reading is called a *parasha*.

Early on in my work with Gidon, I remember walking with him down Ha-Nevi'im St. (Prophets St.) in Jerusalem, trying to understand how this reading plan worked. I remember asking him:

"So if one portion is read per week, does that make fifty-two portions?"

He smiled and said, "Not exactly."

I suddenly remembered that about one out of every three years is a leap year on the Hebrew calendar, which adds one extra month to the calendar. Realizing my mistake, I then tried to correct myself:

"Oh, so are there fifty-six portions, because of the extra 'leap month' of Adar II?"

He smiled again and said, "Not exactly."

---

[1] *Simchat Torah* is a joyful celebration among Orthodox Jews where the Torah scrolls are taken out of the ark and the reading of the last *parasha* in Deuteronomy is followed by the reading of the first *parasha* in Genesis. As such it marks the end and the beginning of the year-long reading cycle and is accompanied by dance, song and celebratory drinking.

That "not exactly" has taken some getting used to, and only after going through the full reading cycle a couple of times, did it start to make more sense. The Torah is separated into fifty-four readings rather than fifty-six which would normally be required during a leap year. Gidon answered "not exactly" because the week-long Passover and Sukkot celebrations have their own special readings that suspend the weekly progression through the Torah for that week. In addition, during each biblical holiday an additional book of the Bible is read.[2]

But keeping it all straight is pretty easy, because our free Root Source newsletter[3] each week lists the Torah portion reading for that particular week. We put that first every week, as a way to honor God and put Him first.[4]

In addition to the Torah, there is also a weekly reading (usually about one chapter) from the Prophets, or Nevi'im. This is called the Haftarah reading.[5]

Not to be left out of the mix, the books of the Writings, or Ketuvim, which include Job, Psalms,[6] Proverbs, Ecclesiastes, Song of Solomon, Ezra, Nehemiah, Daniel, Esther, Ruth, Lamentations and Chronicles, are added to the Torah and the Prophets (the Nevi'im) to comprise what Christians call the Old Testament. The Torah-Nevi'im-Ketuvim (T-N-K) is an acronym that the Jews call the Tanakh. Since Tanakh is not fully known outside of Judaism, you may also hear Jews refer to the Tanakh as the Hebrew Bible, or the Hebrew Scriptures. The canons of the Tanakh and the Old Testament are the same.[7]

---

[2] In addition to the Torah, five other books called the Five Scrolls (Megillot) are commonly read during the year:
During Passover, the Song of Solomon is read.
On Shavuot (Feast of Weeks, or Pentecost) the book of Ruth is read.
On the Fast of the 9th of Av, Lamentations is read.
During Sukkot (Feast of Tabernacles), Ecclesiastes is read.
On the Feast of Purim, the book of Esther is read.
In the Hebrew Bible, these scrolls appear in exactly that order, ordered from the first month of the biblical year (Nissan or Aviv) to the final month of the year (Adar). Why scroll? It is said that these books are deep and many layered, and even as a scroll only opens to a portion of the text at any one moment, so is much of their wisdom hidden from view.

[3] https://root-source.com/amember/signup

[4] The https://www.chabad.org/ website is the best I've found for understanding the holiday readings.

[5] For more on the Haftarah readings see: https://en.wikipedia.org/wiki/Haftarah. Early on I mistakenly pronounced them "Haftorah" readings, which they are not. While I've looked, we cannot use the Haftarah readings today, often in Isaiah, to determine when during the year Jesus read Isaiah 61, as recorded in Luke 4:18. For those Christians who quickly point out the absence of Isaiah 53 from the readings, I recommend Nehemiah Gordon's podcast on the topic as the most common-sense view. https://www.nehemiaswall.com/tag/isaiah-53

[6] Passages in the Psalms are also central in Jewish life. The Hallel (praise in Hebrew) are read on festivals (Psalms 113-118); the Hallel Pesukei Dezimra are prayed daily (Psalms 145-150); and the Great Hallel (Psalm 136) with every verse ending with "and His mercy endures forever" is read on Pesach (Passover) and every week on Shabbat.

[7] The additional fourteen books in the Catholic Bible (the Apocrypha), such as the first and second Books of the Maccabees, are not included in the Tanakh. The ordering of the books between the Tanakh and

But the focus of this chapter is the reading of the Torah by the Jewish people, in lock-step, weekly.

Three Books that Might Help

I have found great enjoyment in reading the Torah along with the Jewish people. In addition to the scriptures themselves, I often pick up a commentary to go with the reading. Allow me to share some ideas for such commentaries.

The first year I read the Torah through, I focused on the *ArtScroll Chumash*.[8] The word *"chumash"* is Hebrew for "one fifth," which refers to the Five Books of Moses. *ArtScroll Chumash* is a well-thought-out English translation that uses words that are consistent with traditional Jewish understanding of the Scriptures. It also includes an almost verse-by-verse commentary that chooses some of the most often cited commentaries on each verse from dozens of famous rabbis throughout the ages.

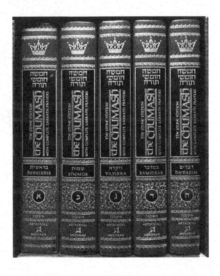

I did not obtain my *ArtScroll Chumash* in early fall when Orthodox Jews begin reading Genesis each year. Instead, I waited until early December to ask for it as a Christmas gift![9] But once it arrived at the house, I couldn't wait, and asked my wife's permission to open my Christmas present early and to start studying! I then

---

the Old Testament is different, as are our chapter divisions. For chapter and verse ordering differences, download the pdf at this short link: https://bit.ly/verse-compare

8 https://www.artscroll.com/Books/9781422617977.html

9 This true story never fails to get a laugh among Orthodox Jews!

discovered for myself, what Dr. Marvin Wilson, author of *Our Father Abraham*[10], had often said over his career: that to study the Scriptures with the Jews is "always interesting and often complementary."

The *ArtScroll Chumash* I use is a five-volume set — one book for each of the five books of the Torah. While reading a Torah portion straight through, might take only an hour, to go through every word of the ArtScroll commentaries meant that the Torah portion study would take at least four hours per week.

The second year I read through the Torah along with the Jewish people, I obtained a book by Sondra Baras called *Shabbat Shalom*.[11] She wrote a brief essay that can be read in just five minutes, usually tying that Torah portion to something related to biblical Zionism,[12] and the development of the heartland of Judea and Samaria.[13] Root Source also published her video lessons for each of the Torah portions available to students.

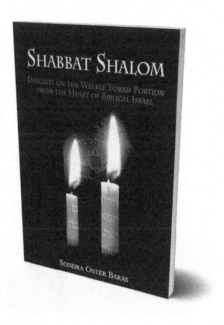

In my third year read-through, I used a jewel of a book, that was birthed and edited by Britt Lode, a Christian woman from Norway. Her book, *The Light from Zion*,[14] brings together the work of twelve rabbis, each writing on several Torah portions during the year.

This book is larger and longer than *Shabbat Shalom*, but not overly so. Most essays only take about 10-15 minutes per week.

Those writers include: Rabbi David Aaron, Rabbi Dr. Nathan Lopes Cardozo, Rabbi Levi Cooper, Rabbi Yehoshua Friedman, Rabbi Moshe Goldsmith, Rabbi Moshe D. Lichtman, Rabbi Gedalia Meyer, Rabbi Chanan Morrison, Rabbi Zelig Pliskin, Rabbi Chaim Richman, Rabbi Shlomo Riskin, Rabbi Naphtali (Tuly)

---

[10] https://amzn.to/3eGBRsW
[11] https://amzn.to/2IPqQa8
[12] Religious or biblical Zionism is the belief that God through His biblical prophets supports the return of the Jewish people to, and the development of, Israel.
[13] Sondra's well-run organization that allows Christians to fund specific projects in Judea and Samaria — e.g. security cameras and children's playgrounds — can be found at: https://www.cfoic.com/
Each project has very visible signage declaring that the funding was from Christians.
[14] http://www.lightzion.com/

Weisz, Gidon Ariel, and Rabbi Abraham Isaac Kook.

Gidon Ariel helped Britt Lode bring this book to life in 2016. Her motivation is stated in the introduction:

> *God wants our obedience and our hearts, that we walk humble [sic] with Him… So the question is who can teach us how to walk the paths today? Who can teach us everything that God has commanded us? It is a very long time since the revelation at Sinai where Moses received the commandments from God, so where can we find the knowledge and wisdom about them today? Baruch Hashem (thank God) God has organized everything very well in His Kingdom. The King Himself has entrusted the tribe of Judah, the Jews, with the very words of God. He gave them the authority and mandate to administer and take care of the law (Genesis 49:10). And He has kept the Jews alive… They did not "get lost" like the other ten tribes. They have preserved the Torah very well, not even one generation has failed in protecting and keeping the wisdom and treasures of the Torah and in passing it on to the next generation. Today's rabbis are the representatives for the Torah, the law, in our times. They are our connection to Moses and Mount Sinai.* [15]

In Conclusion

Today, my wife and I read the Torah in step with the Jewish people. We find the study of the Torah to be enriching on a number of levels.

Here are some of the things that I have noticed over the years:

- Because millions of people are reading these passages in the same week that I am reading them, I feel part of something much *larger* than myself.

- Because generations upon generations have been reading these passages every year, over time I feel part of something much *longer* than my own lifetime.

---

[15] Lode, Britt, *The Light from Zion*, (Jerusalem, Israel: Gefen Publishing House, 2017), 24.

- The detailed instructions concerning the building of the tabernacle and the service of the priesthood are starting (emphasis on *starting*) to reveal their beauty and intent.

- I am discovering just how much of the rest of the Bible is hidden in the Torah. You may have heard it said that everything in the New Testament can be found hidden in the Old Testament. But have you ever heard it said that everything in the Tanakh is found hidden in the Torah? The Torah is the seed for everything else in the Bible.

- The Hebrew Calendar is God's Calendar. I have begun to see how the work God does on the Earth is synchronized with the calendar He created. The result of my Torah study has caused me to feel much more "aligned" and less surprised with the work that God is doing on a larger scale, throughout the year.

- The Jewish people have long known that the events in the larger world in a given week are often found and explained right in that week's Torah portion. I believe that this positions them to have an attitude of expectation. Can it be presupposed and sometimes predicted?

- And finally, I've heard it said from the Jews that not only do they read the Torah each week, but the Torah reads them (collectively).[16]

All the points above boil down to a single sentence:

The annual Torah reading cycle of the Jewish people is the largest, longest-running Bible study in the entire world.

Shalom.

Asking Gidon

Gidon, where and how will a traditional Jew read or hear the Torah portion for that week?

About halfway through the weekly Shabbat morning service in the synagogue, the Torah Scroll is reverently and ceremoniously taken out of the protective Holy Ark, and brought in a procession to the reading table located in the center of the synagogue. Then a reader will chant the first "aliyah," the first

---

[16] Long before I heard that, I had heard a Christian teacher, Dr. Bill Taylor, say something similar: "We do not just read Psalms, the Psalms read us."

Cantor and Reader of a Torah Scroll in Tel Aviv Israel.

of seven readings of that week's *parasha*. At each aliyah,[17] a member of the congregation or a guest is called up to the Torah and reads along with the cantor.[18]

Have you personally seen cases where the events of that particular week in Israel, as spelled out clearly to you, make that week's Torah portion a lens by which to understand the events of that week? Do any past examples come to mind?

This happens all the time! In fact, it is the main way a congregational rabbi will come up with a topic for his sermon; he simply reads the weekly portion and a weekly newspaper, and connects the dots! For instance, the weekly reading on April 25, 2020, was the Torah portion called *Tazria/Metzora*, (one of four double-readings that happen in non-leap years.) That week we were in the midst of the COVID-19 pandemic, during which we were in various levels of quarantine, sitting alone in our homes. Our weekly reading in the Torah included an entire chapter about precautions taken for those who have a certain kind of skin disease.[19] We read in LEVITICUS 13:46: *"he shall live alone; his dwelling shall be outside the camp."* (NASB). Clearly people all over the world

---

[17] The Hebrew word "aliyah" meaning "to ascend" is used here to mean "ascend to the platform on which the Torah scroll resides, in order to read from it." It also means "to immigrate to Israel" as discussed in chapter 15.

[18] The cantor is the primary person who helps read (actually sing) the words of the prayers that are prayed.

[19] While that skin disease is widely considered to be Leprosy, that opinion, as with many things in the Jewish world, is a point of debate.

who read that verse on that week would be thinking about its relevance to COVID-19.

For those Jews who spend a lot of focus on the Torah, have you ever heard of the idea of reading the Torah portion right away, at the very beginning of the week, as a way to get a "head start" on understanding those events that might happen in the coming week?

There is a commandment that all Jews must read the weekly portion twice, and in addition read a translation of it. This is called "*Shnayeem Mikrah Ve-Echad Targum*" (twice scripture and once translated).[20] Today, when most Jews in Israel know the original Hebrew of the Bible better than any other language, especially better than the Aramaic that the original and most traditional *Targum* is written in, the fulfillment of the "translation" part is often done by reading a commentary, usually that of Rashi (Rabbi Shlomo Itzchaki), the most popular of all commentators. It is common that people will read the first Aliyah with its Rashi commentary on Sunday, then the second Aliyah with its Rashi on Monday, and so on, concluding on Friday night with the seventh Aliyah.[21] Then, on Shabbat morning, we follow along with the cantor and complete our second scripture reading.

Within the Jewish community, connections between current events and the weekly Torah portion and the Bible in general can often be found going around on Whatsapp, Facebook, or other popular social media ☺

---

[20] The Targum is an Aramaic paraphrase of the Hebrew text.
[21] Because the weekly portion can be anywhere from two to six chapters long, it is customary to break the reading into seven pieces, spread throughout the week. Even when they are read at home, not from a raised platform, the term Aliyah is still used to imply the spiritual elevation that occurs.

CHAPTER 13

Did Jesus Denounce the Torah following Sukkot?

Every year during The Feast of Tabernacles (Sukkot), thousands of Christians from around the world gather in Jerusalem, to attend the annual conference of the International Christian Embassy of Jerusalem (ICEJ). While the largest such gathering of its kind, it hardly compares to the number of Jews who gather in Israel for Sukkot, and also to visit relatives and friends.

The Jewish gathering today was hardly any different from the Jewish gathering in biblical times. Jews would flock to Jerusalem for the feast. Then, after the final feast day on the eighth day of Sukkot, Jews would leave Jerusalem in great numbers to head home. That was the moment in time that the Gospel of John records, in the last verse of chapter 7:

Everyone went to his home... JOHN 7:53

But the chapter that follows immediately begins the story of what happened in the life of Jesus, when He stayed on in Jerusalem following that very same Sukkot. It is the famous story of the woman who was caught in the act of adultery.

What does a story about adultery have to do with the relationship between Christians and Jews? It has *everything* to do with it, because this gripping story, historically, has caused many Christians to walk away from both the Torah *and* the Jewish people in one fell swoop.

We now take up the serious *problem regarding the Torah* that is raised in these verses. And along the way, we will take a crack at proposing a solution to the mystery that has long accompanied this story:

What might Jesus have written on the ground?

It is in this context that I would like to introduce you to yet another woman. In the last chapter I quoted from the words of Christian Britt Lode, the editor of

The Light from Zion. In this chapter I would like to quote from the words of Lesley Richardson,[1] a Christian friend who wrote the book, *Bible Gems from Jerusalem.*[2]

Lesley addresses, head on, the story of the adulterous woman in one of her chapters, and has a view which I have found to be both fascinating and instructive. Rather than speak about her work, I have asked her permission to quote significant portions of that chapter. After her commentary, I will make some concluding remarks.

Lesley Richardson on Jesus and the Adulterous Woman

"Chapter 8 of John's Gospel commences by relating that Jesus then returned to Jerusalem and began to teach in the Temple "early in the morning" — as the light came flooding from the eastern horizon to illuminate the new day that was dawning. Here in the Temple as He was teaching one of the most dramatic scenes recorded in the Gospels unfolded. John's account of this event is only twelve verses in length, but it became one of the best known and most loved passages of the New Testament. The story of the Woman Taken in Adultery is one of the gems of world literature. Within its small compass it is entirely flawless, and its revelation of God's mercy toward sinners as demonstrated through the words and actions of Jesus has captivated generations of readers. However, this exceptional narrative, and most especially Jesus' words, "He who is without sin among you, let him be the first to throw a stone at her," have been misunderstood in various ways. What are some of the problems to be found in many traditional explanations of the text?

"In the first place, many interpreters have viewed the passage through a moralistic lens, arguing it teaches that because all have sinned it is therefore hypocritical for any Christian to presume to pass judgment on another. As the logical consequence of this argument, it would seem that only a completely

---

[1]   You can get to know her, and hear multiple passages in her book at this shortened link to the interview on Root Source: https://bit.ly/Lesley-interview. Lesley's late husband, Canadian Dave Richardson famously wrote the pop song, *Wildflower*. Her late brother-in-law Don Richardson is well known for the book *Peace Child*.

[2]   https://amzn.to/2BlyVDL

righteous person has the right to make a decision concerning sin and guilt — which would ultimately suggest that God alone can act as judge. This is a conclusion which flies directly in the face of a great number of New Testament scriptures concerned with disciplining erring Christians. However, there are other attempts to explain the passage that are even more troubling. Many exegetes will go to great lengths to show how the story demonstrates that it was Jesus' intention to overthrow the Law. Such interpretations reveal a fundamental misunderstanding of the Old Testament regulations, which had been mediated through Moses and had governed the Israelite community for over one thousand years. That great prophet had never stated that a man needed to be perfect in order to judge adultery, or any other crime for that matter – quite obviously, the officers and judges who operated under the Old Covenant system were not without personal sin, yet were still held capable of making crucial decisions concerning justice in the community.

"When the story is read in this way it has the final and most unfortunate effect of "casting stones," as it were, at the Old Testament law, implying that the rules and commandments found therein were harsh and burdensome, and that furthermore they were administered by men who were unfeeling and judgmental. It was the Law which mandated the death of the adulteress (LEVITICUS 20:10), and thus Jesus was seen as granting her unconditional freedom and forgiveness, demonstrating in this way that with His coming, a new age of grace had dawned. And yet, while that was certainly true, the passage is not revealing that it was Jesus' intention to set aside the clear requirements of Mosaic legislation in order to show mercy. Jesus was not arguing on this occasion that adultery was not a punishable sin, nor that one needed to be perfect in order to judge anyone guilty of a transgression. In fact, in this episode of the Adulterous Woman, it can be demonstrated that Jesus not only obeyed the Mosaic Law as those present understood it, but also endorsed it completely.

"It is a remarkable picture John presents, full of the most intense human interest and pathos, which has captured the imagination of numerous artists over the centuries, and compelled them to render the scene at its most arresting moment: the Pharisees and Scribes standing on one side, their faces hard and accusing, Jesus seated over against them, and the woman in the midst. "But," the narrative continues, "Jesus stooped down, and with His finger wrote on the ground … And again He stooped down, and wrote on the ground" (JOHN 8:6b-8). Was this action on His part simply an indication that He, who knew so well what was in the hearts of men, was unwilling to continue looking upon the display of arrogance and hypocrisy on the part of the religious leaders? Or was there some particular significance in the words which He had written?

"The suggestions as to what Jesus might have written in the dust are numerous and full of ingenuity — some say He wrote the sins of the witnesses, or a pardon, others suggest it was the name of the man involved in the adultery who was noticeably absent from the scene. However, perhaps it is not so much *what* He wrote that was significant; rather, the important thing is *that* He wrote, for by this action He was surely alluding to the fact that the Ten Commandments given to Moses were inscribed on two stone tablets "written with the finger of God" (EXODUS 31:18). Regardless of what Jesus actually set down, John was indicating that He (Yeshua) was claiming to be the actual Writer of the Law. This view is reinforced by the fact that He wrote a second time, bringing to mind God's creation of the second set of tablets after the first had been destroyed.

"Nevertheless, there is an Old Testament scripture which has good claim to be the subject of Jesus' inscription in the dust. In light of Jesus' pronouncement at the just-concluded feast, it is possible to imagine that what He wrote upon the earth was the message of JEREMIAH 17:12-13:

> O LORD the Hope of Israel, all that forsake You shall be ashamed. Those who depart from Me shall be written in the dust, because they have forsaken the LORD, the fountain of living waters.

"According to this scripture, those "written in the dust" stand in profound contrast to those who have their names inscribed in the book of life (EXODUS 32:32; DANIEL 12:1). This powerful metaphor is also reminiscent of God's pronouncement to Adam and Eve in the Garden of Eden, "*Dust you are, and unto dust you shall return*" (GENESIS 3:19). It indicates with great finality the fate of those who turn away from the Source of Life.

"Yet Jesus not only knew the hearts of those making the accusation against the woman, He also knew the law of Moses and was presently fulfilling it, in their hearing and in their seeing. He then raised Himself up and made His famous pronouncement, "*He who is without sin among you, let him be the first to throw a stone at her*" (JOHN 8:7). With these words, He acknowledged the valid application of the law of Moses to the situation before Him and ratified the punishment as given in the statutes. However, He did not leave the matter there. In calling for those who carried out the sentence to be "without sin" He was alluding to another Mosaic requirement for the proposed action; namely, that witnesses to a crime should have pure and impartial hearts:

> If a malicious witness rises up against a man to accuse him of wrongdoing then both the men who have the dispute shall stand before the LORD... and if the witness is a false witness you shall do to him just as he had intended to do to his brother. DEUTERONOMY 19:16-19

"The Law made very clear that only an objective, non-malevolent witness could testify in a legal matter and Jesus, through His enunciation of the "without sin" principle, was questioning the validity of the Scribes and Pharisees as witnesses to this particular transgression.[3] He knew they were testifying against the woman not out of a blameless heart of concern for justice in Israel, nor out of zeal for the holy Name of God; rather, their intentions were so maligned that they were prepared to sacrifice another individual, one made in the image of God, in order to attain their purpose [to discredit Jesus or worse]. Moreover, the Law was clear that if the witnesses were indeed motivated by evil inclinations they were subject to the very punishment they had proposed for the adulteress. It is noticeable also that, throughout the scene, Jesus never stood up but rather was sitting: the position of *Judge*.

"As the saying of Jesus fell upon their ears, the accusers of the woman, who until that point had been so vocal, were silenced. Deeply, sharply, He pierced His words into each conscience, bringing a stunned realization of the veracity of His judgment. One by one the Pharisees walked out of the Temple area, the oldest going first, suggesting that those who were most familiar with the Scriptures recognized more swiftly their guilt under the very Mosaic Law by which they had proposed to judge the woman.

"Jesus remained on the scene, still bent over and writing, with the woman standing before him. In Augustine's words, "The two were left alone, *misera et misericordia*" — "a wretched woman and Mercy." Then Jesus straightened up and said to the adulteress, *"Woman, where are those accusers of yours? Has no one condemned you?"* This was a technical legal question, for witnesses were required before guilt could be established and a sentence passed. She answered, *"No one Lord."* And Jesus spoke to her the words which overflowed with His forgiving mercy and love, and which have comforted generations of believers: *"Neither do I condemn you; go and sin no more"* (JOHN 8:11)."[4]

Concluding Remarks

What Lesley has revealed to us is not simply a Jewish Jesus who values mercy, but a Jewish Jesus who does so within the bounds of the Torah. Jesus was not overthrowing, setting aside, or even side-stepping the Torah, nor was He inviting

---

[3] In addition, both Leviticus 20:10 and Deuteronomy 22:22 state: *"If a man be found lying with a woman married to an husband, then they shall both of them die, both the man that lay with the woman, and the woman: so shalt thou put away evil from Israel."* Since the Pharisees only brought the woman to Yeshua, putting her to death alone would have been a violation of Torah law.

[4] Richardson, Lesley Ann, *Bible Gems from Jerusalem, History and Theology in the Feasts of Israel*, (Bloomington, IN: WestBow Press, 2017), 234-39.

us to do the same. Rather, He masterfully revealed how they can be brought together, even as the Psalmist says:

> *Mercy and truth are met together; righteousness and peace have kissed each other.*
> Psalm 85:10 (KJV)

In my opinion, Lesley's words show us that **no Christian can ever denounce the Torah based on this story**. In fact, it is stories like these that even affirm the words of Jesus:

> *Do not think that I have come to abolish the Law or the Prophets; I have not come to abolish them but to fulfill them.* Matthew 5:17 (NIV)

Looking to the Next Chapter

However, what Lesley did not do in her words, nor could she have done so because the text would not allow it, is to absolve the Scribes and Pharisees who brought her to Jesus, from any sin. Indeed, many New Testament passages reveal sin in the hearts of Jewish leaders of that day. And with this reality standing right in front of us, it is time to tackle it. I believe it is an elephant in the Christian living room: a subtle, yet very real reason why so many Christians refuse to have a relationship with Jews today.

Shalom.

Asking Gidon

Gidon, the death penalty and other harsh penalties in the Torah have been suggested by many people as being antiquated. Some Christians also see such penalties as a sign of God's wrath in Old Testament times, as compared to the way God is presented in the New Testament. How do you respond when Christians raise the charge that the Torah reveals a "God of wrath"?

> Actually, traditional Judaism would *de facto* be on the side of the claimants that biblical capital punishment is antiquated.[5] Regarding the contrasting of the God of Wrath in the Old (Jewish) Testament and the God of Love in the New (Christian) Testament, that issue is too complex to be given the attention it deserves in a short answer.[6] Suffice it to say that Jews understand God as

---

[5] https://en.wikipedia.org/wiki/Capital_and_corporal_punishment_in_Judaism
[6] Here is an example of a "too short" answer which does not do the question justice, but would at least be a way to begin a conversation: God has multiple facets. He is both the God of judgment *and* the God of

being unchanging by definition, therefore such an idea is anathema. I do not personally remember ever being on the receiving end of the "charge" that Torah reveals a God of Wrath, but I assume that I would walk away because I do not like to argue with such fire and brimstone types ☺ I think that most if not all of the Christians that I am friends with are as uncomfortable with such a charge against God and His Word as I am.

The Jews have been meticulous about passing down from Sinai, not only the Hebrew Bible, but many stories and much commentary about the giving of the Torah.[7] What has been passed down about the execution of the death penalty within Israel regarding such sins as adultery, dishonoring parents, partaking in sorcery and perversion, and worship of the stars, among others? Were those laws upheld and implemented often?

A good discussion of this is in the Wikipedia article I referred to above. The classic source about this is quoted in that article, and it is worthwhile quoting it here:

> *"A Sanhedrin that puts a man to death once in seven years is called a murderous one. Rabbi Eliezer ben Azariah says, 'Or even once in 70 years.' Rabbi Tarfon and Rabbi Akiba said, 'If we had been in the Sanhedrin, no death sentence would ever have been passed'; Rabban Simeon ben Gamaliel said: 'If so, they would have multiplied murderers in Israel.'"[8]*

---

mercy, *and* they are part of His Oneness. In Hebrew, there are different names for God and they express different aspects of Him. One of our teachers, Rabbi Gedaliah Meyer has a series called "God the Jewish Image" which looks at these names.

[7] Such as Pirkei Avot chapter 1: https://bit.ly/Avot-1

[8] Mishna Makkot 1:10

CHAPTER 14

Scribes, Pharisees, and the Elephant in the Room

I remember hearing of an experiment that took a group of young adults and then randomly split them into two groups. One group was, in this experiment, to become prisoners that would live together in confinement, while the other group was to become their guards, providing for their basic necessities while ensuring that none could escape.[1] As the experiment progressed over a period of days, tensions began to flare between the two groups, and the very feelings that were typical between prisoners and prison guards began to surface. The prisoners began to feel that their treatment by the guards was not fair, and the guards watched as the prisoners' behavior regressed into actions that were "ungrateful and inappropriate." The study showed how physical separation and role separation creates a situation that is ripe for emotional separation.

It is human nature.

But in the case of the relationship between Christians and Jews, or more correctly, the *absence* of large-scale relationship between Christians and Jews, we have the very same situation. Christians and Jews have been separated physically and emotionally for centuries.

With respect to the Christian side of that separation, there is an elephant in the Christian living room, that I believe has been at the root of much

Scribes
Pharisees
+

Scribes, Pharisees, and the Elephant in the Room.

1 https://en.wikipedia.org/wiki/Stanford_prison_experiment

of that separation. An example comes from the story about a woman caught in adultery[2] (as mentioned in the previous chapter). The woman did not accidentally bump into Jesus in a small, back alley of Jerusalem. She was brought to Him by the Scribes and Pharisees as a test, putting Jesus into a seemingly no-win situation. If Jesus "let her off" then He would be charged as violating Torah. If Jesus commanded that she be killed, then He would be shown to be an extremist: harsher and crueler than anyone in Jerusalem.[3] An additional complication presented itself that day, because in fact, Jerusalem was not even self-governing, so any action taken by Jesus would have been under the full scrutiny of Rome — a sticky situation indeed!

Before we proceed to the central point of this chapter, I would like to pause to make a point about the Scribes and Pharisees in the story. In His famous response: *"He who is without sin among you, let him be the first to throw a stone at her,"*[4] not only did Jesus provide a "way out" for the woman, He provided a "way out" for the Scribes and Pharisees too. It was pointed out in the previous chapter that the older Pharisees left the gathering first, providing leadership to those younger men who might not have caught the full intent of His words. I believe that Jesus/Yeshua did not want *anyone* to be hurt, even if their motive was to entrap Him.

Now we proceed to the central point.

Christian Separation

For centuries, we and our Christian forefathers have sat in church on Sundays and heard the stories of the Bible, particularly the stories of the New Testament. And nowhere in the New Testament are there more stories than in the first five books, the four Gospels and Acts. And while the interactions Jesus had were manifold, they often included confrontations with the Scribes, the Sadducees, and especially the Pharisees. This chapter focuses solely on Jesus' recorded interactions with the Pharisees.

We Christians, while being physically separated from the Jewish people in our churches, hear stories about all kinds of interactions between Jesus and the Jewish leadership of the first century from our pastors and teachers. Dr. Marvin Wilson has said, "The problem with most seminaries today is that they teach future pastors to love the Jewish scriptures, but not the Jewish people." And so, while it may

---

[2] John 8:1-11
[3] Recall that in the last chapter, Gidon said that it was quite rare in Jewish practice to ever administer the death penalty, even though such punishment was clearly written by Moses. In chapter 34, this book will attempt to reframe the traditional view of punishment even further.
[4] John 8:7

never be stated directly from the pulpit, we are left to draw the conclusion that:

If Jesus represents all that is good, then by contrast the Scribes and Pharisees of His day represent all that is bad.

And then, by extension, we are left to fill in the vacuum in our own minds, by:

Attributing the attitudes and behavior of the Pharisees from 2,000 years ago, upon the Orthodox Jews of today.

It is a giant elephant in the room, or in the pews, or in our own living rooms, or lurking in the shadows of our minds, whenever and wherever we happen to be reading the stories.

So now what?

Seven Responses

To this situation I make seven responses.

1. First, an original rhyme:

No story has been penned in the annals of men,
more sweet than great foes who become lifelong friends.

These preconceived notions we have been taught, either inadvertently or overtly, build in us a stronghold that is ripe for the tearing down. To the very extent that one has been laden with stereotypes about the Jews, one has been made ripened to have those stereotypes overthrown. And those first true relationships that are formed can become one's sweetest relationships of all.

2. Where are those Pharisees today, anyway?

I have been to Israel over fifty times and have met hundreds and hundreds of Jews who may all disagree with my belief regarding the Messiah, but who still treat me with kindness and respect. For sure, many Jews would and should feel uncomfortable to be around a person whose "Messiah" has been the name under which their own forefathers were persecuted and even murdered. But my point is that I simply don't see the "stories of Jesus' interactions in the New Testament" being replayed in Israel today. I'm not saying it can't happen, but I am saying I've never personally seen it with my own eyes even once.[5]

---

[5] It is also incorrect to assume that the Pharisees of Jesus' day were all of one mind and outlook. This is addressed in a question to Gidon later in this chapter.

3. The proof of change is in the return.

The Jews tell us that their perception of the reason that the Second Temple was destroyed was "the improper treatment of people."[6] They see that somehow the Jews of the first century had lost sight of what it means to care for one another, and love one another. If that was the case, then I argue that the return of the Jews to the Land MUST BE PROOF that this sin has been sufficiently repented of, and rooted out of the people of Israel, to reward them with their return.[7] Am I viewing Israel with rose-colored glasses? Am I closing my eyes to the facts? No, the way that the Jewish community rallies around each other, is a sight to behold. When our gaze lifts up beyond our own churches and fellowship groups, and we look at the larger scale picture of Christian community, the love within the larger Jewish community is at a higher level of caring and intensity than the Christian community. While I didn't expect to see this, I have had to generally admit that on a large scale our "community" among Christians is not at the same level of caring as the Jews have for each other. The nation that was exiled for not being brotherly among their own, is now a world leader in modelling what it means to be brotherly among their own. And that love is beginning to extend beyond the border of Israel as well, in the form of, for instance, IDF emergency disaster relief assistance[8] (with the UN ranking the IDF emergency medical team as 'No. 1 in the world'),[9] caring for Syrian fighters in Israeli hospitals,[10] not to mention attempting to live side-by-side in peace with Arabs everywhere.[11]

4. Jesus confronted His own.

Jesus was more aligned socially and theologically with the Pharisees of the first century than any other religious group. For instance, as compared to the Sadducees, Jesus and the Pharisees would interact freely with anyone, as opposed to seeking out those with wealth, power and influence. In addition, Jesus and the Pharisees clearly believed in the resurrection, while the Sadducees did not. It would have

---

[6] More specifically "baseless hatred." The Talmud suggests the theological reason for the Temple's destruction: *"But why was the second Sanctuary destroyed, seeing that in its time they were occupying themselves with Torah, [observance of] precepts, and the practice of charity? Because therein prevailed hatred without cause."*
http://www.yashanet.com/library/temple/yoma9b.htm

[7] One Orthodox Jew, upon hearing of my opinion, was quick to add that the lack of a Third Temple standing today proves unequivocally that their repentance for "unwonted hatred" is not yet complete. However, I think that even without a Temple, the miraculous rebirth of Israel in 1948, followed by the reunification of Jerusalem in 1967, are signs from God to the whole world that the Jewish People are on the right path.

[8] Short link to article at Jewish Virtual Library: https://bit.ly/Israel-relief

[9] Short link to article at Times of Israel: https://bit.ly/IDF-medical

[10] Short link to the article on the Independent: https://bit.ly/Syrian-fighters

[11] As Chairman of the Knesset in 2006, Benjamin Netanyahu said in a speech before the country's legislature, *"If the Arabs lay down their arms there will be no more war, but if Israel lays down its weapons there would be no more Israel."* Short link to the article on The Atlantic: https://bit.ly/Arabs-arms

been natural for Jesus to spend the most time with the Pharisees. It is natural to spar more strongly in your own group, than outside of it. The Pharisees would have been His preferred subgroup.

5. Jews can criticize their own.

It has been pointed out that when it comes to criticism of the Jews in the New Testament, that such recorded criticism was always between fellow Jews. I am not aware of any record in the New Testament of a Gentile being in any way commended or encouraged to criticize the Jews. Instead we are encouraged to love and appreciate them, and to shun arrogance within us, as directed in ROMANS 11:18.[12]

6. Our Christian reaction to the separation has been to "fix" it.

I believe that much of what we have seen in past centuries regarding the kind of interaction that HAS happened between Christians and Jews, is that of attempting to fix the Jews. What I am suggesting here is that some (not all) of that underlying desire to *fix the Jews*, comes from the negative perception of the Pharisees of the first century that has been taught to us in our formative years. We have been partly trying to fix a stereotype that exists in our own minds, a stereotype that has been preserved by *lack* of relationship.

7. And lastly, is there really any "us" versus "them?"

One of the best sermons I ever heard at my church had as its summary: the attitude we should have in ourselves when relating to the world around us is:

There is no "us versus them," there is only "us."

Yes, the right way to read the stories of interaction between Jesus and the Pharisees, is to let them be a revealing of ourselves. Are there any attitudes in the hearts of any men in the first century that are not present in our hearts today? Is there anything new under the sun? Of course not.

If we need to press the world into good versus bad, with Jesus being the good, then let's be sure and put ourselves properly on the side of the "bad." The Bible says so:

Man's deeds are corrupt and loathsome; no one does good. PSALM 14:1b (TIB)

---

[12] *"...do not be arrogant toward the branches; but if you are arrogant, **remember that** it is not you who supports the root, but the root **supports** you."* Romans 11:18 (emphases mine)

And regarding Jesus being good, He is not silent on that topic either. Remember that time in which a rich young Jew came to Jesus and addressed Him as "good teacher." He responded:

"Why do you call me good?" Jesus answered. "No one is good—except God alone." Luke 18:19 (NIV)

When it came to goodness, Jesus taught us to look up. In the world of Jewish-Christian relations, I'd have to say that…things are indeed *looking up.*

And with regard to Christians throwing stones at the Pharisees of the first century or at the religious Jews of today, perhaps the words of Jesus can still be applied:

"Let that Christian who is without sin among us be the one to cast the first stone." John 8:7b *(paraphrased by author)*

Shalom.

Asking Gidon

Gidon, how do you react to this essay? Did you even know that the stories of interactions with Pharisees in the New Testament can affect the way in which you are viewed by Christians?

It seems to be a very sensible thesis. For Jews, it is a given that what is shared behind closed church doors is often and probably not "good for the Jews." This is probably less the case in modern "feel good" churches, but was, more often than not, the catalyst for historical pogroms in Christian Europe.

The interactions by Jesus with the Pharisees are read as being monolithic in nature, that is that all Pharisees are similar. Tell us about the two schools of Pharisee in the first century, and tell us which school you would have been drawn to personally, if you had lived in the period of the Second Temple.

I believe you are talking about the schools of Bet Shammai and Bet Hillel. I recommend the Wikipedia article[13] that discusses this concept comprehensively. Regarding the assumption of monolithic anything about Jews, the well-known phrase "two Jews, three opinions" comes to mind. Not only did Bet Hillel and Bet Shammai argue hundreds of recorded times in the Talmud,

---

[13] https://en.wikipedia.org/wiki/Houses_of_Hillel_and_Shammai

there is barely a page in the Talmud without a debate. In fact, that foundational encyclopedic work is arguably first and foremost a record of arguments! There are close to one thousand sages quoted in the Talmud, and each is usually mentioned when they are debating someone else. It's hard for me to commit to what I would do if I had been living in the Second Temple period. It's easy to say I would side with Bet Hillel, as they emerged the winners usually. But truthfully, I prefer to make my decisions only after hearing each side present their case, not merely hearing both sides. So you'll have to wait for my answer after I get back from a spin in a time machine.

CHAPTER 15

Playing Aliyah Chess with God

In Hebrew, the word for "to ascend" is *aliyah*. The word can be used as meaning "to go up to Jerusalem" but it is more commonly used in the sense of political Zionism, a movement fathered by Theodor Herzl in the late 1800s, as meaning "to go up to Zion," which is to say, to move to Israel permanently. Therefore, when Jews immigrate to Israel they are said to "make aliyah."

Biblically and culturally, an Israeli never says that they plan to "go down to Jerusalem," even if they live north of Jerusalem. Neither do they say they go down to Jerusalem if they live at a higher elevation than Jerusalem. For there is no such thing as going down to Jerusalem. Being the footstool of the throne of God, Jerusalem is a place to which humans can only ascend.

One of the most famous uses of the word aliyah is in Psalms:

Who may ascend into the hill of the LORD? And who may stand in His holy place?
PSALM 24:3

The word ascend here is *aliyah,* and in the next verse we are encouraged not to go to Jerusalem casually or flippantly:

He who has clean hands and a pure heart, who has not lifted up his soul to falsehood and has not sworn deceitfully. PSALM 24:4

Whose Destination is it?

Indeed the word aliyah is something that people take personally. The *destination* is Israel, or Zion, or Jerusalem, and *one who travels* to that destination is you or me.

But have you ever considered that *the one who travels* to that destination might be God Himself?

For the Lord has chosen Zion; He has desired it for His dwelling place. Psalm 132:13 (KJV)

Orthodox Jew AnaRina (Heymann) Kreisman has turned this simple but powerful idea into an entire ministry called *Align with Zion.*[1] Her idea: if Jews and non-Jews alike were to see Jerusalem not just as the capital of Israel, not just as the center of the biblical world, but also as *the object and desire of God Himself*, then *we will treat her differently*. The "her" is not AnaRina, but Jerusalem, because all cities in the Hebrew language are of the female gender! To *treat her differently* then is to spiritually align ourselves towards Jerusalem, as a physical embodiment of God's desire.[2] Suddenly, "praying for the peace (shalom) of Jerusalem" changes for us. It is no longer just praying for *a place of importance*; it becomes aligning oneself with the very innermost desires of the very heart of God!

AnaRina, who made aliyah from South Africa, grew up praying northward, facing north towards Jerusalem. Today she brings this message of *alignment*, especially to non-Jews. While there is no New Testament verse that asks Christians to face any particular direction when praying, Daniel opened his windows towards Jerusalem and prayed three times a day from Babylon.[3] Today, some Christians find it meaningful to follow in the footsteps of that great prophet Daniel and *align with Zion physically* during their prayers as well. In retrospect I would have to say that I *have* had some important encounters with God while facing east from my home in Austin. And I definitely gaze to the east when I'm thinking about my next upcoming travel, my next *aliyah* to Jerusalem.

An Ascent

One very memorable aliyah I made to Jerusalem actually started from inside Israel. It began at the Aliyah Return Center, south of the Sea of Galilee, shown on the map.

From there, I traveled to Jerusalem by car. My journey to Jerusalem that day, *my aliyah*, actually began more than 600 feet below sea level, since it began near the shores of the Sea of Galilee! From my starting point, the only direction that a person can go *lower still*, is to travel southward down the Jordan River valley. There one eventually reaches the Dead Sea, the lowest point on earth, about 1,400 feet below sea level. Then one makes a sharp right-hand turn, and begins to ascend

---

[1] www.alignwithzion.com
[2] Gidon and I once joined AnaRina's tour of the City of David, and heard her explain her vision for Jerusalem in that context. See guided tour at this short link: https://bit.ly/David-tour-1
[3] Daniel 6:10 is not only the basis for facing Jerusalem, it is the reason why Orthodox Jews pray three times a day.

quickly almost 4,000 feet to reach Jerusalem which is about 2,500 feet above sea level.

The Aliyah Return Center, a ministry originally founded in Canada, helps to acclimate North American Jews who are "making aliyah" to Israel.[4]

While there, I learned something in the Aliyah Return Center presentation room, a room which has been repurposed from its original use as a kibbutz bomb shelter. Sitting on a table by the exit door was a one-page document published by Galilee Calendars,[5] which sells products for Christians. That sheet came from their "Up to Zion" Calendar.[6]

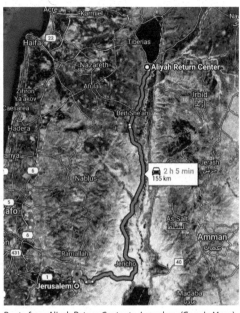

Route from Aliyah Return Center to Jerusalem. (Google Maps).

On this sheet is the best presentation of scriptures on aliyah that I have ever seen, and from that sheet I have captured its table, below.

THE 64 "ALIYAH" SCRIPTURES

1. Deuteronomy 30:1–6	17. Isaiah 49:18–23	33. Jeremiah 30:18	49. Ezekiel 34:11–16
2. 2 Chronicles 30:6–9	18. Isaiah 51:11	34. Jeremiah 31:8–9	50. Ezekiel 36:7–12
3. Nehemiah 1:4–9	19. Isaiah 52:7–12 (NKJV)	35. Jeremiah 31:10–14	51. Ezekiel 36:22–38
4. Psalms 14:7	20. Isaiah 56:8	36. Jeremiah 31:16–21	52. Ezekiel 37:1–14
5. Psalms 53:6	21. Isaiah 60:4–5	37. Jeremiah 31:23–24	53. Ezekiel 37:15–28
6. Psalms 106:44–48	22. Isaiah 60:8–9	38. Jeremiah 32:37–41	54. Ezekiel 38:7–9
7. Psalms 107:1–3	23. Isaiah 66:18–22	39. Jeremiah 32:42–44	55. Ezekiel 39:25–29
8. Psalms 126:1–6	24. Jeremiah 3:14–18	40. Jeremiah 33:4–9	56. Hosea 11:10–11
9. Psalms 147:1–2	25. Jeremiah 12:14–15	41. Jeremiah 33:10–13	57. Joel 2:28--3:2
10. Isaiah 11:10–12	26. Jeremiah 16:14–16	42. Jeremiah 33:23–26	58. Amos 9:13–15
11. Isaiah 14:1–2	27. Jeremiah 23:1–4	43. Jeremiah 46:27–28	59. Obadiah 17:21
12. Isaiah 27:12–13	28. Jeremiah 23:5–8	44. Jeremiah 50:4–5	60. Micah 2:12–13
13. Isaiah 35:10	29. Jeremiah 24:4–7	45. Jeremiah 50:17–20	61. Micah 4:6–10
14. Isaiah 41:8–10	30. Jeremiah 29:10–14	46. Ezekiel 11:14–20	62. Zephaniah 3:17–20
15. Isaiah 43:5–6	31. Jeremiah 30:1–3	47. Ezekiel 20:40–44	63. Zechariah 8:7–8
16. Isaiah 49:8–13	32. Jeremiah 30:4–11	48. Ezekiel 28:25–26	64. Zechariah 10:6–12

Sixty-four scriptures on aliyah.

4 https://www.aliyahreturncenter.com/
5 https://www.galileecalendarcompany.com/
6 Document is available for download at this short link: https://bit.ly/aliyah-64

Did you know that there are at least **sixty-four scriptures** in the Tanakh that detail the promised return of the people of Israel to the land of Israel? Is that not an amazing list of scriptures? That is quite a challenge to those who deny the validity of Jewish Zionism.[7]

The original calendar cites a few other interesting facts:

- The spiritual restoration of the Jewish people is stated **sixteen times** in the Old Testament (Tanakh).

- The pouring out of God's Spirit on Israel and on the nations is stated **three times** in the Tanakh.

- The theme of a worldwide spiritual awakening is stated **seven times** in the Old and New Testaments combined.

But, the most impressive point of all to me is simply this: **God promises the return of His people to the land sixty-four times!**

Sixty-four is eight-by-eight, which is also the size of a chess board.

Chess Board.

---

[7] The Bible contains many promises about the restoration of the Northern Kingdom of Israel, often referred to in Scripture as "the House of Israel," as differentiated from the Southern Kingdom, often referred to in Scripture as "the House of Judah." An explanation of those distinctions has strong merit, but goes beyond the scope of this book. Many strongly entrenched positions are held. My own approach has been to look for the beauty and glory and majesty in God's providential plans to both separate and reunite people groups for His purposes. For more on that, see my chapter 12 in *One in Messiah, Perspectives on Commonwealth Theology Presented at the Denver Convocation 2019*, pp. 307-350, available on Amazon: https://amzn.to/2AxDVEN

With sixty-four different passages in the Bible speaking of aliyah, it is as if God has placed an aliyah chess piece on every square of the Cosmic chess board.

Kings and kingdoms may try to play Aliyah Chess with God. They may tell themselves that God does not exist (atheists), or that if He exists He does not care (humanists), or that He used to care but has since moved on (Replacement Theology adherents), or that He always cared, but He just never cared for Jacob! But in reality, no man, no woman, no power of death and hell, has any chance to separate God's people from His love, and His plan to return His people to His land.

When it comes to Aliyah Chess, God has already won the game because He has a piece on every square.[8]

Shalom.

Asking Gidon

Gidon, the first scripture I quoted using the word *aliyah* was: *Who may ascend into the hill of the Lord?* What does the "hill of the Lord" mean to you?

While there is room to understand the phrase "hill of the Lord" as [all of] Jerusalem, it is usually understood as the Temple Mount.

Do Jews speak of these various aliyah scriptures often in Israel? Are such scriptures considered famous because many of them are being fulfilled in our lifetime?

Some of these scriptures are quoted in ceremonies, like on Independence Day. And from time to time something will happen that will have a few hours of headlines, like a freak rainstorm, and someone will find a verse in the week's Prophets reading (the Haftarah) that seems to hint to that, and that verse will gain traction on social media for a while. But I think that the Jewish People are LIVING the aliyah verses every minute of the day, so we don't "have to" quote them all the time.

I think that there are a lot of "lucky" verses as I call them, that are better known than others, many in the Pentateuch and the Haftarot (as they are read publicly every year), and many in the Psalms (as they are read in prayers, some

---

[8] Various counts exist. Depending on how you count, it can be well into the hundreds. *Let my People Go!*, by Tom Hess, lists 700 related promises: https://amzn.to/3gLxbUr

even daily). I personally know a lot of these aliyah verses because they are in fact beautiful examples of God fulfilling His promises, and I loved focusing on them in my studies in *yeshiva* and in my time as a member of the Bnei Akiva Religious Zionist youth movement.

Very soon the number of Jews in Israel will exceed 50 percent of the Jews in the entire world. When did you personally "make aliyah," and from where? Did you feel you were fulfilling prophecy when you did it?

I "made aliyah" in 1978 when I was fourteen years old from New York. I don't know how strongly I felt that I was fulfilling prophecy at that point, but in a small part I unquestionably was.

Millions of Jews still live outside of Israel. Jewish immigration rates have dropped to a small fraction of the rates of the 1990s when up to 100,000 Russian Jews immigrated per year.[9] Given that all Jews have a "right of return" to Israel, and an open invitation from Israel to immigrate, yet very few are "making aliyah," if you could send a message to every such Jew in the world of three sentences or less, what would you want to say to them?

I'll do that in three sentences or less — in one word even: Come!

---

[9] https://en.wikipedia.org/wiki/1990s_post-Soviet_aliyah

CHAPTER 16

Hearing the Sound of Aliyah

I n the heart of the Jewish quarter in the Old City of Jerusalem is Hurva Square. Facing that square is a little Jewish shop that has been visited by many hundreds of thousands of Christians over the years called *The Shorashim Shop*.[1] The smiling, warm-hearted owner, Orthodox Jew Moshe Kempinski, loves to converse with Christians. If you ask him when he made aliyah to Israel, he will begin with a sound he heard over the radio while living in Canada: the first shofar to sound out at the Western Wall on June 7, 1967, the day Israel recaptured the Old City of Jerusalem in the Six-Day War. I would contend that in that sound, Moshe Kempinski *heard the sound of aliyah.*

But we also learned in the last chapter that *aliyah* happens *every time* we travel to Jerusalem, because Jerusalem is always *a place you ascend* to reach. Therefore, my meeting Gidon on the walls of the Old City Jerusalem, and hearing in my inner ear, "That's your man!" was in a very real sense the *result* of an aliyah. Furthermore, if, as we say in Christian lingo, that my meeting Gidon was part of "God's *call* on my life to travel there," then I suppose it is not too much of a stretch to say that meeting Gidon resulted from "*hearing* the sound of *aliyah.*"

This chapter tells the story of how I "heard the sound of aliyah" and found myself in Jerusalem in January 2014, perfectly positioned to meet Gidon and hear his novel idea that became Root Source. Who might play a key role in that aliyah? As with all things God does, and as we already learned, that key birthing role would be carried out by a woman.[2]

My work with Israel from 1988 through 2012 was primarily in the high-tech field, where at the time non-Orthodox Jews outnumbered the Orthodox by about

---

[1] http://www.shorashimshop.com/
[2] The topic of chapter 4.

ten to one. I had no great interest in spending time with Orthodox Jews until I had that powerful encounter with God on July 16, 2013, the 9th day of Av.

Briefly, here is what happened. After reading history and realizing that as Christians we had broken all Ten Commandments against the Jews, I sat down on the 9th of Av to sort and organize the hundreds of Jewish persecution events I had collected in my research. My idea: show respect for the greatest day of Jewish tragedy and mourning by spending exactly one minute considering each event, putting myself into the situation if possible. But, when I sorted my sheet, I realized there were 500 persecution events! This exercise would take eight hours! Starting promptly at 8AM, by the early afternoon, having reached only the 13th century, I was undone by the horror of what I had seen and was physically unable to continue, never even reaching the worst events in the list. **It was a lifetime turning point.** A response was needed, but it would take weeks and even months during 2013 to plan a meaningful one.

Prior to that point, my primary Christian interest beyond regular church activities was in missions. I knew numerous missionaries and missions experts and analysts. I was the kind of person who could quote to you how many thousands of people groups around the world had fewer than 1 percent of their population who had accepted Jesus. Even before 9/11 happened in 2001, but especially afterwards, I was particularly interested in seeing Muslims reached for Jesus. Already having a fondness for Israel and having at least a basic understanding of the Palestinian issues, I had already reached the conclusion that if there were more Muslims who would respect and honor Jesus, then besides all the other benefits, such a move could help foster better relationships between Muslim people groups and the state of Israel.

In 2011, I joined with my good friend at church, Frank Costenbader, to track some of the emerging trends we had heard about, that were causing more and more Muslims to begin to see Jesus as more than just a prophet in the Koran, but truly the Son of God. The most exciting emerging trend we examined was *Isa Dreams*,[3] the dreams that many Muslims were having of Jesus. While no two dreams were exactly identical, one common pattern was a person having an unforgettable dream, or vision, where a shining man, in glowing white garments appears to them in the night, who may or may not speak, but if he speaks he says something such as, "I am Isa. I am the way to God (Allah)." Interestingly this figure never compared himself to the prophet Mohammed or denounced Mohammed, he just presented *Himself*.[4] The feelings of warmth and safety and peace in the midst

---

[3] Isadreams.org
[4] Notably absent in the reports were cases that the prophet Mohammed was reported appearing in

of those dreams were so strong that many (but not all) Muslims who had these dreams began to discreetly seek out more understanding. Search engine results from Muslim countries for search terms like "Isa al masah" (Jesus the Messiah in Arabic) were growing rapidly we learned.

Anecdotal evidence from missionaries in Muslim-dominated countries was so amazing and consistent that it seemed like God was up to something. One team in Indonesia we talked to had sent people into the deep jungles and simply asked people (in the local language) if they had had any unforgettable dreams. One leader told us that in their efforts over several weeks, one out of every twenty such persons had had such a dream, or at least knew someone close to them who had.[5]

But anecdotal reporting of dreams is not nearly enough evidence to show that Muslims were actually accepting Jesus as savior. Christian missiologists needed to be able to track something more tangible than just *interest* or *inquiry*. One of them, David Garrison, who wrote *Wind in the House of Islam*[6] and is well-known for his analysis of the Muslim world, used the metric of baptisms, and specifically looked to measure "Muslim movements for Christ." In his research he defined a Muslim "movement" as one thousand baptisms within twenty years in a given location. His research had uncovered a fascinating pattern.

Between 610 CE (when Islam began) through 1800, there were zero Muslim movements for Christ around the world. By 1900 there were three. By 2000 there were twenty-five. And since 2000, they have been taking off all over the world, with hundreds of movements already after the first decade of the 2000s. Frank and I had noticed that the reports of Isa Dreams happening in these countries *were also rising fast* in the same time frame these movements were happening. We decided in 2013 that a conference should be convened in Dallas, Texas to look at the evidence. We would bring together those who were studying Isa Dreams, to see what more we could all learn together.

At that point, five authors had written books about Isa Dreams, including David Garrison, whose book was in pre-release. We invited all five authors to the conference and all five accepted our invitation into the first-ever conference held specifically on the topic of "Isa Dreams." Besides the opportunity to share research, we also put together a declaration for attendees to sign, if they were willing, saying that the Church should wake up, and start seeing God's love for

---

nighttime dreams; only Jesus was appearing.

[5] While the number of Muslims (including Muslims residing in America) having these dreams was high, enough to reach into the millions worldwide, we found almost zero evidence of such dreams occurring among Jews. The disparity is striking, real, and consistent. It just isn't happening.

[6] https://amzn.to/2ApAgsN

Isa Dreams Conference.

Muslims as evidenced by His work to reach them in the most remote locations through dreams.

As part of that conference, and as one of the conference organizers, I took the opportunity to present a paper on a topic of interest to me: Early Isa Dreams. I was interested in the question of whether the earliest Muslim movements to Christ had been perhaps triggered by "Isa Dreams." The answer turned out to be YES!

My research on the Christian history of Indonesia showed that the first *recorded* "Isa Dream" anywhere in the world by a Muslim was in 1843, a dream which started a chain of events on the Indonesian Island of Java that resulted in the first Muslim movement to Christ being known to exist by 1883. The movement in Indonesia had been already happening for about ten years prior, but it took until 1883 for the news to *reach the ears* of the Christian world.[7]

As I presented my paper, sitting in the audience were the five authors of the five books on Isa Dreams. One of these authors, the first person to ever write a book on Isa Dreams, was Christine Darg and her husband Peter. She wrote her book, *Miracles Among Muslims*, first in 1999 and then revised it in 2005.[8] This was the same Christine Darg that Gidon called a "mighty woman of God" in the Prologue. She was the woman with whom he had built a good relationship, and who had

---

[7] The Dutch Reformed Church discovered it, having been working in that region for years. The movement escaped detection because it was led by the Indonesians themselves rather than workers officially sanctioned by the church. As such it was not only the first missional movement among Muslims, but the first indigenous one as well.

[8] https://amzn.to/3cnzc6a

been inviting Gidon to speak at her Jerusalem convocations, which were held several times each year.

I had never met Christine before the Isa Dreams conference. And yet, in the next few minutes on the stage, I was going to say something that affected her so deeply, that she was going to rush up to me with her husband, and throw all caution to the wind and say, "Home run!! Would you please come speak at our Conference in January 2014!?" Upon hearing that I was speechless. She had no knowledge that I already had a strong desire to go to Israel — to Jerusalem — and look for ways to be a blessing to Orthodox Jews. Here I was at an Isa Dreams conference regarding Muslims! The last thing I expected to receive at this event was an invitation to Jerusalem!

So it was in her invitation to Jerusalem that I was *hearing the sound of aliyah*. Once in Jerusalem, I met Gidon. He has already told his version of that story in the Prologue; I shall tell mine in chapter 30.

So what could I have possibly said that could have caused her and her husband Peter to throw caution to the wind and invite an unknown like me, right there on the spot, to speak at their next Jerusalem conference?

Hearing The Sound of Aliyah

It was because I told the room something that nobody there had ever heard, or had even considered in their wildest dreams: I made a connection between the First Movement of Muslims to Christ in Indonesia becoming known in 1883, to the First Aliyah of the Russian Jews to the Holy Land, also becoming known in 1883![9]

How did I do it?

First I took the audience to the valley of dry bones prophecy in EZEKIEL 37:7 and read for the audience:

> So I prophesied as I was commanded; and as I prophesied there was a noise [Heb: "qol" for thunder] and behold a rattling [Heb: "raash", for earthquake]; and the bones came together, bone to its bone. EZEKIEL 37:7

After pointing out the Hebrew words for thunder and earthquake, I asked the audience, "Can anybody right now tell me what was the loudest sound that has

---

ever been recorded in human history?"

The room was silent.

"Speak it out please! Does anybody know?" I asked.

Then somebody in the back said:

"Krakatoa?"

"Yes!" I said, "It was the Krakatoa volcano!"

Then I told them that the Krakatoa explosion on August 27, 1883 was a mere 100 miles from the first movement of Muslims to Christ on the island of Java. The sound and shaking must have been terrifying there, because those who were closer would have had their eardrums ruptured instantly! As a testament to how loud that sound was, that deafening "pow" reached the island of Rodigues near Mauritius 3,000 miles away, where residents reported hearing "cannons firing offshore" in the direction of the volcano. No ships were in sight. Unbelievably, pressure waves circled the world seven times over the next five days. Barographs, which were recently invented, would record these pressure waves as they circled the world. Tsunamis from that event reached every continent in the world. And the skies around the world would be somewhat darkened for the next five years![10]

After destroying itself in the eruption of 1883, a new peak of Krakatoa is rising above the sea, twenty-five miles east of Java, Indonesia.[11]

---

[10] https://en.wikipedia.org/wiki/1883_eruption_of_Krakatoa
[11] Image attributions for all photos and graphics may be found at the end of the book.

At the conclusion of my conference presentation I proposed that the Krakatoa explosion could have been part of the fulfillment of Ezekiel 37, heralding the return of the Jews as well as the awakening of Muslims to Jesus.[12] Regarding the Jews, I would learn later that the Valley of Dry Bones verses were already considered by some Jews to have been fulfilled in the story of the rebirth of Israel out of the horrors of the Holocaust of WWII. Those Ezekiel 37 verses even today crown the main entrance into Yad Vashem, the Holocaust museum in Jerusalem. And regarding the Muslims, that first movement among Muslims in Indonesia had already crossed the 1,000 baptism metric by 1883, reaching 3,000, and would grow to 15,000 by 1920.

The Krakatoa part of my presentation in the fall of 2013 *was the reason* Christine Darg birthed the idea to invite me to speak at that upcoming January conference in Jerusalem. She told me that, in her experience, Christians who work in Muslim missions often take on the adverse attitudes of the Muslims that they work with and side against Israel. In her mind, the fact that I saw the word of God as important to both people groups *simultaneously*, was a breath of fresh air. I would speak on Monday January 6, 2014, and would meet Gidon the very next day. Over time I would become a regular contributor to their future conferences.

I believe that God sent a message to the whole world in 1883 that something was happening. It was the beginning of the first wave of aliyah that would eventually culminate in the rebirth of Israel in 1948. A verse can have multiple fulfilments. I think it is "just like God" to fulfill his scriptures in multiple ways, including its literal fulfillment. We will propose yet another fulfillment of this verse in chapter 24, but for now, let us simply stand in awe at the idea that something as important as the rebirth of Israel should begin with the loudest sound in recorded history.

Our God does not do anything second-rate!

In the last chapter we said how foolish it would be to play "Aliyah Chess with God." In this chapter we conclude by saying that "Hearing the Sound of Aliyah" is not going to be difficult at all — as long as God is the one doing the talking. Just ask Moshe Kempinski of the Shorashim Shop.

Shalom.

---

[12] Note that this was the first of many Muslim movements yet to be recorded.

Asking Gidon

Gidon, in the Arabic world, very strong emphasis and importance is placed on dreams, and the desire to interpret them. Are they at all important among Orthodox Jews?

Interesting question. Of course, the Hebrew Bible is quite full of dreams, and the Talmud relates to dreams a lot as well. But I am not familiar with any Jewish community today that assigns any importance to dreams at all. I would say the interpretation of dreams in Judaism is rare.

Yad Vashem cites the Ezekiel 37 passage, the Valley of Dry Bones prophecy, at its entrance. Is this connection well-known and well-accepted among Orthodox Jews in Israel?

I don't know if surveys asking this question are conducted frequently, but to me it is pretty obvious. The Hebrew Wikipedia article about the Vision of the Dry Bones (much more expanded than the English article) has a whole subsection about how it is perceived in Zionism, and I remember the Chief Chaplain of the IDF always quoting it at Holocaust Day and especially Independence Day ceremonies. Here is a cool photo essay I found: root-source.com/drybones/

In this chapter I raised the idea of the Krakatoa volcano eruption being a sign from God that the return of the Jewish people to Israel was finally starting! What do you think about that idea?

Explosive! Seriously, until you discussed it with me, I had never heard of this Krakatoa volcano, and it seems that no one save one other person in the room when you referred to it during your lecture did either… I don't think that every noticeable occurring phenomenon is a requirement for the fulfilment of a prophetic divine occurrence, and certainly isn't a proof. But it can be cool, and introduces the possibility that there are millions — infinite! — things that God placed in the universe that are part of His exquisite puzzle, that may one day be discovered by man, and yet may never be.

CHAPTER 17

The "Evil Speech" Speech

The last two chapters have talked about *aliyah*, that is, getting to Jerusalem. This one discusses something very practical and important that I learned from God once I arrived there.

I prefer talking about good things. But, there comes a time when we must allow the light of God to shine on those places that are not good and right, where we are missing the mark, and expose them. I am speaking about myself.

Rest assured that we will not "go negative" for the rest of this book — we have many beautiful topics to discuss. But I need to share with you a weight that I carry. You can be the judge of whether that which I carry is my own opinion, or is also from the heart of God.

Talking about the Negative

Have you ever noticed that it is extremely difficult to talk about negative things, and not stumble in the process? In fact, the variety of ways in which one can stumble in such a case is itself quite large. And so it is with the feeling of stepping up to the edge of a cliff, that I make a few opening remarks on the topic of *negativity*.

The world today seems to be handing out PhDs right and left on negativity. Public figures seem to compete for the title of how vicious they can be to each other. Yet the ranks of *public figures* are small compared to the rest of us. Compared to such people, most of us are simply floating on the ocean of communication and thought while public figures cast giant boulders at each other from afar. Each boulder then slams down into the water near their opponents, while the rest of us are rocked by the waves of their monumental bombardments.

But if we look carefully, we should be able to find a smaller body of water, perhaps a lake or maybe even a little pond where *we* become the *public figures*. We may not be players in our local government, but when it comes to our churches, our congregations, and certainly our homes, we become those public figures.

Gidon's "Evil Speech" Speech

With that image in mind, I would like to tell you about my early days with Gidon Ariel. We were discussing the possibilities for what Root Source might become, and what problems Root Source might solve. In the end we decided that the first course that needed to be taught — with Gidon as our first teacher — was going to be on prayer. We ended up calling it *Pray Like a Jew*.[1] But that was *not* the first idea that ever bubbled to the surface. The *first idea* was about "evil speech." Here's how it happened.

While I don't remember precisely what sparked the conversation, I remember almost exactly where we were — driving in the neighborhoods of Jerusalem — when Gidon first gave me the "evil speech" speech. I suppose that I was doing my "marketing thing" and trying to consider how certain people would react to the *idea* that would become Root Source. Did I ask Gidon a question about somebody he knew? Did I begin to tell Gidon a story about somebody I knew? I don't know, but what I remember is that he told me that in Judaism, they are *taught not to speak evil* about others.

I was stunned.

Gidon went on to explain that the term **lashon hara** (literally "evil tongue") is considered to be a very serious sin in Jewish tradition. He said it is fine to speak positively about a person, but especially when a person is out of the room, one must not speak in a derogatory way about them.

I remember asking: "Then how do you communicate the truth about a situation, if you cannot say anything negative about them?"

I'll reveal his answer in a moment. But first, let me quote the passage that Gidon explained to me concerning the sin of **lashon hara** and why it is so memorable to the Jewish people.

> *Miriam and Aharon spoke against Moshe because of the Cushite woman he had married: "He married a Cushite woman!"* NUMBERS 12:1 (TIB)
>
> *As the cloud withdrew from the Tent, there was Miriam stricken with snow-white*

---

scales! When Aharon turned toward Miriam, he saw that she was stricken with scales. NUMBERS 12:10 (TIB)

Miriam was one of the most important persons in the ranks of Israel. Without her, Moses would never have become the son of the princess of Egypt. Miriam was a prophetess herself. She was a leader of the people. She is legendary for singing a song to the people after the crossing of the Red Sea:

And Miriam chanted for them: Sing to Hashem, for He has triumphed gloriously; Horse and driver He has hurled into the sea. EXODUS 15:21 (TIB)

And yet a person of her stature was massively humbled in the sight of God and all the people because of what she said about her brother. As Gidon began to tell me about these things, I began to have two significant thoughts.

First, what he described was *way, way* different from what I saw happening in the Church. We who "know" that we are not supposed to gossip, have defined that sin so narrowly that we have been tearing each other down almost constantly in the vein of simply "relating the facts."

Second, I realized that this is a very good example of "the fear of the Lord" in operation; the good kind of fear. If Jewish schoolchildren are taught that the sin of evil speech can result in disease of the skin, that can be a very strong deterrent.

That's when I said to Gidon:

"I think this is the first teaching you should give on Root Source."

In the end, we decided to go in a positive route and just look at the whole topic of prayer. But I never forgot the power of the contrast I was seeing between the practice of the Jewish world and the Christian world as I know it.

Bob's "Evil Speech" Speech

We are killing each other with our words today. Our culture in America has become divisive and vicious. If that's true, then according to the New Testament:

For the time has come that judgment must begin at the house of God: and if it first begin at us, what shall the end be of them that obey not the gospel of God? 1 PETER 4:17 (KJV)

In the Christian world, we are hurting each other with our words today as well. We are not standing out from the culture as much as we should. If the culture is at fault, we cannot claim that as an excuse. God will not withhold judgment from the house of God before He judges the larger cultural problem.

If God would grant me one request — one answered prayer, one sin to fix in the Church, one area of life in which I could pray that we can raise our standard to the level of Jewish teaching around the world — I think my request would be that we would be rid of the sin of evil speech. Why?

Because it prevents growth in every other area. The "speaking against" our brothers and sisters not only tears them down (whether they hear it or not), it tears us down in the very same moment. It is a double destruction. And it holds back the *blessing* that God would otherwise desire to give. Actually, Gidon adds that the Talmud Arachin 15b[2] says that evil speech is a triple destruction. It kills three: the one who says it, the one who is spoken about, and the one who hears it!

I wonder how much skin disease, physical and emotional irritation and related factors that we observe in our friends and family and ourselves, might not be a result of evil speech.

And so, as we embark on a discussion of things that are not right in the house of God, I also carry the responsibility to do so without engaging in evil speech.

Gidon Answers my Question

I promised you an answer to the question I asked Gidon:

> "Then how do you communicate the truth about a situation, if you cannot say anything negative about a person?"

I don't even remember how Gidon answered that question in the car. But I suppose that I don't remember it because his answer wasn't highly satisfying *at the time*. Yet I got my answer over time while working with him daily, and by watching him walk it out in his life.

Now before I reveal this answer, please remember two things. First, this is my first attempt to describe in words what has been inculcated in me over these years. I'm probably not going to do it justice. Second, even as Gidon's words in the car could not adequately describe the answer, neither will *my words* adequately describe the answer. Now with those caveats, here is what I learned.

- Gidon doesn't make sweeping generalizations about people. He doesn't categorize them or label them, unless it is positive.

---

[2] https://bit.ly/Arakhin15b

- He treats a negative situation as having a lack of the positive. For example, he might have said in the early days of Root Source: "I just don't think they are going to be able to make time to meet with us right now."

- When it is absolutely essential to describe a characteristic that is lacking (it's actually quite rare that this is essential), it is described in the kindest way possible, or from the standpoint of the difficult situation from which they have come.

- Gidon refers to the future optimistically. Nobody is ever written off, ever! "Let's give it some time and then we will try again," is something I can hear him say.

- He puts the best face on something that is lacking. Is he just a positive person? No, I really think it is more than that. I think it is a decision.

On my part, I have learned that my role in such a situation is:

- Remember that **not every question that comes into my head needs to be asked out loud**. Have you ever considered this in your dealings with other people? Evil speech often comes as a result of **the answering of a question**. I know that in many, many cases Gidon *could* say more about a given situation. But do I really *need* to know? What if I ask him a question that were to touch on some inner frustration he carries? Is such a question building up God's kingdom?

- It really comes down to *trust*. Can I trust that Gidon's perspective on a situation, for instance regarding the Jewish world, is sufficient?

And likewise, when the situation is reversed and involves the Christian world, Gidon allows me to characterize a situation in a way that is respectful to the Christian world. He does not press me for intimate details, except when the situation is all-positive! He loves a detailed story with a beautiful ending!

In speaking these kind words about Gidon's character, I suppose if you are like me, you might be wondering: Is Gidon the norm in the Jewish world, or is Gidon somehow "better than average" in this matter of **lashon hara**?

If I asked Gidon that question, my guess is that his answer would be what I heard him say on camera once: "I'm inspired by the positivity of my friend Yehudah Glick, a man who has made a career out of making a decision to never say anything negative about anybody."

In other words, Gidon's kind deflection to my question would carry within it the real answer that was needed: "Is that even the right question to be asking?"

Shalom.

Comment to Gidon

Gidon, while I can think of many questions, given my own advice to think carefully about what questions I ask, I am going to simply make a positive comment instead. When this chapter was first published online in the form of a blog post, many Christians either commented, or told me privately, that it impacted them deeply in their own lives. For this and for all of us, I would just like to say "Thank You" for living this out in the way that you do.

Aww shucks 😊

CHAPTER 18

Unoffendable

In the last chapter we dealt with a topic which is a real problem in the Church. In this chapter we take up a topic that is also a problem in both the Church and the rest of the world.

Offense!

Offense and its consequences are endemic to the human condition, but in this chapter I will choose to limit my remarks to those who, like me, are followers of Jesus/Yeshua. I believe that *offense* is the most effective *counter-punch* that the enemy has in his arsenal to use against Christians.

It seems that the enemy generally has a two-pronged tactic in what he does. The first tactic he uses is to *keep us from knowing the truth.*

For example, I would contend that the evil of Replacement Theology is a truth that the enemy would prefer that we never know, never recognize as sin, and never repent of in any way. I had lived fifty years of my life before even considering it!

But if we are to learn the truth about something, whether Replacement Theology, or something good such as the Jewish roots of our faith, the second-pronged tactic of the enemy is to tempt us to take offense at others who do not share our viewpoint.

For example, suppose you are a Christian who learns the truth of how painful the symbol of the Cross of Christ has been in the history of the Jewish people. Therefore, on your next tour to Israel you decide that you will not wear a visible cross, as you might normally do at home. Next, you speak to the leader of your tour group, suggesting that they educate the group about this fact and ask the others to refrain from wearing their crosses visibly. The leader now responds to you. Not only are they not willing to make this a tour requirement, but they will not even let you make such an announcement yourself as a suggestion from your personal conviction. At this point, the secondary tactic of the enemy kicks in, and you are tempted by the enemy, or as the Jews would say, by the evil inclination (*Yetzer Harah*), to *take up an offense.*

This example is hypothetical, but it is a window into a much bigger problem in the Church that happens in more ways than we can possibly count. Here are several larger categories of offenses:

- Those in the Hebrew Roots or Jewish Roots movement can take offense at Christians in traditional churches who reject the Torah,[1] the Sabbath, and the feasts of the Lord, and whose Sunday morning services appear to be about performance and "show".

- Those in traditional Christian churches can take offense at those in the Hebrew Roots movement who reject holidays like Christmas and Easter, and whose separation from traditional churches makes them appear to be self-righteous and haughty.

- Those in the Messianic streams can take offense when traditional Christians ask, in so many words, *why they can't be more normal,* like regular Christians.

- Those in politically conservative evangelical congregations take offense at politically liberal mainline denominations, and vice versa.

- Protestants take up offenses against Catholics, and vice versa, for various sins in the present, and in the past.

Once an offense has been taken up on any side, the enemy leverages it for great harm. As it is written:

> *See to it that no one falls short of the grace of God and that no bitter root grows up to cause trouble and defile many.* HEBREWS 12:15 (NIV)

But if we are at least *aware* that this is a huge tactic of the enemy, then we at least have a chance to see it coming, and thereby refuse to allow that poisonous root to spring up in ourselves.

Unoffendable

But how does one stop oneself from slipping into the trap of taking offense?

---

[1] The term *rejecting the Torah* here means to reject the applicability and observance of the commands in the Pentateuch on the basis that they are irrelevant, outdated, or in direct contradiction to the freedom that was gained through the death of Christ.

I'll tell you the path that has helped me. (Notice I said *helped*, not solved!) What has helped me is to realize that Jesus/Yeshua was **unoffendable**.

Have you ever been taught that? I had not. But I was at a wedding in 2017, and had felt the strong sense that a set of problems one of the groomsmen was facing was actually the need to forgive the people who had wronged him in the past. I spoke with him about the importance of being willing to forgive using the verses that immediately follow the Lord's prayer:

> *For if you forgive other people when they sin against you, your heavenly Father will also forgive you. But if you do not forgive others their sins, your Father will not forgive your sins.* MATTHEW 6:14-15 (NIV)

Just then the groom's father, a devout Christian who happened to be standing nearby, said:

> "That's right, and did you know that Jesus never took up an offense? He was unoffendable!" He went on to say, "I just read a good book about it by Brant Hansen."[2]

What is the connection between unforgiveness and offense?

> **To refuse to forgive is an *example* of — if not the *heart* of — taking up an offense against someone else**.

As soon as the groom's father made that comment, I immediately remembered a story that had happened some twenty-five years earlier. A friend of mine at church had had a profound experience with the Holy Spirit, where he was sort of "caught up" into heaven during our Sunday morning meeting. Then, in our small group-gathering later that in the week he shared what had happened to him: there before him was Jesus, greeting him with the widest range of assorted fruits and vegetables of the earth, spread beautifully on tables with gleaming white tablecloths. Jesus held out His hands towards the nearest table, and gestured to my friend, as if to say, "would you like to enjoy some of these foods?" I can't remember if my friend said that

---

that particular table had fruit or vegetables on it, but what was amazing is that my friend said back to Jesus:

"I don't want *anything* on that table! I'd like something *else*!"

Those of us listening to this story were open-mouthed and aghast. He didn't even say "Please!" But the part of the story that I most remember was my friend's description of what Jesus did next. He said Jesus simply turned towards another table, without the least bit of offense, and said, "Well, how about these over here? Would these be better?"

When he told this experience that evening, several of us were telling him: "Are you crazy?! Don't you know that you were turning up your nose at God's own creations? Why didn't you at least try something that was offered? Why didn't you speak more kindly in return!" All our friend could say was, "It didn't seem to matter."

So that wedding day, when I put together in my own mind that memorable story of Jesus twenty-five years earlier, and the groom's father telling me about the book called *Unoffendable*, I suddenly realized that I didn't have to read the book at all![3] All I had to do was to go back and read the gospel accounts with a new eye, with the view that:

What Yeshua said towards others never came out as a byproduct of a personal hurt. It was just the best possible response in that situation.

If you do that too, I promise it will change your perception. Instead of seeing "offense and righteous anger," you will see a much larger view of love.

Conclusion

All is not right with the Church and the world. We are permeated by offense. We look on as people not only take offense, but invent new ways and reasons for the taking up of offenses against others.

In the light of this evil age, our only response is the opposite. May we all find God's grace to resist offense, until perhaps one day we too might attain a love that is itself *ever-present* and *unoffendable*.

Shalom.

---

[3] My wife and I actually ended up purchasing the book later. It sits on our coffee table.

Closing Prayer

Would you be willing to pray this prayer with me?

Heavenly Father,

Our world is full of offence given, and offence taken.

May we be those who exercise self-control in how much we say and the words we say. May we be those who are given wisdom by the Holy Spirit regarding what to say and when. May our speech be "seasoned with salt".[4]

May we also be those who grow in the area of how we receive the words that are spoken in our hearing. May we be, like Christ, unoffendable. May our responses, upon hearing those things which are not easy to hear, be responses which make a situation better. May we find the paths through stress and strife that will bring responses which are in line with God's will, and bring glory to Your name.

Amen.

Asking Gidon

Gidon, has the expression "being unoffendable" ever come up in your hearing in Jewish discussions?

Not using that exact phrase, no.

Is there any often-repeated phrase or quote in the Jewish world about the need to resist taking offense?

What comes to mind is: "*Al Tikach Lalev*" — don't take [it] to heart."

Does any particular person stand out in Jewish history as "not taking offense" in a situation when others might?

A certain contemporary rabbi comes to mind, Rabbi Zelig Pliskin, who is the author of dozens of important self-help books, including a re-writing of the classic laws of Evil Speech entitled *Guard Your Tongue*.[5] I had the delight of

---

4   Colossians 4:6
5   https://amzn.to/2U18QQR

sitting in on a lesson he once gave about being offended and how it is never right. Students approached him and tried to stump him, to see how he would react if such-and-such a thing were to happen to him. He gave a reason not to be offended in every example.

Another slightly less contemporary rabbi who comes to mind is Rabbi Shlomo Zalman Auerbach of blessed memory, who never was caught without a smile on his face.

Another rabbi that would be mentioned on the topic of not taking offense was the subject of the bestseller *A Tzaddik [righteous person] In Our Time*,[6] Rabbi Aryeh Levin, who would also probably be the person mentioned when most Israelis would be asked "who is a *tzaddik*?"

And finally, historically, a famous story is told of Hillel, when someone lost a bet that he would be able to make Hillel angry.[7]

---

[6] https://amzn.to/2XQBiWP
[7] Talmud Shabbat 30b and following: https://bit.ly/Shabbat30b

CHAPTER 19

One Word, Two Worlds

One word divides the Jewish world and the Christian world.

No, it is not the word you are thinking about. It is not the word *Jesus*, which itself is really the Hebrew word for *salvation*. There is virtually no disagreement that such a person named Jesus/Yeshua walked the Earth. There is no dispute that He died in Jerusalem. The disagreement is in the significance of those events.

Of all my thousands of discussions with Gidon, one stands out clearly. I can remember exactly where we were walking, leaving the Old City through the Zion Gate, walking alongside the Hinnom Valley, and then crossing that valley to walk up the other side, when he and I both stumbled on something important. It was a word — a very important Hebrew word that seems to carry within it that great controversy that divides Christians and Jews.

Hinnom Valley today.

One Word

Would you like to try to guess it? Here a few hints that might allow some to guess it, each hint getting you closer to the answer.

Hint 1: It was spoken by Abraham.

Hint 2: It was spoken about God.

Hint 3: The word was spoken in what is now Jerusalem.

Hint 4: More specifically, it was spoken on Mount Moriah.

Some of you may be able to guess it now!

Need another hint?

Hint 5: There might have still been a knife in Abraham's hand when he spoke it!

Need another hint?

Hint 6: It was spoken after the ram was sacrificed to God.

The word is *Yireh*.

This is the word that forms part of the word *Jerusalem*. This will be even more obvious if we write Jerusalem phonetically as: *Yireh-shalom*.

The conversation between Gidon and me had drifted to Abraham's "almost-sacrifice" of Isaac. Gidon may have been saying something about how GENESIS 22:14 is a key verse from which the name of "Jerusalem" is derived, *Yireh*.

He then dropped the bomb on me without realizing it when he casually added that *Yireh* means:

"The LORD will see."

And I replied, "don't you mean to say:

'The LORD will provide'?"

And Gidon replied, "What makes you say that?"

I answered, "Because that's what my New American Standard Bible says, and this is one of the most literal translations out there." That translation reads:

Abraham called the name of that place The LORD Will Provide, as it is said to this day, "In the mount of the LORD it will be provided." GENESIS 22:14

Then, to strengthen the point, I told him that as a kid I used to sing songs about *Jehovah Jireh*, the God who provides for our needs. Today, songs have continued to be written on that same theme. For instance:

Jehovah Jireh, Jehovah Jireh, My provider, His grace is sufficient, For me, for me, for me.

Another popular song we often sing at our church begins like this:

Jehovah Jireh, won't you come and give us life?

Gidon said, "Hmmm, I don't think so. The root of *Yireh* is *raah*, which means 'to see.'"

As we were walking, Gidon did some checking online using his smartphone, and said that it might be possible to also translate the word "to make manifest," but it definitely does not mean "to provide."

The Israel Bible (TIB), which has often been quoted in this book,[1] is a version which derives most of its text from the very well-known Jewish Publication Society (JPS) version. The Israel Bible translates *Yireh* using the word *vision*, as follows:

> *And Avraham named that site Adonai-yireh, whence the present saying, "On the mount of Hashem there is vision."* GENESIS 22:14 (TIB)

Why does this one little word deserve an entire chapter on its own? Using the analogy of music, sometimes an entire orchestra is held silent while just one instrument plays one very long note. The note hangs in the air. All ears are drawn to it. And every other musician must wait for its completion before anyone else can play. This chapter is that single note, a single Hebrew word *Yireh* that hangs in the air.

Why does it matter?

Because this little word, *Yireh*, contains both the **problem and the solution** for us as Christians, in helping us understand why the Jewish people don't see *salvation* the way we do.

As Christians, we have come to see God (the Father) as the God who provides us *His Son*, the greatest gift ever given! That story reached its pivotal climax in Jerusalem! God *has provided* a sacrifice for us, allowing us to be accepted into His household, His family, and for our sins to be forgiven. Without a doubt, **Jerusalem is the place** where God *provided* a way for us to come into relationship with Him.

And yet Jews relate to that verse through the verb of *seeing*. Specifically, the words spoken by Abraham are "God (the four-letter name of God YHVH) will *see*." What's the implication?

---

[1] The decision to include this version has multiple reasons behind it, including to expose readers to some Jewish translations; to bring more attention to this new version published by Orthodox Jew, Rabbi Tuly Weisz; and sometimes a different wording keeps us from reading verses too quickly without thinking about them.

For Jews, **Jerusalem is about what God sees, not about what God provides.**

The Torah has many facets, and there are certainly dozens of ways to unpack this verse. But for the purposes here, I would like to propose the following summary of this particular facet from the Jewish point of view, as I see it:

> *Jerusalem is the place it is today, a place of hope for all nations, because a man, Abraham, was so moved by the walking out of his obedience unto death (of his only heir), that it was revealed to him that God was much more involved in the affairs of this world than he ever thought possible, and that the world did change, has changed, and continues to change forever, not because of what Abraham saw and didn't see that day, but because of what God sees.*

The lesson for us regarding understanding the Jews, is similar. I would state it as:

> *Let us not look at them and determine "what we see" and "what we do not see," but rather let our peace, our shalom, be based upon asking God to reveal to us what He sees. It matters not what we think we see. What matters is what God sees.*

This one lesson, this one idea, is one I would suggest is worth pondering long after this book's final chapter.

Selah.

It Begins Early

I would like to share one other difference that crystallizes, for me, the difference between Christians and Jews. It is the difference between the first song that is learned by Christians and Jews respectively.

The first Christian song is one that is taught to our kids in Sunday School. For most kids it is *Jesus Loves Me*.[2] The first verse goes like this:

> *Jesus loves me this I know*
> *For the Bible tells me so*
> *Little ones to Him belong*
> *They are weak but He is strong.*

In his class on prayer,[3] Gidon mentions that one portion of the morning prayer

---

[2] This song has had great impact upon the Christian world. For instance, theologian Karl Barth, when asked how he would summarize the essence of all his books, once replied, "Jesus loves me this I know, for the Bible tells me so." Short link to article on Christianity Today: https://bit.ly/Barth-Jesus

[3] https://root-source.com/channels

service is often sung by Jewish kids. For most kids it is *Adon Olam*. The first verse goes like this:

> *The Lord of the Universe who reigned*
> *Before anything was created*
> *When all was made by His will*
> *He was acknowledged as King.*[4]

Notice the differences?

Do you see in the Christian song how Jesus is *providing* Himself to us — His love and His strength. He is meeting our needs for love and strength, because we are not sufficient in ourselves. But in the Jewish song, the focus is on God's preeminence and abilities before He even created us. These Jewish verses describe for me a majestic God who is looking outward intently and with great purpose on His plans to do something marvelous.

There you have it! The difference in perspective between Jews and Christians is unmistakable right from the very first verse of possibly the first-learned song in our respective kids' education.

Selah.

Last Word

We wanted this book to focus mostly on what we share, rather than what divides us. But this departure in our perspectives, this one word — *Yireh* — can give us something important to ponder in the days ahead!

Yireh-Shalom.

Asking Gidon

Gidon, I don't expect that conversation we had near the Hinnom Valley was as memorable to you as it was to me. But at that moment, I thought that someday I would need to write about this. It was one of the seeds, in fact, for this entire book. What is your reaction to this chapter? Do you scratch your head wondering how Christians could ever "get that" from

---

[4] This link helps teach the song: https://youtu.be/G4eEhrTyI9E
Here is a nice arrangement: https://youtu.be/nvOtcWEFWo8

that Abraham story?

I am impressed Bob by your ability to internalize some of these teachings and to utilize them further with your own input. I think that this chapter about the words and concept of *Adonai Yireh* is not the last word but the first word in shared learning about them by Jews and Christians. (I still don't have an answer about how *Yireh* can be translated as "provided!")

Putting *Yireh* and *Shelem* together makes Jerusalem. What exactly *is the definition* of Jerusalem from the Jewish standpoint?

At this point, Jerusalem is only the name of the city. Really, putting *Yireh* and *Shelem* together, to mean "[He] will see completeness," is only one midrash on the word. Another could be "*Ir Shalom*," meaning City of Peace.

Adon Olam is, to my way of thinking, a fairly complex song.[5] What is the thinking (because I've learned enough to know it isn't random) about why such a complex song would be the first one taught to young children?

That's a great question. There is value for setting sights high in Judaism, even for little children, such as assigning them to sing the most esoteric theological song, even if they cannot possibly understand it. Another well-known tradition is for children to begin their Bible studies (at least ritually, that is, not spending too long on it) with the first few verses of the Book of Leviticus, which discusses sacrifices and purities. The famous explanation for this is "Let the pure ones come and study pure topics."[6] Only then, after they have been given a distant target to strive for, do they start with Genesis.

---

5   https://youtu.be/G4eEhrTyl9E
6   In other words innocent children.

CHAPTER 20

The Great Divide

t the halfway point of a football game, each team goes into the locker room and their coach speaks to them. The coach speaks *whatever he feels the team needs to hear*, even if it isn't what they *want* to hear. You are now in the middle of this book, and I would like to do the same. You see, many Christians see themselves as being on one team, with Orthodox Jews on the other, and view the object of the game being to "win" everywhere possible on the issue of Jesus/Yeshua being the Messiah.

The "Jesus is Messiah" issue is admittedly the greatest of our divides. It is a question whose answer has no middle ground. But, if we are a team, **then our team is making a big mistake in the way we approach** *the great divide* **that separates us**.

Before explaining the mistake, let me stress that I am speaking *collectively* to Christians in this chapter. What any individual Christian does on any given day — how you obey the command of Jesus to "follow me" — that I leave between you and God.[1] Rather, I speak to the collective team.

We begin by switching metaphors away from football.[2] Let's talk about marriage!

A Marriage Story

My wife and I spent seven years of our lives working in Christian marriage ministry. She was first to be drawn towards it, being stirred inside by a belief that there *must* be more to our marriage than what we had been experiencing.

---

[1] Jesus/Yeshua Himself warns us to *"judge not that we be not judged"* (Matthew 7:1, ESV paraphrased), and Paul asks, *"Who are you to judge the servant of another?"* (Romans 14:4).

[2] Several worldwide sports describe themselves using the word *football*, and thankfully they all have halftimes!

On the other hand, I felt pretty satisfied. I thought to myself: I am committed to her, and she is committed to me; I love my wife and she loves me; both her parents and mine were in stable, loving relationships in their marriages. It seemed therefore, that we had a good foundation. "So why wasn't that good enough for her?" I thought.

We went to an information session to learn more about a certain kind of marriage course called Married for Life,[3] and heard some couples talking about what they had gained from going through this course. My wife eagerly wanted us to join a course, and asked me for my opinion, forcing me to reveal my thoughts! So I told her I envisioned this course as five to seven couples sitting around a living room talking about what was wrong with their marriages. Even worse, I thought the idea of us revealing each other's faults in front of a bunch of strangers was revolting![4]

Fast-forward a few years.

We had taken the course *several times* now and been so enriched by it and appreciative of it, that we had become leaders ourselves. We were part of a community of leaders and felt loved and accepted both as individuals and as a couple, had experienced the joy of seeing marriages get saved (or enriched) greatly, and seen amazing miracles of healing and growth happening in the lives of couples around our city. We had learned how to talk about our own faults too![5]

The Point of the Story

Why am I telling this story? It is to reveal to you a perspective — not the perspective we had at the beginning, but a perspective into which we grew. Let me illustrate by explaining what would happen at the first session of the class.

Here we are, leaders of a marriage class that is about to start in our home. The door opens and in walks a couple. We greet them and invite them to sit down on a couch in our living room. They are the first to arrive for the class. They look at us a bit nervously, and we look back at them, smiling and trying to make them feel at ease.

The point is this: we know something. We know something that they don't know.

---

3 https://www.2equal1.com/
4 Actually, it was only the thought of her sharing my faults that was completely revolting!
5 The Married for Life course has stood the test of time, being taught for decades in America and in scores of countries around the world.

And what we know is so universal and applicable, that it really doesn't matter how good their marriage is, or what their background is, or to what stream of the Christian faith they belonged. What we know without any doubt is that they have a preconceived idea:

- She thinks their marriage can improve if *he* will change.
- He thinks their marriage can improve if *she* will change.

It is human nature, is it not? When we think about the places of pain in our marriage, do we not think first about the pain we feel from our spouse? We wish for them to change in the way that they treat us. Everyone has such desires, and those desires are not necessarily wrong!

But as we continue speaking with the couple we also know something else. We know what solution is going to be proposed to them in this marriage course — the same solution that was proposed to us when we went through the marriage course for the very first time.

The Solution

As teachers of a marriage course, we know that our job in teaching will only be complete when we have successfully reframed their entire perspective of their marriage from *horizontal* to *vertical*.

The making of a great marriage happens when each spouse goes vertical with God, to deepen their own relationship with God, but at the same time each chooses to focus their attention in the marriage on being a better husband to their wife, or a better wife to their husband.

During our time in marriage ministry we have learned a few expressions that often help crystalize some of these ideas in the couples. For instance, we teach that:

- Your spouse is not your enemy!

This means that in the eyes of God, He is FOR the relationship, not rooting for one spouse to win so that the other spouse will lose. Our real enemy is the evil inclination within us. Our real enemy is Satan who desires to destroy this relationship in every way possible. And one of the most common tactics of the enemy is to get both partners in a marriage to look upon their spouse as "the problem," or "the enemy."

Another expression we teach is:

- Pray it on them, don't lay it on them.

The idea here is that verbalizing the flaws and deficiencies in your spouse, the places where their behavior in the marriage is not meeting your standards, or not meeting biblical standards, **is NOT an effective way** to get them to change. Yet God still cares about our hurts, and so it is perfectly reasonable to take your concerns privately and directly to Him and ask that He guide and convict the other in due time.

A third expression we often use is:

- Let go, and let God.

Each person in the course is going to have to *let go* of judgments, conclusions and "taking up offenses" against their spouse.[6] For instance, we teach couples not to wait for their spouse to ask for forgiveness, but to go to God directly and forgive their spouse for their mistakes. We also teach that couples are going to have to *let go of the idea that they can make their spouse change.* For instance, while the New Testament teaches husbands to love their wives, and wives to respect their husbands,[7] it in no way condones a husband to demand, coerce, cajole, or manipulate his wife to respect him, nor to point out her deficiencies in doing so!

Our course teaches that they are going to have to find a place of peace in the carrying out of their own roles and responsibilities before God. In a Christian course like this, the *letting go* is very much entwined with trusting in the power of the finished work of Christ on the Cross.

Covenant is Key

After God called my wife and me to get more involved in things involved with Israel, at first we saw it as a new calling. But we quickly realized that *both marriage and* a healthy understanding of Israel are based on a single foundational principle: *covenant.*

The transformation of a married couple in the marriage course we just discussed can be summarized using covenantal language:

We must help each spouse to reframe their perspective of marriage away

---

[6] Here is an explanation of *"taking up offenses."* Conflicts and failures between people are inevitable. But, it is all too common for us to fall into the trap of allowing the failures of the other party to begin to build up an emotional wall between us, resulting in a sore, hurting place that festers inside our hearts and prevents close relationship. It doesn't mean that the failures of the other party shouldn't hurt, but it's how we respond to that hurt that determines whether "an offense" has been taken. The Psalms can help us vocalize our hurts to God without sinning. I once counted 120 psalms that touch, at least briefly, on various kinds of pain; of these, Psalms 77 and 88 are especially noteworthy.

[7] Ephesians 5:22-33

from just focusing on the actions of the other, into seeing both themselves and their spouse as together being in direct covenant relationship with God.

But at some point it dawned on me that I could summarize the work of God, as it relates to Christians and the Jews of Israel, in a similar way:

> We must help Christians reframe their perspective of Israel away from just focusing on the actions (or inactions) of Israel, into seeing *Israel as already part of a covenant relationship with God*, in addition to Christians being in covenant relationship with God through Christ.[8]

Bringing it Home

So now we circle back to the opening statement of this chapter. I wrote:

> *But, if we are a team, then our team is making a big mistake in the way we approach the great divide that separates us.*

Here is how I see it. Christians are thinking about the Jews just like that couple who had walked in the door of our living room is thinking about their marriage. We Christians are preoccupied with what the other party — the Jews — are doing wrong.

- We focus on what they don't believe.

- We focus on what they don't see.

- We are convinced that it is the Jews who need to get their act together and fix themselves.

- We falsely believe that the greatest problem preventing the return of Christ is that the Jews don't recognize Jesus/Yeshua as the Messiah.

- We falsely believe that "if they would only change their minds about Jesus being the Messiah" then a great relationship between us would finally be possible.[9]

---

[8] One of the divides in the Christian theological world is the question of how and whether the covenant with Israel differs from the new/renewed covenant spoken of by Christ. Let me tell you what I believe. I believe that *that* issue divides Christians too much already. I believe that every verse of the Bible is true. And I believe all readers of this book ought to enjoy it regardless of their opinion on that question.

[9] This is ridiculous. You don't build strong relationships at the drop of a hat. And even supposing all Jews were to suddenly agree with us that Jesus is the Messiah, our Christian track record of turning on our own is so predictable, and our desire for power and control so seductive, that I am afraid if it happened any time soon the resulting conflicts would be disastrous. Christians don't seem to appreciate the danger here. They assume that "the Messiah will fix everything," including the inter-group relationships. To wait

Even worse, I see that we Christians have even gone so far as to *take up an offense* against the Jews, in regards to their "being blind." Today, while I was editing this chapter, Gidon forwarded to me an email discussion that he had just finished having with a Christian woman. Her last email exchange with Gidon said exactly this:

> *There's no language barrier... The Scripture is very clear for all and you're blind... Or you don't want to see more... But do what you want... I'm not wasting my time... You will see when Jesus will come... He will judge correctly. Sorry. I was just trying to open your eyes... Spiritually... Never mind. Let's finish this. Jesus will remind you about me one day* [Name withheld. Spacing and punctuation preserved.]

That is not an isolated case. Back in 2015, I published an interview with Nehemia Gordon in 2015 on the topic of *why Jews don't see Jesus in ISAIAH 53*.[10] We got some wonderful comments, but most were harsh, and some made me want to take a shower. I finally disabled all comments on that video. It became quite clear then that many Christians are *outright offended* that Jews do not recognize Jesus as the Messiah.

So what should we as Christians do about the "great divide" between Christians and Jews?

My answer to that is the very same answer that you would get from attending a marriage course in our home.

The Christian focus on how the Jews need to change is not going to make our relationship better, but worse. We need to stop what we are doing, and go in a different direction.

Instead, why don't we as Christians turn to God above, and recognize:

- The Jews are not our enemy. They are not even on an opposing team, because God has made covenant promises to them which He has not revoked.

- Pray it on them, don't lay it on them. We need to stop telling them what we believe they are doing wrong or can't see. And we should pray blessings on them publicly and privately.[11]

---

for the Messiah to solve that is simply childish.

[10] https://youtu.be/3GuSg7S-lrQ Ever heard about the Murphy's Law of YouTube? Neither have I, but if there was one, it would be: your most popular video will be the one in which you didn't comb your hair.

[11] When it comes to the desire that Jews might see Jesus/Yeshua as the Messiah, that desire can be taken directly to God in prayer, but I would suggest we pray an even larger prayer: that we might learn to

- Let go, and let God. They are His Chosen ones.

- Let's get to know each other, and find ways to work productively together where possible. Orthodox Jews do all kinds of things to make the world a better place. It is easy to find some project Jews have already started in which you might come alongside and help.

All this is done to sanctify the name of the One True God. The Jews pray to "The Lord God, King of the Universe." Christians can agree with that prayer 100 percent! And perhaps our perception of that King might be different in our hearts, but that doesn't prevent great cooperation.

Because marriage involves two parties, and because marriage is based in covenant, it has been an extremely useful illustration in this chapter. But let us not press that illustration too far. We cannot expect that describing Jewish and Christian relations in the context of marriage would be agreeable with most Jews, nor to most Christians. Indeed, we began this chapter speaking of two teams playing football. So let us also end there.

Are we two teams? And is the object of the game to "win" everywhere possible, on the question of whether Jesus/Yeshua is or is not the Messiah? I believe we need to let go of this image of our Great Divide. We need to let go of the idea of a *Team Christian* and *Team Jew*.

Both Christians and Orthodox Jews

- want to sanctify God's name,

- want the redemption of all things, and

- know that a Messiah will be part of that great, great story.

The divide is not as great as we think. I strongly believe that *from the perspective of God*, we are on the same team.

Team Christian? Team Jew? How about one team: Team God!

Shalom.

---

see the Jewish people as God truly sees them, not how we've been *taught* that He sees them, as was discussed in the previous chapter.

Closing Prayer

Would you like to join me and pray into some of the points covered in this chapter?

Heavenly Father,

We thank You for Your Jewish people and the great work which You are doing in and through them in the nation of Israel and around the world. We acknowledge Your covenantal promises to them and that they are Yours, Your chosen people.

We ask for Your forgiveness for any offense that we have taken up against Jews not seeing the Bible, or history, in the same way we see it. Specifically, please forgive us for taking up an offense when a Jewish person (or anyone else for that matter), does not recognize Jesus/Yeshua as the Messiah. Please remove our sin, and renew our hearts in true love for the Jewish people as they are, right now before You. Forgive us for the ways in which we have brought hurt and pain to the Jewish people by attempting to fix them (and even worse), while simultaneously ignoring our own problems.

Regarding our own problems we pray:

> *Search me and know my heart; test me and know my anxious thoughts. See if there is any offensive way in me, and lead me in the way everlasting.* PSALM 139:23-24 (NIV)

Finally, please show us more of Your plans and Your purposes for Your Jewish people. We ask to see them as You see them and to walk in Your unconditional love, and find ways to accept, respect, honor and cherish those who are the roots of our faith.

Amen.

Asking Gidon

How do you respond when Christians meet with you and want to evangelize you towards Jesus?

First of all, it doesn't happen often, probably because most Christians who want to meet with me are mature enough to see that a meeting with me is an opportunity to learn something in a friendly environment and not to proselytize. But yes, I do sometimes meet people who seem to think "maybe I can say something that he will consider and perhaps move him towards Christianity," and then they turn a private conversation with me towards ISAIAH 53 or something similar. But more commonly, it comes up in the Q&A period of a speaking event with Christians. In those cases, my response to them is usually along the lines of:

- "Why are you trying to convince me of something without establishing a relationship with me first?"

- "Would you take a girl out on a first date, sit her down, and then start telling her the things you want to change about her? Is she a person who you want to get to know, or is she just a platform for changes?"

- "I would request that you view me as another person like you, made in God's image, a person to have a relationship with."

Gidon, you once mentioned to me a principle in Judaism that you wished was a guiding principle for Christians during their evangelism activities. Will you explain this please?

The principle you are asking about was first mentioned by me during an uproar in Israel that happened regarding Christian evangelical efforts directed at Israelis. Now, first, I do not oppose Christians sharing the gospel in other nations, especially in Muslim nations, but I do not in any way approve of any Christian missionary activities directed at Jews, in Israel or anywhere. That being said, I do understand that many Christians read the New Testament and believe that they must also evangelize in Israel; that trying to do so is the Great Commission, "a good deed" or even a commandment, what we in Judaism would call "a *mitzvah*."

Here is the principle: *Mitzvah HaBa'a Ba'aveira.* Literally that means "a commandment achieved through means of a sin." If a "mitzvah" requires a sin to fulfill it, then you should not perform the mitzvah. You must wait until it can be achieved without sinning, and if such time never comes, then you are exempt from that commandment.

In our case, it is hard for Christians to understand the situation in Israel with all the complex history, but what I am about to say is not opinion, it is fact: the sharing of the gospel to Jews right now in Israel is offensive to millions of Jews. It is *illegal in Israel* to do so to children without their parent's consent, but the principle of *Mitzvah HaBa'a Ba'aveira* is not talking about conforming to the law of the land, but rather *sin* in the eyes of God. The sin in question is offending others.[12] So let's say a Christian evangelistic effort gets a handful of converts, but in the process deeply offends millions of Israeli Jews. Now Judaism is not a proselytizing religion, but even if it were and the situations were reversed, our leaders would say to us: "Stop and wait!" on the basis of *Mitzvah HaBa'a Ba'aveira.*

---

[12] Leviticus 25:17 *"one shall not aggrieve his fellow, and you shall fear your G-d, for I am Hashem your G-d."* https://bit.ly/Leviticus25. Both Paul and Jesus made efforts to avoid offending others (1 Corinthians 8:13; Matthew 17:27).

CHAPTER 21

Does God ever Bait-and-Switch?

L et us begin with the answer. No! God does not use the tactics of a sleazy marketer. (I was a marketer, so I have the right to criticize my own kind!) But sometimes what God does is so strange, I once accused God of *acting* like one.

Other than an outright lie from a salesperson, probably the most obnoxious tactic in sales and marketing is *the bait-and-switch*. It is also highly effective. Here's how it works. A newspaper insert contains an ad for an incredible deal on a new product, such as a car. That deal is good enough to get you off the couch and down to the store. Once there, you learn that the advertised product is sold out, or has severe limitations that make it unacceptable, like buying a car in Arizona without A/C. But now that you have already invested the time and energy to visit the store, the salesperson shows you alternative products, always at a higher cost.

While God is not a sleazy marketer, I propose that God once used a strategy that was strangely similar. Come along for a ride in this chapter as we look at the case of the Blood Moons, and what happened with them.

A Bit of Background

Total Lunar Eclipse of January 2018.

Total lunar eclipses, which happen whenever the Moon is completely hidden behind the Earth's shadow, occur on average about once a year.

But, my how things have changed. Because while these events used to be called *lunar eclipses*, that term has now been relegated to the scientists. In popular lingo, lunar eclipses have now become known as **Blood Moons,** the origin of which goes back to a 2008 discovery made by Pastor Mark Biltz,[1] who connected a pattern of four lunar eclipses with the nation of Israel.

Have you ever noticed that those who discover something usually play a large role in naming it?

In March 2008, Mark, a Christian (Hebraic Roots) pastor knowledgeable in astronomy, happened to see on the Internet a total lunar eclipse over the Temple Mount in Jerusalem. Being interested and appreciative of the Jewish roots of our faith, and the Hebrew Calendar,[2] he realized that every full moon (and therefore every lunar eclipse) must occur at the middle of the month on the Hebrew Calendar. He also knew that the major biblical holidays of Passover and Sukkot (Feast of Tabernacles) also occurred at the middle of the month.[3] He wondered to himself how often it might happen that a total lunar eclipse fell on either Passover or Sukkot. He went online and checked the lunar eclipse pages at NASA,[4] one of the best sources of such information, and saw that up to four lunar eclipses can happen in sequence, each of them six months apart. This series of four eclipses is called a *tetrad*, and Mark noticed that some of these tetrads were falling on years that were very important in Jewish history: around the time of the establishment of Israel in 1948 and the Six-Day War in 1967.

I had known of *tetrads* myself for about thirty-five years because of my interest in astronomy, but Mark also knew much about the Hebrew Calendar in 2008, when a lot of people, including me, were unaware of it. Mark quickly noticed that these tetrads sometimes happened on *the Feasts of Passover and Sukkot in two successive years*: 1949/50 and 1967/68, and that another of these tetrads was coming soon in 2014/15.

God had designed these feasts Himself, and God had specifically told Israel that the feasts should be celebrated six months apart, every year. God also set up the placement of the Earth, Moon and Sun to create eclipses. God even designed the orbit of the Earth in such a way that when a tetrad happened on the feast days, the sequence of four eclipses *had to start on Passover*. So the sequence of four eclipses that the world witnessed in 2014/15 was:

---

[1] https://www.esm.us/
[2] Others use the term biblical Calendar or Jewish Calendar.
[3] The word Sukkot is the word for a shelter, or booth, thus it is also rightly referred to as the Feast of Booths. Gidon once made a nice introduction to the holiday here: https://root-source.com/blog/gidon-explains-sukkot-in-israel/
[4] https://eclipse.gsfc.nasa.gov/lunar.html

- Passover 2014
- Sukkot 2014

- Passover 2015
- Sukkot 2015

Four Blood Moons

2014	2014	2015	2015
April 15	**Oct 8**	**April 4**	**Sept 28**
Passover	Sukkot	Passover	Sukkot
Nissan 15	Tishri 15	Nissan 15	Tishri 15

The dates of the Four Blood Moons in 2014/15.

Now Mark was not the first person who noticed that these tetrads can happen on the feast days of Passover and Sukkot. In my research I found a website (no longer active) that posted this information back in the 1990s. But Mark was the first person to say:

"This is *not a coincidence* — it is important to biblical prophecy."

In addition, it seems that Mark was the first person on earth to refer to this special sequence of four total lunar eclipses falling on Passover and Sukkot in two successive years as: "Blood Moons." He derived this name by connecting these eclipses to the famous verse in Joel:

The sun will be turned to darkness and the moon into blood, before the great and awesome day of the LORD comes. JOEL 2:31

The New Testament also describes the Sun turning to sackcloth, and the Moon becoming like blood after the sixth seal is broken in REVELATION 6:12.

Perhaps you first heard about the Blood Moons through Pastor John Hagee,[5] like I did. Pastor Hagee learned about them from Pastor Mark Biltz,[6] but published his own book first which became a bestseller.

The Blood Moons story ended up taking on a life of its own, even bursting out of Christian media and into the secular media. And when the final Blood Moon came and went on September 28, 2015, without any abundantly clear answer to what the "something" was in John Hagee's often repeated claim: *Something is about to change!*, the secular media laughed, and most of the proponents were suddenly silent.

The Blood Moons were a colossal bust!

The Angry Mob

In 2013, well in advance of the Blood Moons, and before they were being covered at all in the press, I set up a google alert for the term "Blood Moons" that allowed me to watch the entire media scenario unfold in front of me one day at a time over the next three years. I watched as the various camps seemed to divide on the issue like this:

- Christians who were already interested in end-times prophecies gravitated to this teaching very quickly to learn about it. They divided into two camps:

  ○ Those who believed it *was a sign from God* were a combination of excited, interested, and fearful about what might happen to Israel and their own nation during this period of the Blood Moons. John Hagee's quote was: "Something is about to change!" After the Blood Moons, many people in this camp felt **let down**. The "changes" were not commensurate with the "buildup." Others in this camp were just downright **angry**.

  ○ Those who were interested in the End Times, but *did not believe this was a sign from God*, first tried to ignore it, but eventually had to weigh in on it. Many articles and videos came out on it from the prophetic community, and from pastors and Christian leaders. The objections to it ranged from "date-setting is unbiblical" all the way to "the Bible never talks about FOUR Blood Moons." None of these people have changed their minds after the Blood Moons. Every one of them would certainly assert: "I called it correctly!" The Blood Moons

---

5   *Four Blood Moons: Something is About to Change:* https://amzn.to/3004dKS
6   *Blood Moons: Decoding the Imminent Heavenly Signs:* https://amzn.to/2XJJ8kQ

People Interested in End Times		
Before	Blood Moons are a Sign from God	NOT a Sign from God
After	Let Down, Angry	I was right! It was hype!

How people reacted to the Blood Moons if they were previously *interested* in the End Times.

for them have become a **poster child for hype** and a **teaching moment** for their flock.

- On the other hand, there were many Christians who were **not previously interested** in end-times prophecy who would hear about "the Blood Moons." They divided into four camps:

  º People who were already interested in Israel, and who were curious to learn about the Blood Moons because they had to do with Israel. This perhaps deepened their understanding of the feast days, and is a **positive outcome**.

  º People who were interested enough in learning about the topic, such that it actually spurred them on to learn about both the topic *and* about Israel *and* to understand the feast days. **This is an extremely positive outcome!** The Blood Moons put Israel on the map for many Christians, forcing them to start the process of learning about their Jewish or Hebrew roots. I myself was one such person!

  º People who had either never heard about it, or simply ignored it completely, because they didn't care about end-times prophecy, or they didn't care to learn any more than they already knew about Israel. Well over **90 percent of Christians** worldwide probably fell into this category.

  º People who had been "burned before" with theories of the End Times, and dismissed the entire event as "here we go again!" These people felt validated for dismissing this theory and next time around will be even more resolute in their dismissal.

People NOT Interested in End Times but wanted to investigate		
Before	Unfamiliar with Israel	Familiar with Israel
After	Learned something about Israel	Deeper Understanding of Israel

People NOT Interested in End Times but did NOT want to investigate		
Before	Ignored	Heard and quickly dismissed
After	Ignored	Felt validated in their dismissal

How people reacted to the Blood Moons if they were previously *uninterested* in the End Times.

The Silver Lining

Are the Blood Moons now the latest in a long series of prophetic-hype disasters in the Christian world?

Yes, they are.

So then, is there any silver lining to this whole story?

Yes, I believe there is. It seems that God is quite content to "get what He wants" even in ways that are unusual, indirect, or not in the manner to that which we might have initially approved.

I believe that God is pleased that in the process of this Blood-Moons mania, hundreds of thousands of people, if not millions, have learned about the feast days of Passover and Sukkot, about how they are part of God's calendar. I believe God is pleased that many people made a connection between something awe inspiring in the heavens — like lunar eclipses — to two of the most important feasts that

God ever invented: Passover and Sukkot.[7]

The Blood Moons cause the Old Testament, as it is referred to by Christians, to be studied, and they sparked debates about how they might connect to the Bible. All told, the Blood Moons turned the attention of millions to Israel, to the Bible, and to what it had to say about the future. This is not a bad thing.

This is surprisingly similar to the *Bait-and-Switch* tactic: get the customer to come into the room for one purpose (the *bait* that interests them — to learn about the end of the world), and then show them another thing (the *switch* that the salesperson cares about — to learn about Israel). This doesn't seem to be the first time something like that has happened. For example, 3,000 years ago many people came from all over the world to meet Solomon and hear his wisdom (the bait), and yet many of them came away with a larger appreciation of the history of Israel and the *God* of Israel (the switch).

God usually wins in the end. No, God *always* wins in the end!

Meanwhile, now that the Blood Moons have passed, and the next Blood Moons tetrad is more than 500 years away, we can all go back to having *lunar eclipses*. These eclipses continue to be signposts in the sky that can inspire awe, and spur us on to praise the Almighty God! Yet thanks to Mark Biltz and John Hagee we don't call them *lunar eclipses* any more. Much of the media now calls them by their newest name: *the Blood Moon.*

Shalom.

Asking Gidon

Gidon, in our book and free online classes, we took a completely different approach on the Blood Moons than did the major players mentioned above. Yet for the 99 percent of Christians who heard about the *Blood Moons*, but never happened across our free videos, many of them were, or still are, perplexed and angry by the lack of a clear fulfillment to the Joel prophecy. That so many Christians see the Blood Moons as a "giant bust" personally saddens me. Does it sadden you?

---

[7] Besides the commonly held view among Christians that since Christ died on Passover He will return on Sukkot, the other reason Sukkot (and not just Passover) is critically important to the nations, is the future requirement that all nations will observe it, Zechariah 14:16-17.

Not so much. I am proud to be associated with you and to have helped to get your theory out there, a positive theory in contrast with the less-positive ones of Biltz and Hagee. But I don't think the angry, let down, and "here-we-go-again" groups grew so much, and on the whole I think God will bring about the End Times as He sees fit, with the skepticism of some Christians not burdening Him.

During the time when millions of Christians were talking about the Blood Moons, were the Jews of Israel aware of what was going on in the Christian world? Were they alarmed?

I don't think the Jews of Israel had any idea about this. Maybe one or two Hebrew bloggers found some Israel365 News articles and put something up, and of course the skygazing community made sure that the mainstream media knew that an eclipse was coming so they'd announce it once or twice, but Jews and Israelis are used to Christians predicting End Times, and at most will smile and nod. Remember, we Israelis aren't just observing cryptic signs of the End Times, we are living them!

Some Jews (often Jews of a more liberal persuasion) have criticized Christians who are interested in biblical prophecy, that we have an agenda for eagerly awaiting, and even hoping for war for the Jewish people, e.g. the Gog and Magog war, in hopes that such war might bring about the return of Christ, at the expense of Jewish casualties. Have you personally heard that view expressed by Jews in Israel? If a Jew posted that kind of comment on your Facebook feed, how would you respond?

Unfortunately this position is the mainstream one here in Israel. Remember, Jews are preprogrammed to be suspicious of Christians, so to deal with their cognitive dissonance they chalk up positive things that Christians do to such beliefs.[8] I am grateful that the faith of Christians who love Israel for other reasons stays strong in spite of such ingratitude, and I believe that soon that faith will overcome all suspicions of Israelis. I've been on Facebook for over a decade, and thank God have very few friends with commenting privileges who post negative stuff. So I will deal with such an eventuality when it happens ☺

---

8   Regarding Gidon's use of the word "preprogramming" consider this. Imagine a people group that was persecuted by more than fifty successive generations of Christians. Imagine what impact that might have on their outlook.

CHAPTER 22

Red Wine, Blood Red Moons, and Salvation

The word *salvation* is about as loaded a word as you can get in Christianity. "Are you saved?" "Do you have eternal life?" "Do you know where you are going when you die?" These are central questions that Christians, especially we evangelical Christians, associate with *salvation*. And these very questions have been asked by Christians for hundreds of years as we have sought to spread the Gospel around the world.

The *Blood Moons*, however, are quite new to the lexicon of Christianity. While they took the Christian prophetic world by storm in 2015, they might have remained completely ignored by the Orthodox Jewish world were it not for Tuly Weisz and Israel365 News, whose editorial approach seemed to be not *"why* to cover it," but "why *not?"* Tuly was the very first Orthodox Rabbi who I ever found writing about the Blood Moons, and that was in the spring of 2014 at the time of the first of the four Blood Moons.

Letting go of the Blood Moons

I became aware of the four Blood Moons in January 2013, a full year before they began. I felt called to study these strange Blood Moons with vigor and purpose as strong as any other call that I had ever experienced in my life. Yet, a mere six months later, by the "Ninth of Av" in 2013, I had an encounter with God that would redirect me even further. In the weeks following that experience, my heart slowly, carefully and resolutely decided to give up on, and let go of, all my research and discoveries regarding the Blood Moons. I cancelled my book plans.

Then out of nowhere one day came a thought that we were all looking at the Blood Moons "upside down." We were all standing on the Earth, gazing up at these four eclipses thinking:

"Wow, these four eclipses must be really important to biblical

prophecy because they are happening on God's Feast Days,"

when we should have been thinking from God's perspective. We should have been looking down on the Earth from the Moon thinking:

"These four feast days on earth must be especially important to God because of these four eclipses."

A feast is not designed by God to be a time for all to fear, it is designed by God to be a time of joy and celebration! All of a sudden, I realized that the Blood Moons were bearing witness, they were a sign of God's covenant love for His chosen people.

However, by that time, I had already made a promise to God to *let go* of the Blood Moons. Therefore, I began to look for those to whom I might pass along my research, and resolved not to make a single dollar on these Blood Moons personally. By the fall of 2013, even before the first of the Blood Moons had happened, I had already changed my entire focus. I would travel to Jerusalem instead to look for Orthodox Jews for whom I might "be a blessing," as alluded to in GENESIS 12:3.

Earth from the Moon.

> *I will bless those who bless you And curse him that curses you; And all the families of the earth Shall bless themselves by you.* GENESIS 12:3 (TIB)

My invitation to Jerusalem came from Christine Darg as already mentioned in chapter 16, and because of that, in January 2014 I met Gidon.[1] Gidon had been invited to advise Christian intercessors on how to pray as "watchmen on the walls." That day he shared his idea for what would become Root Source.[2] I then heard the Holy Spirit say of Gidon, "That's your man," so I figuratively "grabbed onto his cloak"[3] in January 2014, and helped him launch his vision. I was happy to be Gidon's consultant behind the scenes, but that was not enough for him; he

---

[1] Watchmen and Women on the Walls convocation, put on by Christine Darg, co-founder with Peter Darg of Jerusalem Channel and Exploits Ministries. https://jerusalemchannel.tv/
[2] http://www.root-source.com
[3] Zechariah 8:23

wanted a full-fledged partner. For weeks he kept insisting on this until I finally took it to prayer and realized that God was speaking *through him*. I relented, and we spent the next year preparing and launching Root Source as partners.

All the while, I carried my Blood Moons discoveries in my heart, occasionally mentioning them to Gidon. He listened but said little. Once everything was working on our website and our teachers were in place, it was time to start our marketing in earnest. Gidon and I met with Tuly Weisz to see if his company Israel365[4] could help us market Root Source. Their initial advice seemed good and promising. Then, imagine my surprise when I discovered that *this was the very same Rabbi* who one year earlier was the first Orthodox Jew to have ever written about the Blood Moons!

What a joy it was for me to now also share with Tuly the idea that the Blood Moons were not a sign of *harm* to Israel or the world, but a sign of *good* to Israel and the Jewish people! I wondered if Tuly or his company might want to use my research to proclaim a more hopeful message about them to the Jewish people? Gidon then said,

> "The Blood Moons could be a great marketing idea for Root Source!" He then looked at me and said, "Why don't you create some video lessons on the Blood Moons?"

I immediately responded with two objections:

> "But Root Source is *Israeli Jews teaching Christians worldwide*, and I'm not a Jew! Wouldn't they rather hear about this from you rather than from me?" I then added, "Also, I have promised God I would never make any money on the Blood Moons."

Gidon smiled and said,

> "First, you won't be like a regular teacher. And second, we won't charge for your material. Let's give your teachings away for free, and in the process you can tell Christians about Root Source."

I really had no comeback to this, and I had to agree in my heart that this sounded like a great marketing idea.

Tuly suggested that Israel365 develop a companion ebook[5] as well, and that they

---

4 http://www.israel365.com
5 Years later I learned that the Blood Moons 101 ebook produced by Israel365 was based on a massive PowerPoint presentation that had been compiled by Donna Jollay.

market our free lessons to their large email list.

We ended up releasing six lessons[6] on the Blood Moons back in the spring of 2015. They were a hit, and many people were being transformed and encouraged by that message. After that success, Gidon came to me again and said, "Let's work on a book together, that combines your ideas and mine." Two years earlier I had let go of my book idea, but now here was Gidon asking *me* to join *him*! I promised God that I (a Christian) would not write a book. But here was an Orthodox Jew suggesting that we do one together.[7] Thus, *Israel FIRST!*[8] was released in the fall of 2015 covering the Blood Moons, the Shemitah, the promises in GENESIS 12:3, and the Jubilee.

The Blood Moons – What we Published in 2015

Our published message in 2015 regarding the Blood Moons went like this:

The Blood Moons are *not* a sign of trouble, but rather a cause for celebration.[9] Rather than standing on the ground, looking up at the sky and proclaiming, "Those Blood Moons are significant because they fall on feast days," we need to be looking down upon the Earth and saying "Those feast days are significant because of the Blood Moons." Gidon then wrote down his personal view that they were a sign that the Jewish people needed to *change their minds* about Christians who were repenting for the sins of their past.[10] Gidon and I were in agreement that the Blood Moons seemed to be a sign from God, a sign for good and not harm. Some video lesson viewers then pointed out this verse to us:

> His line shall continue forever, his throne, as the sun before Me, **as the moon, established forever, an enduring witness in the sky.** Selah. PSALM 89:37-38 (TIB, emphasis mine)

Not only were the Jewish people continuously in God's hands, as evidenced by the Moon, we revealed that every time the four Blood Moons appeared in the sky,[11] the Jewish people had moved *out of harm's way* and advanced towards their restoration as a people in their own land. The Blood Moons **were a cause of celebration**, in the Blood Moon years of 1967/68, 1949/50, 1493/94, and also all

---

[6]   Short link to Blood Moons part 6 on Root Source: https://bit.ly/BloodMoons6

[7]   I still prayed about it, but God quickly gave me the green light. Apparently He wanted me to give the research to Gidon as an offering. I didn't expect that it would ever be given back to me in such a way (Luke 6:38). My mouth was open with surprise.

[8]   http://www.israelfirstbook.com

[9]   Ariel, Gidon & O'Dell, Bob, *Israel FIRST!*, (Jerusalem, Israel: Root Source Press, 2015), 75, 90, 268.

[10] The topic of chapter 1.

[11] Jeremiah 31:35-37

the way back to the earlier occurrences of the Blood Moons in 1428/29, 860/61, 842/43, 795/96 and 162/63 CE.

Our biblical pattern for festive celebration was clearly defined in the entire book of Exodus! In particular, we studied the series of feasts highlighted by the Blood Moons: Passover, Sukkot, Passover and Sukkot. Just as the four Blood Moons happened over two years, so also were those first four feasts spread over the first two years in the wilderness. They were the critical period in which Israel was not only **saved out** of slavery in Egypt, but began to **move towards** their destination to Israel.[12] And to top it all off, in our book we even revealed an exciting (yet admittedly a long shot) idea, wondering if it was possible that four Blood Moons actually appeared in the sky during the first two years of the original Exodus!

That is what we thought we knew in 2015 regarding the Blood Moons. But hold on, because something (in our understanding) is about to change.

The Blood Moons – What we think Today

Today, some years later, I only see more evidence towards our theory, not less. Therefore today, I would like to take another step forward and suggest that:

The four Blood Moons are not only a sign of the original Exodus, but a sign of the salvation of Israel.

Four Wine Cups at Seder Dinner.

I admit, that sounds like a pretty big claim! But, maybe the real problem is us.

---

[12] If you are thinking the word redemption might be appropriate, I agree. But have patience, the chapter's not over.

Maybe most Christians, including myself, have been looking at salvation in too narrow a sense. Perhaps we should consider salvation more in the ways that Jews see *redemption*, which is in Hebrew: *geula*.

Before I present the case to Christian readers that **Exodus is the story of the salvation of Israel**, I would like to remind you that many passages in the New Testament speak of *salvation* in all three tenses: past, present and future. This is well-known in Christianity:

- **He HAS saved us (regeneration)** – *"For by grace you have been saved through faith; and that not of yourselves, it is the gift of God;"* EPHESIANS 2:8

- **He IS saving us (sanctification)** – *"Therefore we do not lose heart, but though our outer man is decaying, yet our inner man is being renewed day by day."* 2 CORINTHIANS 4:16

- **He WILL save us (glorification)** – *"who are protected by the power of God through faith for a salvation ready to be revealed in the last time."* 1 PETER 1:5

And then there is the dimension of *joint responsibility* between God and us for *our* salvation:

> So then, my beloved, just as you have always obeyed, not as in my presence only, but now much more in my absence, **work out your salvation with fear and trembling**; for it is God who is at work in you, both to will and to work for His good pleasure. PHILIPPIANS 2:12-13 (emphasis mine)

Now with this larger view of salvation in mind, look carefully at the following elements of the physical story of the Exodus, and see if you cannot find many of these elements in your own theology of salvation as a Christian:

- Israel is miserable and stuck in slavery.

- God sends help, but not with immediate impact. In fact, things in Egypt get a lot worse before they get better.

- After the plagues are finished, God's offer is much more complete — a whole new way of life and to return to the Promised Land.

- God speaks both directly through miracles, and also through men — Moses and Aaron.

- The people learn a name of God that they previously did not know.

- The people must exercise faith in God in many stages, and especially during the Passover. Their faith is tested many times.

- Death "visits," but "passes over" the houses of people who place blood on the doorposts.

- The people begin a journey with God to learn of His ways and to have their entire way of life changed forever.

- God never relents from His promise to ultimately take them to the Promised Land.

Do you see what I see? I see in each of the items above the very same principles of past, present and future salvation as described in the New Testament — not a narrow sense of salvation, but a larger sense of salvation as detailed by Christian theologians.

If you have tracked with me so far and can accept it, **you should still have one big question** left in your mind: If salvation is played out in the story of the Exodus, how can I possibly propose to connect *salvation* to the *Blood Moons*?

How is the Exodus story connected to our theory of the Blood Moons? It is a very good question, and here are my three answers.

First, Moses demands that Pharaoh let the people go **so that they can go celebrate**! They are to go celebrate a feast to the Lord after a three-day's journey outside of Egypt!

> *Afterward Moshe and Aharon went and said to Pharaoh, "Thus says Hashem, the God of Yisrael: Let My people go that they may* **celebrate a festival** *for Me in the wilderness."* EXODUS 5:1 (TIB, emphasis mine)

Second, when God institutes the feasts in EXODUS 12, and says that they will be celebrated "for all time" (verse 14), He goes on to further clarify in EXODUS 13:10 that they should be celebrated "from year to year," which in the Hebrew literally means **"from days to days."**

The Blood Moons come in a sequence of four consecutive total lunar eclipses over two years. The celebrations are from Passover in one year to Passover in the next, and from Sukkot in one year to Sukkot in the next. The Blood moons cover that interlocking sequence perfectly.

And finally, we have **"The Four I Wills"**. Before the journey ever started, God tells Moses what His ultimate purpose of the Exodus really is by making four unilateral declarations of not only His intention, but the final result. These declarations are known as **The Four I Wills** in EXODUS:

> Say, therefore, to B'nei Yisrael [the sons of Israel]: I am Hashem.
>
> *1. I **will** free you from the labors of the Egyptians and deliver you from their bondage.*

2. ***I will*** *redeem you with an outstretched arm and through extraordinary chastisements.*

3. *And **I will** take you to be My people,*

4. *and **I will** be your God.*

And you shall know that I, Hashem, am your God who freed you from the labors of the Egyptians. EXODUS 6:6-7 (TIB, emphases mine)

The Jewish people even today during the annual Passover Seder meal, pour four cups of red wine to celebrate their redemption: one for each of the **Four I Wills**. I believe that these four cups of red wine, blood red wine if you will, parallel the four blood red moons that God placed in the sky — moons that when they ever happen, can ONLY begin on Passover, never Sukkot.[13]

Summary

The Passover Seder is a *celebration* of life even while the angel of death is close at hand. It is the first organized celebration of salvation in the Bible, and I believe the Blood Moons are a further witness to God's ultimate purpose in that salvation, which are described in the **Four I Wills** of the Exodus story.

In the next chapter, we will move on from the Blood Moons take up a discussion of a type of salvation that we rarely if ever consider as Christians: national salvation.

Shalom.

Asking Gidon

Gidon, how important to you are the Four I Wills, and the corresponding four cups of wine in your own Passover Seders in Israel? Do you drink all four cups completely?

These four "I wills" are very well known in Judaism, and are part of the many "fours" that are very prominent in the Passover Seder. We do drink all four cups completely! Which is why sales of low alcohol wine are considerably higher just prior to Passover in Israel!

---

[13] I want to acknowledge Lesley Richardson as the first Christian to explain the **Four I Wills** to me.

Do Orthodox Jews use the word "salvation" in the telling of the Exodus story? What does that word mean to Jews, if not generally then at least in the context of the Exodus story?

The word salvation can probably have numerous translations in Hebrew. The most popular one is probably *yeshu'ah*, which appears in the Bible a surprisingly few times, only nineteen according to the tora.us.fm concordance,[14] mostly in Psalms and Isaiah (whose name actually means "God is my salvation"). As you mentioned in this chapter, the four "I Wills" do not use the word *yeshu'ah*, so the terminologies used there are more popular in the Passover context.

What do Jews mean when they refer to *geula*, that which is typically translated as *redemption*, and how does that word differ from salvation in Jewish understanding?

I don't know that the biblical word *yeshu'ah* has a significantly different meaning than *ge'ulah* (which has closer to a hundred appearances in the Bible), usually translated as redemption. I think that the concept of redemption in Jewish thought has a more nationwide and even worldwide connotation, while *yeshu'ah* has a personal, individual connotation. Make of that what you will ☺

Gidon's last answer leads us right into the next chapter!

---

[14] Short link to the Hebrew concordance: https://bit.ly/yeshuah19

CHAPTER 23

National Salvation and Christianity

This book contains essays that are attempting to offer some observation or insight about things that are happening at the intersection of Christian/ Jewish relations. This chapter's topic is a lot heavier on the observation than the insight.

How should Christians think about *national salvation*?

In the previous chapter we discussed the similarities between the story of the Exodus and the idea of personal salvation as understood by Christians. While many aspects are comparable, this chapter discusses four aspects of salvation that do not compare easily.

First, the Exodus story is the birth of a new nation. A large family enters Egypt and hundreds of years later, a nation named Israel — the Israelites — make their Exodus from it. As we saw in the last chapter, God promised to free them, redeem them, take them as a people, and to be their God. Because Israel was chosen corporately, not one person at a time, it makes sense that their salvation is to be corporate as well.[1]

Revelation at Mount Sinai.

---

[1] The *chosenness* of Abraham, Isaac, Jacob, and ultimately the nation of Israel is not a major topic of this book. Gidon, for his part, will only allude to *chosenness* in his first answer of this chapter. I wonder, do we Christians really understand *chosenness*? A friend once suggested the following question to be a good *chosenness conversation starter*: Was the rebirth of Israel in 1948 an act of the United Nations, or an act of God's chosenness?

Then what of Christians? Yes, it is true that national concepts do appear in the New Testament. But I think I could argue that there is heavier practical teaching in the New Testament on manifesting a spiritual kingdom on earth, than building an earthly kingdom.[2] Even if you disagree with that, I think everyone can agree that to the extent an earthly kingdom is portrayed, it is not a kingdom that is wholly separate from the idea of *Israel*. Is it any wonder, then, why Replacement Theology was like a "forbidden fruit" that was tempting and inviting, and was plucked from the tree and offered from Christian to Christian for 2,000 years?

Now the fact that the New Testament primarily emphasizes a non-political spiritual kingdom is not to say that the New Testament does not strongly develop the idea of "the nations." It does.[3] But, much of the instruction in the New Testament was on how to bring a spiritual, heavenly kingdom down into the here and now — "thy kingdom come" — in whatever nation in which one happened to reside.

Second, the newly formed nation of Israel had physical adversaries. Israel had to defeat physical adversaries such as Pharaoh and his army, as well as the Amalekites, and many others along the way. The New Testament does not ask us to go out and start our own new nations, and wage physical battles against any enemies who would hinder that effort. Instead it asks us to try to live peaceably in whatever nation in which we find ourselves. We are told that our battle is not to wage war against flesh and blood, but to use spiritual tools to do battle in the heavenly realms against spiritual enemies.[4] We are also taught to fight sin in our own lives, to overcome it, and to become ever more like God Himself.

Third, the nation of Israel was on a physical journey to a physical Israel. The nation of Israel was on its way to a physical land that had already been given to them by God. The New Testament teaches clearly that we Gentiles can become spiritual descendents of Abraham,[5] that we can be grafted into the olive tree that is Israel, and that we can be brought into what Ephesians also refers to as the commonwealth of Israel.[6] Yet many Christians find their hearts being drawn to the land of Israel physically, wanting to actually live there. A few may achieve that, but most must be content to visit on tourist visas. This topic could take us into

---

[2] John 8:36

[3] First, the word Israel is never modified in its meaning compared to its use in the Hebrew Bible, as both a place and a people. Neither did the resurrected Christ in any way criticise His disciples for asking *when* the kingdom might be restored to it (Acts 1:6-7). Second, the word *ethnos*, while it is more often translated as Gentiles, is still translated nation, or nations, dozens of times. Third, the book of Revelation goes out of its way to retain the concept of "nations" as distinct from "tribes, peoples and tongues" (Revelation 7:9), both now and in the age to come (Revelation 22:2).

[4] Ephesians 6:12

[5] Galatians 3:29

[6] Ephesians 2:12

many different areas of thought, such as the topics of sojourners (or *ger)*, the ten tribes, Israel's immigration policy today, and the definition of a Jew. Some writers zestfully tackle these topics publicly and in print,[7] while it seems other writers or ministries have made a decision to never touch these topics at all. I don't fit into either category, by the way.[8] But, for the majority of Christians today, the land of promise is a place called Heaven.[9]

Fourth, the nation of Israel was brought to Mount Sinai to enter into covenant. The nation of Israel was asked by God at Mount Sinai if they would be willing to enter into a national covenant with Him. According to Scripture, the entire nation committed itself to obey those commandments.[10] Today, those who believe that Jesus is the Messiah are sharply divided on what the Mosaic commandments mean for us. Numerous positions are taken. I suppose that they range from, on one extreme: a Christian must keep all the commandments (as is possible to keep) to be "saved"; and on the other extreme: the Old Testament and all its commandments (including the Ten Commandments) were fulfilled and therefore made null and void by the Resurrection of Christ.[11]

Today, I would suggest that the most common position among all Christians worldwide is that we Christians should keep the Ten Commandments, and to follow everything written in the New Testament. The irony of this most common view is that most Christians are not aware that the New Testament has over 1,000 unique commandments in it,[12] many more than the 613 commands in the Torah![13] But the middle ground is quite large and growing. Many Christians find themselves drawn to keep some aspects of the Torah given at Sinai: Shabbat, keeping the biblical feasts of the Lord, and restricting diet towards only eating meat that is biblically clean. While they often differ on the details and the biblical justification of their particular choices, the fact that hundreds of thousands — if not millions — of non-Jews are being "drawn" to move towards such practices is the most important observation of all! Something is going on here, and while I do not know, I wonder if it has something to do with the subject of this chapter, an inner longing for a larger, national salvation.

---

[7] In the Orthodox Jewish world, I appreciate the approach of Hanoch Young with his website kolyehuda. com who addresses the Ten Tribes topic openly, but without proposing a reconciliation plan.

[8] After five years wrestling with various aspects of it, I finally wrote about it in 2019, I'm just not taking it up in this book. See chapter 12 in *One in Messiah, Perspectives on Commonwealth Theology Presented at the Denver Convocation 2019*, pp. 307-350, available on Amazon: https://amzn.to/3cmmJzl

[9] Hebrews 12:22-23

[10] Exodus 24:3

[11] If you know of a more extreme position in either direction, please write to me!

[12] Short link to 1,050 New Testament commands compiled by Christian Assemblies International: https:// bit.ly/1050commands

[13] I suppose that most Christians today, if they are honest with themselves, consider most of the New Testament commands more like suggestions and guidelines, rather than hard-and-fast commandments.

So to summarize, what we just covered are four additional elements of the "salvation of Israel" that appear in the Exodus story, but are not embraced in the Christian idea of salvation. What do we do about these additional elements?

First — Do No Harm

I consider myself to be a "learner" in all these topics. I do not have hard-and-fast conclusions about all of them. I have not found any follower of Yeshua yet who has views that fully answer all my questions in any of these four topics, much less all of them combined. I often find that the more certain a Christian becomes, the more certain they are that they have "worked it all out," the less comfortable I get. But what I do feel very strongly about is the need to "do no harm" in my process of being a learner.

For me that comes in the form of both a Commandment A and a Commandment B, which are my personal instructions that I believe I have heard from the Lord (and from Scripture).

- Commandment A while learning: **Honor the Israel of the "here and now."**

The evidence is overwhelming that the Israel of the here and now is a miracle of God. Gidon considers that Israel today refers to three entities: a land — the Land of Israel; a state — a Jewish political state that has a flag and law and borders etc; and a people — the Jewish People. That works for me. I therefore consider that my first commandment in the work I do regarding Israel, is to honor the ongoing work of God in these three aspects of Israel.

- Commandment B while learning: **Stand against Replacement Theology in the nations**.

If I believe that God is at work in Israel, I must also believe that God is at work in the nations of the world as well. By nations I also mean the territories, the various nation states (Mexico, Ghana, etc.) and all the ethnic people groups distributed around the world, and the spiritual work of God in those various nations through Christ. But I see my main job in the nations, as it relates to Israel, as standing against Replacement Theology, which has led to massive sin against the Jews. What that means practically, is that while I remain a learner on those four big topics above, I will not hesitate to "call out" and "stand against" anything that looks and feels like Replacement Theology in any current nation of the world.

Now having revealed to you my two commandments of learning, I will venture into a final topic regarding national salvation: which nation on earth, if any, has been built on the idea of national salvation?

Second — What about the United States?

Because I know the USA better than other nations, I find it easiest to discuss it. But if your nation has a story that might be similar, you may find these questions relevant to you, as well.

Was the United States built around *national salvation* as in Exodus?

On this topic I am also still thinking, still learning. In such cases I try to think it through by trying to make the case *for* and the case *against*.

The Case For

1. The founders at Plymouth Rock considered themselves as having made an Exodus from the tyranny of England.

2. The fact that a relief portrait of Moses hangs in the halls of Congress[14] is testimony to what has been often written in conservative journals: that the Pilgrims were seeking to escape slavery in Europe, to find their freedom, and that they took on that task under the direction of the Christian Bible (both Testaments).

3. In addition, during the development and deliberations regarding the US Constitution, the Bible was by far the most often quoted reference source.

4. The Bible was taught early on, and Hebrew was taught at early collegiate institutions.

5. Many of the earliest arrivals spoke about coming to create a "new Israel" where they could worship God freely and build a new kind of community.[15]

6. Much of our principles of democracy and legal code is based on the Torah.

The Case Against

1. While many, if not most of the early founding fathers were Christian, there was no religious requirement placed upon those early founders. Secular views were present, and some of the strongest voices in the Constitutional

---

[14] Moses' relief portrait is one of twenty-three profiles of historical figures noted for their work in establishing the principles that underlie American law. The eleven profiles in the eastern half of the chamber face left and the eleven in the western half face right, so that all look towards the full-face relief of Moses in the center of the north wall. Short link to the relief portrait plaques on Architect of the Capitol: https://bit.ly/23reliefs

[15] For the historical record on this, see *The Light and the Glory*, by Peter Marshall. https://amzn.to/37nJpyv

process were secular.

2. Secular views are fully protected whether they be the minority or the majority. The Constitution stated that no laws should be made concerning religious practice, that which we commonly call "the separation of church and state."

3. The Constitution, not the Bible, dictates how the nation is to be governed, and such governance was to come up from the people in the form of elected officials. Thus, as John Adams saw so clearly: the governance of this nation was not able to work if the people were not themselves moral.[16]

4. The Ten Commandments are no longer taught, mandated prayer in public schools is gone, per the Constitution under the establishment clause of the First Amendment.

So on which side do you, dear reader, fall? Is the United States a candidate for national salvation, or not?

In the first book I wrote with Gidon, *Israel FIRST!*, we observed the trends, and held present-day events up to the light of God's Word, and made a number of predictions. But there is one prediction I made, about which I am much less sure today: that the United States is on the path to complete destruction *unless the nation repents soon*. It's not that I've changed my mind about the importance of repentance — we must still repent! The part that I am no longer sure about is whether the continued existence of the United States is a *conditional* existence. I am now thinking that it is possible that if the United States sins so long and so badly that we are "sent into exile," that such an exile would *not* spell the ultimate conclusion and destruction of our nation. I am thinking it is possible that if we, like Israel, are sent into exile, that our future descendants, if dispersed, could be gathered again later. Furthermore, if our descendants are not regathered as an entity called the United States, then at least those who are Bible-believing, pro-Israel, Jew-respecting Christians will one day be invited to make an exodus to the nation of Israel; that is to say, being regathered out of exile into the land of Israel.[17] It seems that Scripture strongly hints at a regathering of those who desire it from all around the world into Israel, but even if correct, I don't see it happening anytime soon.[18]

So which is it? Is the United States a nation whose "national salvation" is contingent

---

[16] https://wallbuilders.com/importance-morality-religion-government/

[17] Avi Lipkin created a political party in Israel to prepare for this future influx of Christians into Israel. Short link to article on Jerusalem Post: https://bit.ly/Lipkin-Bloc

[18] Jeremiah 16:14-15 promises an influx to Israel so big that people will stop talking about the original Exodus from Egypt. How that promise could dovetail with the "two sticks becoming one in God's

on repentance, or is the United States a nation of destiny that, like Israel, God considers to have already made His decision that "the United States will be saved," even as He said the same thing about Israel.[19] And if you live in another nation, you have the very same question before you as well. Every nation has its story.

Regardless of your position on this question, or your own journey towards answering this question, we can all agree on this: the United States today is in a great struggle. I see the struggle as between

1. the belief in the One True God and living by His principles that are set out in the Bible, and

2. the belief that certain smart/successful people have progressed in their capability to "know the good" way we should go, and are asking (if not demanding) us to follow *them* rather than God.

Those choices are clear. One choice is choosing the Tree of Life and the other, the Tree of Knowledge of Good and Evil. Is there anything new under the Sun?

May God save every nation on the Earth!

Shalom.

Asking Gidon

Gidon, you mentioned in the last chapter that you see salvation as more of a national issue than a personal one. In your view, does that national salvation happen "on the way" to the coming of the Messiah, or only after He arrives?

From what I have heard and read, I understand that Christianity is heavily focused on personal salvation, being personally saved by the Savior, usually understood as being a *quid pro quo* for accepting that Savior into one's life.

Judaism has no such concept! Our relationship with God is based on our being a member of His chosen nation, or of His chosen human race.

The enjoyment of one's life thanks to pursuing a relationship with God can be a byproduct of that pursuit, but many other factors go into quality of life,

---

hand" prophecy in Ezekiel 37:18-23 is not addressed in this book. See my chapter 12 in *One in Messiah, Perspectives on Commonwealth Theology Presented at the Denver Convocation 2019*, pp. 307-350, available on Amazon: https://amzn.to/3cmmJzl

[19] Romans 11:26

discussed in answers to the question "why do bad things happen to good people?" A relatively simplistic answer is that a person's reward for good behavior in this world will be given in the next world, but this answer is not without difficulties.

In any case, Jews envision that the coming of the Messiah, God's human representative on earth, will happen when He decides that the time for the final scene of history has come. That Messiah will be the King of the Jewish people, and the King of the whole world.

The concept of Salvation is usually used in Jewish context as a synonym for Redemption — that final stage of human history. So "national salvation" is a synonym for "Messianic age." We think more in terms of "the Messianic Age" as opposed to just an individual messianic King arriving from "out of the blue" as it were. The fact that so many messianic prophecies have been realized in our age, before the Messiah's arrival, is a clear sign that we are in that Messianic Age.

But since you specifically asked about salvation, the Jewish nation is "saved" when it no longer is subject to the whims of malevolent non-Jewish kings and perhaps values. In my opinion it is clear that we are part of the way there with the establishment and success of the State of Israel, but we are not all the way there yet.

It turns out that I happen to be writing this answer to you on Israel's Holocaust Memorial Day, exactly one week before Israel's Independence Day. The contrast between these two days screams out an answer to the entire world of what Israel's "salvation" looks like.

How does the Day of Atonement, the holiday of Yom Kippur, fit into the Jewish idea of national salvation? Is Yom Kippur the day in which the nation as a whole is forgiven by God and saved from exile?

The concept of national redemption seems to be a point (or era) in Jewish and world history, while Yom Kippur occurs annually. However, the concept of *teshuva*, repentance, figures prominently in both.

Yom Kippur is our most intense day of prayer all year, with five prayer services occurring throughout that day. In one of those prayer services there is a part called *Kedushah* (holiness), which eventually reaches its pinnacle moment as we collectively pray:

> *"Holy, Holy, Holy, is the* LORD *of hosts, The whole earth is full of His glory."*
> ISAIAH 6:3b

However, just before we begin the *Kedushah*, we sing/pray a poem in which is the most sombre moment of the day, where we reach the point in that poem when we pray: "On Rosh Hashanah it is written and on Yom Kippur it is sealed, those who will live and those who will die [in the coming year]." Yet, just following that serious pronouncement, we pray: "But in spite of God's decision, repentance, charity and prayer may cause God to annul the bad decree." So repentance is woven tightly into the primary message of Yom Kippur, even at one of the awe inspiring moments of the day.[20]

What are a few things that Jews do personally in the days and weeks leading up to Yom Kippur to prepare for that national holiday?

Special prayers are added to our regular prayers, and special forgiveness prayer sessions (Hebrew: "*selichot*' — forgiveness prayers) are added as well. During this period people make a point of reviewing that which has happened during the year, and asking for forgiveness from one another.

One of the prayers added towards the end of our morning and evening prayer service during the twenty-nine days of the month of Elul is PSALM 27. It begins with:

> *The* LORD *is my light and my salvation; Whom shall I fear? The* LORD *is the defense of my life; Whom shall I dread?* PSALM 27:1

Despite what I said two answers prior, that we are a corporate nation with a relationship with God, that does not mean that we avoid praying passages such as PSALM 27 that twice mentions personal salvation! I hope this encourages readers to see the answers I give, not as the complete word on anything, but a starting point of discussion.

---

[20] It is commonly thought that this Yom Kippur poem inspired the Leonard Cohen song "Who by Fire." https://youtu.be/EgMaBreDuF4

CHAPTER 24

A View Too Small: Resurrection

This book covers topics that live at the intersection of the Christian world and the Jewish world. I hope that I have been able to reach my goal in many of the preceding chapters to make you *think about something* that you may have never considered before!

Beginning with this chapter we start a series of chapters in which I don't believe we (as Christians) are *wrong*, but for which our current view is just *too small*. The first of these topics is: *resurrection*.

In choosing this topic I feel like a sprinter who wears sprinting shoes to a marathon! In other words: we *are not* in for a slow start!

But the reason I want to begin with the "big kahuna" of *resurrection* is because readers may still recall my comments in chapter 20, *The Great Divide*. In that chapter I may have left some readers wondering if I have betrayed my own evangelical heritage by telling Christians that it is more important that we get right with God ourselves, than it is to evangelize the Jews of Israel. That approach never dealt with that great unknown that lies beyond the veil of death for the Jewish People. In so doing am I forsaking the ministry of the Gospel of Christ as I have been commanded in Scripture? On the other hand, as detailed in chapter 16, I have worked for years in researching and in support of various worldwide gospel ministries towards Muslims. Why do I strongly support missions overall, but not in Israel?

A View too Small

I believe that when it comes to Israel, we Christians are generally underestimating the power of God to fulfill His promises to His chosen people.

The tragic history of Christianity is that we have viewed the "lack of response" by Jews to the announcement of Jesus as the Messiah as an ever-present indictment of them, and an indication that God has forsaken them. And yet this historical mistake, that led not only to Replacement Theology and persecution of Jews, flies in the face of what Paul boldly proclaimed in Romans:

> *All Israel will be saved.* ROMANS 11:26a

This verse sends Christian theologians into a tailspin trying to explain how the word "all" means something less than "all." One solution they latch onto is to define "Israel" as something less than "all the Jews." I have personally heard this verse twisted around so violently as to use it as *proof* that Messianic Jews are the "true *Israel*" because only Messianic Jews are *saved*! I consider this view a new twist on the old theme of Replacement Theology, which inevitably results in finding some way to exclude the vast majority of Jews from the promises of God.

Others read this verse and focus on the future tense "will be saved" and define it in this way: All the Jews who are alive and on earth at the time that Yeshua is revealed to them as the Messiah, and believe in Him — *those* Jews will be saved, but all those who died before that time are lost.

Please consider the implications of that idea! Do you realize that at this very moment, less than 10 percent of Jews who ever lived are living on earth right now? Have you considered that this interpretation of "All Israel will be saved" is condemning 90 percent of Jews to a lack of salvation?

Such an interpretation cannot possibly fulfill that verse. It is a view too small.

Yet how do we as Christians reconcile the gap? How do we as Christians believe Jesus when He said *"No one comes to the Father except through me"* (JOHN 14:6, ESV), and also believe the declaration of Paul that *"all Israel will be saved"* (ROMANS 11:26)?

The answer I would propose to you, towards a larger view, is through the idea of *resurrection*.

Resurrection as a Solution

Earlier in the same chapter in which Paul tells us that "all Israel will be saved," he tells us that our own salvation was dependent on the nation of Israel as a whole not recognizing Jesus:

> *By their transgression salvation has come to the Gentiles.* ROMANS 11:11b

But with regard to that which is still to come, Paul strongly hints at resurrection when he says:

> *If their rejection is the reconciliation of the world, what will their acceptance be but* **life from the dead**. ROMANS 11:15 (emphasis mine)

What I am saying is that we Christians have worn down a path in our minds to read these scriptures as intending "the smallest fulfillment" that can possibly fulfill them. Yet three verses earlier Paul exhorts us to imagine the *largest* fulfillment we possibly can!

> *Now if their [Israel's] transgression is* **riches** *for the world and their failure is riches for the Gentiles, how much more will their* **fulfillment** *be!* ROMANS 11:12 (emphases mine)

We are being exhorted to think big, not small.

We Christians fall into the same trap in the Old Testament when we read about the Valley of Dry Bones in Ezekiel:

> *Then He said to me, "Prophesy to the breath, prophesy, O mortal! Say to the breath: Thus said Hashem: Come, O breath, from the four winds, and breathe into these slain, that they may live again." I prophesied as He commanded me. The breath entered them, and they came to life and stood up on their feet, a vast multitude.* EZEKIEL 37:9-10 (TIB)

As was mentioned in chapter 16, a verse from this very passage is inscribed near the entrance of Yad Vashem, the Holocaust Memorial in Jerusalem. Indeed, through the unspeakable horror of the Holocaust, the nation state of Israel has come back to life in the land originally given to it by God: Israel. I don't have any problem with Christians proclaiming that this verse has been fulfilled in the rebirth of Israel in 1948; I only have a problem if Christians proclaim that it is the ONLY fulfillment of this verse!

Again, there is a tendency to read the Bible in a way that is too small.

If you read it as being fulfilled in the death of six million Jews and the rebirth of Israel, then to what end do you ascribe the countless Jews who walked into the gas chambers of Auschwitz while singing the Shema?[1] Is the very Messiah, who in the New Testament would "leave the ninety-nine to recover the one,"[2] not going to recover those who were calling on the Name of Adonai at Auschwitz? The

---

[1] Deuteronomy 6:4
[2] The Parable of the Lost Sheep, Matthew 18:12-14.

solution that I see, one that preserves the integrity of everything written in the entire Christian Bible, is *resurrection*. Perhaps these same people will be resurrected by the Messiah in the future, and given the chance to welcome Him [Jesus] into Jerusalem with the greeting: *"Blessed is He who comes in the name of the Lord."*

> *For I tell you, you will not see me again until you say, 'Blessed is he who comes in the name of the Lord.'"* MATTHEW 23:39 (NIV)

In the New Testament, the Greek word for resurrection is *anastasis*, which literally means "a standing up" or "a resurrection." The very first appearance of this word in the life of Yeshua is recorded in the words spoken over Him by Simeon, a devout Jew in the Temple who said to Joseph and Mary:

> *"Behold, this [Child] is appointed for the fall and rise [anastasis] of many in Israel."* LUKE 2:34b

The translators chose the word "rise" in this case, but in every other case in the New Testament, *anastasis* is translated *resurrection*. I believe this verse is a reinforcement of the prophecy of the resurrection of Israel as spoken about in EZEKIEL 37. The vast multitude of Israel will both *rise up* and *come back to life* on this earth.

Much more could be said on this topic. My purpose is not to convince you, but simply to introduce the idea of *resurrection as a solution* to readers who are trying to reconcile the idea that Jesus is the only way to the Father, and God's promise that "All Israel will be saved." Now surely Jewish scholars would diverge with us about how salvation is and will be accomplished in the Jewish People, but I am speaking to Christians and the Christian-mindset here.

However, there is one place in which both Jews and Christians wholeheartedly agree. Unlike the Sadducees described in the New Testament, Orthodox Jews today firmly believe in resurrection. It may surprise you to learn that:

Jews pray for resurrection twelves times a day!

Contained within the eighteen blessings of the Amidah in the Jewish prayer service[3] is the second of those blessings about God's Might which can be translated as follows:

> *Your might is eternal, O LORD, Who **revives the dead**, powerful in saving, Who sustains the living with loving-kindness, Who **revives the dead** with great mercy, Who supports the falling, heals the sick, frees the captive, and keeps faith with those asleep in the dust. Who is like You, Almighty, and who resembles You, O King?*

---

[3] Short link to download document here: https://bit.ly/Siddur-weekdays

*Who can bring death and give life, and can make salvation blossom forth! And faithful are You to **revive the dead**. Blessed are You, LORD, Who **revives the dead**.* (emphases mine)

Not only is a future resurrection prayed four times, but salvation is affirmed twice! The Amidah is prayed in all three prayer services: morning, afternoon and evening. Therefore, *resurrection* is proclaimed at least twelve times per day by every Orthodox Jew!

The prophecy in EZEKIEL 37 talks about a breath of life that must be breathed upon the dry bones. From where does that breath come? It comes from the *four winds*.[4] While we Christians absolutely believe in the resurrection of the dead, we do **not** often pray for it. On the other hand, millions of Jews pray this very blessing daily all over the globe, and they pray it individually and whisper it through the gentle breath of their mouths. (The Amidah is whispered gently, only loud enough so that the person praying can hear it!)

It must be through the combined prayers of the Amidah that God will accomplish resurrection and salvation for Israel, as if it were all the combined breaths of all the prayers ever prayed that will come rushing down upon those bones from all directions: the four winds!

It is time for us as Christians to enlarge a view that has not been wrong, but has been way too small. We need to see a larger role for the might of God, believing and perhaps even praying WITH the Jews the very prayer they are already praying *twelve* times a day.

Twelve times a day? Indeed, *all Israel* will be saved!

Shalom.

Asking Gidon

Gidon, if a Rabbi were holding a lecture on the topic of *resurrection*, what kinds of things might you expect to hear in such a lecture? Redemption? Messiah? The world to come?

Well, all three of those terms, even all four of them if you include resurrection also, are part of the same package. Which is in contrast to Christians, who I

---

4   Ezekiel 37:9 is followed by the promise in verse 14 that this Spirit gives life.

understand can be quite argumentative with each other. For example, whether the future is premillennial or postmillennial, Jews recognize differences of opinion with regard to what order these will happen in, but are content to wait for them to happen to make a final decision. So the answer to your question would certainly be "the End Times."

While Christians tend to speak more in terms of heaven, it seems that Jews speak more often about the world to come. How do you say that in Hebrew, and what kind of things come to your mind when you think about that phrase?

The World to Come in Hebrew is *Olam Haba*. I think what comes to mind is "complete and final reward." This is based on the teaching of the Sages in the Talmud tractate Eruvin page 22a[5] on the verse in DEUTERONOMY 7:11. Rabbi Yehoshua ben Levi said:

> What is the meaning of the verse: "And you shall keep the commandments, and the statutes, and the judgments which I command you today to do them"? It means: …Today is the time to do them, but only tomorrow, in the ultimate future, is the time to receive reward for doing them.

Putting aside who the Messiah might be when He comes, is there any traditional view on how the Messiah is to be greeted or welcomed?

This topic is not a topic in which there is a long-recorded tradition. But as a matter of fact, this question has been asked within the last fifty years, and a collection of blessings has been proposed to be used to greet the Messiah. Most of these blessings, when taken individually, are quite ancient; it is their compilation together for this purpose that is relatively new. While variations do exist, for your convenience here is a table that includes one list of six blessings with brief explanations, as compiled from this site: https://www.yeshiva.co/midrash/25315.

---

[5] https://bit.ly/Eruvin22a

BLESSING	EXPLANATION
Blessed are You, the Lord our G-d, King of the universe, who has granted of His wisdom to those who fear Him.	This blessing is said upon seeing an outstanding Torah scholar, which the Messiah certainly will be.
Blessed are You, the Lord our G-d, King of the universe, who has granted of His honor to those who fear Him.	The blessing said upon seeing a Jewish King.
Blessed are You, the Lord our G-d, King of the universe, the Master of secrets.	This blessing is made when one sees over 600,000 people gathered in one place at once. The blessing expresses our awe at G-d who has created such a multitude of people, all different from another, yet understands the needs of each one. Presumably, when the Messiah comes, the entire Jewish nation will gather in one place, thus prompting the recitation of this blessing.
Blessed are You, the Lord our G-d, King of the universe, who has given us life and sustained us and allowed us to reach this occasion.	The well known "Shehechiyanu" blessing, made upon experiencing good tidings, joy or a new event.
Blessed are You, the Lord our G-d, King of the universe, who has redeemed Israel.	The definition of our end-times hope, executed by the Messiah.
Blessed are You, the Lord our G-d, King of the universe, who is good and does good.	The blessing recited upon hearing exceptionally good news.

CHAPTER 25

A View Too Small: Torah

Here is another topic about which I don't believe we (as Christians) are totally *wrong*, but for which our current view is just *too small*. I believe our view of the *Torah, the first five books of the Bible,* is too small.

Let us begin with a story.

What Makes a Great Business?

My wife was recently telling me about a local exercise studio that was sold and how much it had changed. On the surface, it seemed as though nothing had changed. The building was exactly the same. The pricing hadn't changed. But over time membership started dropping with some of the staff leaving as well. Why? We agreed the change had to be attributed to the new owner.

This caused me to recall some of my past experience in the world of high-tech startups in Silicon Valley, California and in various startups in Israel. It was known that in the very best startups there was a certain kind of culture that was present, a culture that could be boiled down into just two aspects regarding the work environment.

1. *Involvement.* The leadership involved the employees in the workings of the company whenever possible. Employees felt encouraged to work hard, innovate, and were continually asked "is there a better way to do things?" Employees felt like part of a large family. They felt included in the discussions, they felt they had a voice, and they felt their voice would at least be heard, even if their suggestions might not ultimately be acted upon. In other words, company decisions and policies would need to be made, but there was some give and take, and employees could be part of the process. Naturally the earlier you joined the company, the more influence your own voice might have. Over time, a company's culture solidifies and is established at all levels. Nevertheless, the opportunity to

be part of one of those companies in the early days and help shape it can be a thrilling experience even if you are not in leadership. Such people feel intensely part of the community.

2.   *Vision.* Through many different kinds of interactions and forms of communication, the leadership believed and instilled in the employees a sense of vision and purpose for company direction. The leadership would speak often about how their company is on a mission to change the world, or improve the world. Employees bought in to the vision and worked long hours, both in the office and at home, and were often so engaged in the vision and purpose of the company that they would continue thinking about the products and the problems they faced even at night and on weekends. Sometimes the best ideas would come to employees at the most unexpected times.

No company is perfect, but in companies that fit what I describe above, I can assure you that such companies have people *eagerly wanting* to join them.

So why then was a fairly young exercise studio suddenly losing business? Because while the original owner did (1) and (2) very well, the second owner viewed the business as "something to manage." In the words of my wife: "The entrepreneurial spirit in that business has been lost."

Too Small a View of Torah

What does *involvement* and *vision* have to do with my claim that our view of the Torah, the Law, i.e. the first five books of the Bible, is *too small*?

Yes, many Christians see the Old Testament as an absolutely necessary part of the Bible. Yes, many Christians see the value of the Torah in helping us understand our Jewish Roots. Yes, many Christians have learned that the best translation of the word *Torah* is not *law* but rather *teaching or instruction*. But, even so, I think that we Christians are missing something huge, because we are viewing the Torah as a way for God to *manage a nation*, rather than a way for God to create and encourage an *entrepreneurial spirit*!

Simply put, we are viewing The Torah as a way that God (the Commander) gets His will done on earth (the control).

This view is too small!

God is the greatest entrepreneur that ever existed, or ever will exist, and the Torah is full of entrepreneurial spirit!

Let us look at the two previous items again, this time with Mount Sinai in our minds.

1. *Involvement.* God did not deliver the Ten Commandments just on stone, as if it were an operational manual from the Human Resources department, but He presented it directly to the people! Amazingly they both *saw* and *heard* the words personally, and the Jews say that everyone heard the commands in their own language.[1] The fact that they were terrified shows that this was probably the greatest, most awesome "sound and light show ever created" to reveal what the Great Entrepreneur had in mind! Indeed, even after Moses took on the primary role of messenger between the people and God, God was still interacting with the people through Moses. Individuals and the problems they brought to Moses would help refine the details of how the Torah was to be kept in the larger community. Occasionally God even added new commandments[2] to the *written* Torah based on their observations and questions, such as when the daughters of Zelophehad questioned the male-only inheritance ruling.[3]

2. *Vision.* The giving of the Torah was not about command and control, to keep the people from being too unruly in the desert; the Torah was about creating a brand new culture on earth. We think about *Jewish* culture and *Jewish* practices, but these things we see today were invented by God directly. They are an expression of none other than God's culture and God's preferred practices. The first big milestone of the vision was to fulfill what had been promised to Moses, that the people would come to the very mountain where the burning bush had stood. The next great milestone was to get the people ready to enter the Promised Land — not just to enter it, not just to conquer it, but to build in it a new kind of community, different from every other nation on earth, with the potential to stand the test of time. This community had the potential to live forever and not collapse as empires do when they are created in the image of man.

Too Small a View — Two Examples

Let's now look at two examples of mistakes that Christians can make, when we view the Torah as too small.

The first one involves the perception of God in traditional Christianity. If we

---

[1] Exodus 20:18, 22

[2] Moshe Kempinski of the Shorashim Shop once remarked that when Christians hear the word *commandments* they hear the word *burden*, and when Jews hear the word *commandments* they hear *swimming with God.*

[3] Numbers 27:1-11

see God at Mount Sinai as a "command and control" kind of God, and then we read about the grace and mercy of Yeshua as shown in the New Testament, then we unintentionally act as if God has changed, even though the Bible clearly says He does not![4] This leads theologians to various forms of dispensational thinking, where God's manner of interacting with mankind changes over time, as a result of the coming of Christ. The terms used for this thinking, like "The Age of Law" versus "The Age of Grace," are taught as axiomatic because of the formal theological labels that accompany them.

My point here is bigger than "whether you know and use such labels." It is to beware of any kind of thinking that pushes the Torah into either a status of being old and outdated, or harsh and restrictive. Paul says the Torah is our tutor.[5] If so, it is a good tutor, not an outdated one from a bygone era.

But our second example affects followers of Yeshua in the Hebrew Roots movement. Some followers of Yeshua celebrate the feasts of the Lord on days that are not aligned with the Hebrew calendar that the Jews are using. How did this happen? In recent decades, certain followers of Yeshua have studied the history of the Jewish calendar and every mention of the calendar in the Torah, and have *taken issue* with the way the Jewish people are interpreting and implementing the Torah's commands. The Jews, they say, are in error, and to correct the problem they wait another month to observe the feasts.

The complaint these followers have against the Jews is that they are no longer relying on human observations of the moon for their calendar as implied in the Torah and as it was done in the Temple periods. Rabbi Hillel II and others that followed him figured out a formula for the Jewish Calendar in about 358 CE.[6] This allowed Jews around the world to keep the same calendar everywhere without a centralized authority in Jerusalem — an ingenious solution during the Exile. But even though it was a brilliant move, over time it has drifted slightly. Yes, Jewish scholars know about this drift, but most Jews don't even notice, and even fewer are pressing for a worldwide change!

But to take issue with the way the Jews are following the Hebrew Calendar, is itself a mistake. It reveals that we as followers of Yeshua are *misunderstanding* the Torah on at least two levels. First, it misunderstands how God *involves His people* in the development and interpretation of the Torah. For a deeper understanding of this

---

4 Malachi 3:6; Hebrews 13:8
5 Galatians 3:24
6 https://en.wikipedia.org/wiki/Hillel_II#Fixing_of_the_calendar

principle, I suggest a Torah teaching given by Gidon Ariel,[7] in which he describes that the very first commandment given to the nation of Israel is a commandment involving *shared responsibility* between God and man! It is regarding the keeping of the Hebrew calendar! The implication is clear: God adjusts to the decision of the people, but He does not adjust to the decision of every person! In other words, **God expects the people to come together as a community and work and live together under a single calendar**.

So if a friend of mine questions the Jewish calendar today and wants to live by a corrected calendar, my response to them is this: "Even if you are *right*, you are *wrong*."

I tell them that "You are wrong because you are separating yourself from the calendar that the Jewish people have set." It doesn't matter if the current system is slightly off — God is adjusting to their community decision. Two competing calendars do not please God, and it creates separation between followers of Yeshua and the Jewish People. When the Jewish people are ready to make a community decision to change it, at that time we should change *with them*.

You may individually choose *not to observe* a certain day on the Hebrew Calendar. That's fine. But if you *observe* a day, don't separate yourself from the community decision.

Summary

I doubt if people are *consciously* trying to be hurtful to the Jewish People. We just don't understand the Torah. Unless we learn directly from the Jews, we will be reading the Torah apart from the Jews, and trying to interpret the commands precisely and correctly. But that is a view too small. We are missing the bigger point of:

1. God's *involvement* with His people in the interpretation of the Bible.

2. God's *vision* to create a new culture that would inspire the World.

God is pretty good at His work! I would say that He did a pretty good job getting a new entrepreneurial effort off the ground and inspiring the people to go take the Promised Land, and to build a community that had lasting potential. Indeed, the Jewish people have lasted for 3,500 years with this very culture, and now they are back in the Land.

---

[7] https://youtu.be/jK_Z2ei0zbc. This link takes you to the same video: https://bit.ly/Gidon-Torah

Silicon Valley has produced some amazing companies over the last fifty years, and likewise the nation of Israel is well known for having a culture that fosters many successful startups.

But it is time for us to celebrate that about 3,500 years ago *God founded a startup of His own.*

The Israelites who left Egypt were the original *Startup Nation!*

Shalom.

Asking Gidon

Gidon, I defined Torah as the first five books of the Bible. But I know that when you say the word Torah you may be referring to up to three different ideas, depending on the context. What are they?

As I wrote in *Israel FIRST!*, the multifaceted word Torah encompasses a number of things. It includes the Pentateuch (the Five Books of Moses), the entire Tanakh (the Old Testament), and the orally transmitted laws, stories and ideas given to the Jewish people at Mount Sinai together with the Written Torah. It also includes any idea that any student comes up with related to any of these, from the time of Moses over 3,000 years ago to this day.

As you mentioned in your own story in the Prologue, a school of Jewish learning for Torah is called a *yeshiva*. About how many yeshivas operate in Israel today?

Depending on how you define them, there are probably close to 2,000 yeshivas in Israel today, ranging in size from 10 to 6,000 students. Altogether there are probably about 150,000 students in Israeli yeshivas today studying at least half a day, 5 days a week. By the way, back in 1941 before the re-establishment of Israel, there were just 28 yeshivas in this land.

One of the most amazing phenomena in the demographics of the students is the exponential growth of serious Torah study among women. This trend, which would certainly astonish the sages of old, is very healthy to spiritual growth, as I have had occasion to personally witness among my own daughters.

What are a few of the differences people might see if they walked into a yeshiva, versus the typical college atmosphere with classes, lectures, homework and exams?

I don't think a single yeshiva student spends any significant amount of time in a yeshiva without hearing that Torah study is incomparable to academic study. In yeshiva, we are studying God's ideas, fulfilling God's will. The number one value in modern Judaism is *Limmud Torah Lishma* — studying Torah for its own sake, not in order to get any reward, like a diploma. See this article about the concept of the Torah being the Jewish People's "portable homeland:" https://njjewishnews.timesofisrael.com/portable-homeland/

In what way do YOU think Christians are viewing the Torah as "too small"?

The Torah is often described as a window into God's infinite nature. If it is infinite, how could anyone's view of the Torah be anything but too small?

CHAPTER 26

A View Too Small: Community

Here is another topic about which our view is *too small*: Jewish Community. As Christians we can learn something from the Jewish practice of community life. But first, a disclaimer: I do not have much experience with Christian community as practiced outside of the western Church, beyond nations similar to the United States; I speak only to those in the western Church.

Something Important Here

Community life is a massive topic and one that touches us way down deep in our hearts, minds, and souls, even if we don't realize it. Here are two examples:

1. Of all the books written by the German Christian theologian Dietrich Bonhoeffer, his most cherished was the book that he wrote in 1938 called *Life Together*.[1] In it he described the early days of Christian men living together in seminary, seeking to pursue God daily.

2. The final God-inspired blessing given by Balaam, whom King Balak had hired to curse the Jewish people while looking down upon them from a mountain, begins:

   How fair are your tents, O Yaakov, Your dwellings, O Yisrael! NUMBERS 24:5 (TIB)

In his Root Source lessons "Pray Like a Jew,"[2] Gidon Ariel notes the fact that one of the very first prayers Jews pray in the morning quotes this non-Jew, Balaam, an outsider of Israel. Gidon also speaks of a commentary that says one of the reasons the tents were beautiful, was that every tent was positioned so that its entrance was not facing the entrance of any other tent! It is simultaneously a picture of both

---

[1] https://amzn.to/3duEG05
[2] https://root-source.com/channels/

community and respect for privacy!

We think of the forty years in the desert as a lot of wandering, angst, and death, but the Jewish view is that this season was the season of the closest knit community life in the history of Israel. Imagine: everyone in an entire nation living within a day's walking distance of everyone else, for forty years! One Torah had been established, and although a rebellion surfaced,[3] Moses' leadership was continuous for forty years. He was loved and respected. Everyone had a role to fulfill within the nation, whether to prepare the next generation, or to prepare to enter the Land themselves. And the divine presence of God was visible continuously over the Tabernacle — to the nation and their enemies alike.

My Early Perspective on Christian Community

When I was twelve, our family left the Baptist Church in order to participate in the charismatic renewal that was emerging in the 1970s. Because none of the churches in Clearwater, Florida were participating in that renewal, my parents started a Sunday morning meeting in our home. I was suddenly thrust into participation in a close Christian community. Over time, my parents and older brother and sister researched the New Testament scriptures for clues of what it meant to "do church" in the first century. For example: the New Testament never mentions more than one church in a city, even though today we tend to speak about multiple churches even on the same intersection! I grew up believing that there is only one church per city.

A question began to form in my mind: If there was only one church, then why did I feel *very connected* to those Christians who met in our home, but not connected *at all* to the rest? Over time, our family suggested that we should not be so isolated. As a result, many of the people who came to our house on Sunday morning, began to attend a second gathering in another location on Saturday night, which came to be known as the *Saturday night meeting*. Here, Christians of various "fellowships and churches" came together to participate in the charismatic renewal as a larger group. Those meetings included not just prayer and song, but teaching and fellowship as well. But while I have many fond memories of those evenings, the administration of that larger meeting by a diverse set of co-leaders eventually became discordant. I learned just how difficult community life could be.

As I look back on those days today, I realize that my Saturday night meeting experience lowered my expectations of what could be attained to, within a

---

[3]   Korah's rebellion, Numbers 16.

Christian community. I settled for less. When I moved to Austin, Texas in the 1980s, I got married and we joined a non-denominational church that was somewhat charismatic. But in its structure, this church behaved much more like the Baptist Church that I grew up in than the free-for-all meetings of the 1970s.

An Evolved Perspective on Christian Community

In 2012, something changed. In a time of personal prayer for our church, I sensed God's leading that He wanted to form a group of men in our church. While the name of our church was Hope Chapel, I sensed that this group should be called *Men of Faith*. Why faith? Because as men, our key challenge was passivity, and faith is what motivates men to step into their calling. We invited men in the church to come together to create *Men of Faith*, to stand up against "passivity," and grow up into spiritual leaders and prayer leaders in the church and in our homes. I was not *the* leader, I was one of *four* co-leaders. We agreed that all leadership decisions would be made through consensus. In addition, the group was under the authority of the pastoral staff, from whom we invited critique and oversight. We met every other Saturday morning for four years without having a regular pattern to the order and content. In fact I would venture that no two meetings were exactly the same, but the feedback among all was that these meetings were being guided by the Holy Spirit, and the activities we embarked upon were pleasing to God.

The *Men of Faith* group was fully established before I ever met Gidon Ariel, and even before I was interested in the Jewish Roots of our faith. I thought we had a really great community of men put together in *Men of Faith*. And we did!

But a page did turn when I met Gidon.

An Introduction to the Jewish Perspective of Community

Through Gidon, I was introduced to Jewish community life, and I began to see just how *small* my view of Christian community really was.

For starters, Gidon lives within walking distance of a synagogue, which every other family in his community attends. He knows every family. There are Whatsapp groups (a smartphone app invented in Israel that has spread worldwide) that allow Jews in Israel to do many creative things in their community, such as coordinating almost spontaneous carpools. But more than just coordination, people routinely borrow many things from each other as needed — including their cars. I once watched a man on Gidon's street ask another man to borrow their family car to drive to Jerusalem (a 45-minute drive each way). He asked as if he was needing to borrow a cup of sugar.

Our men's group was doing well to pray for two hours every other week. Gidon prays over an hour a day *every day* — and not alone, but in groups of ten or more men. Our prayers were more impromptu, though often derived right out of Scripture. Jewish prayers are standardized for each occasion, and also built from Scripture. I estimate our participation in *Men of Faith* was about 10 percent of the men who attended our church. In Gidon's community, being established as a religious community, I would estimate that 90 percent of the men of the entire community participate daily. Over time, I watched as men in our group began to step into more leadership in their homes, and some of the men got invited to join the official governing board of the church. But I was also impressed by the way the Jewish men seemed to be enjoying their prayers together in their spontaneously formed groups of ten or more, and were fully engaged in the spiritual life of their homes. While men praying together in my church community was desirable, in Gidon's community men praying together was woven deeply into the culture. It was the way of things.

Seeing many, many dimensions in which the Jewish community was bigger, stronger and more committed than my Christian community, did set me back a bit. I definitely gained a bigger vision of what was ultimately possible within our Christian community overall. I began to read New Testament verses with new eyes.

> *And if one member suffers, all the members suffer with it; if one member is honored, all the members rejoice with it.* 1 CORINTHIANS 12:26

It is easy to visualize that happening in a small, group, Christian setting. But thanks to the Jewish People I began to start to imagine this at the level Paul intended: that there is only "one church in each city."

Here is the key point. It is not that most of what I see happening in Gidon's community is completely foreign to any of our western Christian experiences; **it is that Jewish community is happening in and among a much larger group of people than I have ever seen**. It's like everyone is part of one massive family. And they are!

But while the difference between Gidon's level of community life compared to mine was huge, one day something occurred to me that raised my spirits greatly: almost everything that God had led us to do in *Men of Faith*, was also happening, albeit on a larger scale, in the Jewish community. We were on the right track! And if we were being led by God's spirit, then it also showed that God must be blessing these Jewish practices also.

One God over all.

Pressing the Boundaries of Community

What do Jews think about our Christian community? My experience is that the Jews are prone to believe the best about us. But there is one thing that WE DON'T DO that baffles them. Why do Christians in one part of the world not do more to rescue Christians in another part of the world who are being persecuted, even slaughtered? Why don't we care more for our own? It is ironic that the best film I've seen about Christian persecution was produced by a Jewish non-profit![4] In our city, it was Jews that approached Christians suggesting that we partner to raise awareness of this worldwide problem.[5]

Better than any other group I know, Jews do come together in the face of tragedy. We can discern this by self-critique of Jews about their own people. A Jewish friend, Yehudah Katz[6] recently wrote to Jews in his own community about their "coming together" not long after the death of one of their community members:

> No one of us can say that we don't have the vessels and capacity to get together. We have done it before and this week we have done it again. Why? Why? Why does it take a tragedy to unite us?

Yehudah is appealing to his own community to be even more closely connected on a daily basis! He is not complaining about the level of connectedness during tragedy! This quote shows just how much further down the road the Jews are than we Christians, and perhaps every other group.

But perhaps the most interesting example of all is the attempt to form a new kind of Jewish/Christian community. Jeremy Gimpel and Ari Abramowitz are Orthodox Jews, and each other's best friend. They break all stereotypes. Fearless and friendly, they have done it all over the years: TV, radio, politics, music, and of course military service.[7] And a few years ago they felt moved to start something that they proudly admit: "We don't even know what this is." Their location is the Arugot Farm, a hilltop and valley near Ma'ale Amos in the heart of Judea. When I first visited, there was only one small house. They took me down to a hillside cave that David and his mighty men must have used. We prayed together there for their new project.

Ari and Jeremy say that now that Jews have returned to the land of Israel, "G-d

---

[4] https://faithkeepers.clarionproject.org/about/
[5] Not only was the event a success, but many Jewish-Christian relationships were established that allowed creative cooperation in the years to follow.
[6] https://www.facebook.com/yehudahkatz/
[7] Even today, Jeremy is Ari's reserve duty commander in the IDF.

is changing our hearts and replacing fear of the nations with love."[8] For years, they have explored ways to fulfill the prophecy of Isaiah *"for from Zion the Torah will come forth, and the word of God from Jerusalem."* (ISAIAH 2:3b, paraphrased by Ari). To that end, they recently invented a new community paradigm called *The Land of Israel Fellowship.*[9] It brings Christians and Jews together in regular online meetings, building a kind of community — something in Hebrew referred to as a *chaburah* — for learning and Hebrew prayer. Its biblical basis is the famous "ten men" passage in ZECHARIAH 8:23.[10]

Summary

The topic of Jewish community life is huge. We cannot hope to cover it fully; only to introduce it in a brief chapter like this one. I know I have only just scratched the surface.

I have no clear answers on how Christians can get to this level of community life. But I do know this: we must not settle for what exists. The redemption of all things is not complete until God redeems the concept of community and brings it to His ideal state.

Let us recognize that the Jews have something, and have realized a degree of community life that on average, is well beyond the current expression of the western Church.

Well beyond!

Shalom.

---

[8] You may have noticed in Ari's paraphrase he wrote the word "G-d" instead of "God". Many Jews, when writing or speaking in both English or Hebrew, are very cautious when referring to God or writing His name. According to Jewish law, if one of God's names is written on a piece of paper it cannot merely be thrown away or discarded, it must be buried out of reverence and respect. This is rooted in the second commandment, not to use God's name in vain. Therefore they choose to write God's name omitting a letter, as a reminder that God's four-letter name (YHWH) is so holy it is not spoken, but replaced with Hashem (literally "the name") in general conversation, and replaced with Adonai (literally "Lord") in Torah study or prayer. But Ari would never demand (nor even request) a Christian to modify their use of "God" when writing to him.

[9] The organization is http://thelandofisrael.com/

[10] One of their most oft-repeated sayings is: Jews are called Jews because they came from Judea. They honor that truth by having sold everything they owned to move there. They actualize (more than most Christians I meet) what it truly means to "live by faith."

Asking Gidon

Gidon, have you gotten so used to the level of community you have in Israel that you take it for granted?

Actually, I am much more communal than average. I think that our community could be even closer knit than it is.

Please describe your community. First, tell us what comes to mind when I say "your community?" Besides prayer, carpools, and coming together in a tragedy, what other aspects of community life are meaningful to you?

When I use the term "community," I am thinking of the small village I live in, called Ma'ale Hever. We all have common values and common goals. There is a certain nature of family between us, and that feeling begins with the common knowledge that *everyone here* has made a choice to live together, outside a big city. Some tangible examples of that feeling include:

- We have a salaried person who is responsible for social events which occur frequently, a few times a month.

- We have a packed schedule of Torah classes for all age groups.

- We have a community charity chest from which our rabbi has discretion to distribute funds to residents in need.

- Every child knows every adult like an uncle or an aunt.

If you, and your wife and kids were to spend a year in America within walking distance to a local synagogue (so that those basic spiritual needs were met), what would you miss the most about your community life in Ma'ale Hever in Judea, Israel?

I think that Orthodox Jewish communities are similar in enough ways that they are pretty interchangeable for most people. Obviously people are creatures of habit and usually don't like to change too much, but an Orthodox community helps make a change of location much smoother.

Chapter 27

A View Too Small: Secularism

Here is another topic about which I don't believe we (as Christians) are *wrong*, but for which our current view is just *too small*. Secularism.

Secularism is defined by Merriam-Webster as *"the indifference to, or exclusion of, religion and religious considerations."* I believe our view of secularism is too small, because we think of it in terms of what it is protesting against (religion), rather than seeing it as a religion — an "anti-religion" religion if you will — which is the topic of this chapter.

Secularism in modern history was born in a period when the Church had great power and control over society. Secularism questions the existence of God, questions the authority and legitimacy of the Bible, and envisions a better world than the one where the Church's great power led to abuses such as the Inquisition. More than 400 years later, secularism is still on the rise. Rabbi Berel Wein has called it "the greatest enemy of both Judaism and Christianity."[1]

What Does Secularism Want?

I have been observing what those who identify with the secular movement want to see changed in our society. Here in America, those desired changes seem to have been building up, like water behind a dam. Since the ruling of the US Supreme Court on gay marriage in June 2015, many other desired changes, like waters behind the dam, have all been released into the arena of public debate.

The debate on the gay marriage issue has also shifted. It is no longer about whether it is right or wrong, but the extent to which those who stand with a biblical

---

[1] Wein, Rabbi Berel. *5000 Years in 5 hours, The Crash Course in Jewish History.* Set of 5 CDs, CD series S425D. CD 5, C0422.

definition of marriage will be allowed to follow their conscience.

What I wish was still being debated, is how the gay marriage ruling squares up with the law of Moses. The law of Moses was given to us by God. But alas, the debate about gay marriage simply won't take place at Mount Sinai in the public sphere. The battle won't be fought there. Instead, secularism wants to reframe every battle and fight every fight in a different location entirely: the Garden of Eden.

The Garden of Eden?

I have observed that the issues that are being debated right now are so fundamental, that most, if not all of them, can be found in the first two chapters of Genesis! For instance, the battle over gay marriage is a battle that is framed at the conclusion of Genesis 2:

> Hence a man leaves his father and mother and clings to his wife, so that they become one flesh. GENESIS 2:24 (TIB)

Secularism is an "anti-religion" religion because its purpose is *progress* that destroys Judaism and Christianity. They will attack us in the very beginning of our book. They hope that anyone who actually sits down to read God's account of creation will be appalled at the out-dated and backward notions it conveys, and quickly reject both Old and New Testaments.

But secularism is also an "anti-religion" religion, because it elevates man over God. **Therefore, secularism is also the religion of Self.** How do you join the "membership rolls" of the religion of Self? You join it by turning *against* the Bible.

What then is the next major target of secularism, now that it has taken new ground regarding the biblical definition of marriage? Let us listen in as the religion of secularism convenes to discuss their internal strategy. "Where can we strike against the Bible next?" asks a leader. "Stay away from Sinai!" someone shouts. "Stay away from Noah!" says another. "Go earlier still!" says a shrieking voice hidden from view in the shadows.

So let us look just two verses earlier from the last verse we quoted in Genesis:

> And Hashem fashioned the rib that He had taken from the man into a woman; and He brought her to the man. Then the man said, "This one at last is bone of my bones and flesh of my flesh. This one shall be called Woman, for from man was she taken." GENESIS 2:22-23 (TIB)

The next major target of secularism is masculinity; about God having designed a man to take the leading role, a first-mover role in his connection to woman. Secularism also attacks those women who have a desire to manage the affairs of their household, including the undervalued job of raising children.

But that target is not satisfying enough. Secularism shifts its focus even earlier, going back a further seven verses in the Garden of Eden:

> *Hashem took the man and placed him in the garden of Eden, to till it and tend it.* GENESIS 2:15 (TIB)

Secularism puts Self on the throne. A person's career journey — his work — is not to be seen as "God placing" us into a role that benefits His will. Instead, secularism compels us to find a plan of our own making. And if it's successful we will have ourselves to thank!

But there are additional targets to be had by moving still earlier into Genesis chapter 1.

For instance, we have the attack on procreation:

> *Hashem blessed them and Hashem said to them, "Be fertile and increase, fill the earth and master it."* GENESIS 1:28a (TIB)

In secularism, God's command to mankind to be fertile and increase is ignored. In secularism, Self is on the throne. Children have to be tolerated, but don't have too many or they might interfere with your financial standard of living, or your career aspirations.

But more battle targets are found in the prior verse. How about an attack on the definition of gender?

> *And Hashem created man in His image, in the image of Hashem He created him; male and female He created them.* GENESIS 1:27 (TIB)

The essence of secularism is Self. Self is on the throne. Do you self-identify as the opposite of your biological sex? Then you make the call. God's decision in how He elected to create you is now irrelevant.

The battle continues eighteen verses earlier:

> *Hashem said, "Let the water below the sky be gathered into one area, that the dry land may appear." And it was so. Hashem called the dry land Earth, and the gathering of waters He called Seas. And Hashem saw that this was good.* GENESIS 1:9-10 (TIB)

Secularism eliminates the possibility of taking the matters of "climate change" to God in prayer. God says that if we really want wisdom about complex issues we can ask Him. The Bible actually describes great environmental upheaval occurring before the Messiah arrives. But what I take issue with is the idea that we can come together without God and take control of our planet and fix "climate change." In fact, I smile when I hear secularists talking about the need to "save our planet." That's apparently what the religion of secularism considers *salvation*.

What is Secularism's Ultimate Aim?

Where is secularism heading, if it can obtain everything else it wants? I suppose that its ultimate aim is to raise itself up against the knowledge of God completely — to ban God entirely from our nations.

> *In the beginning God created the heavens and the earth.* GENESIS 1:1

Secularism already rejects God. But I am afraid that ultimately secularism will never be satisfied until **The People of the Book** also reject Him. The first stage in that process is that you agree never to speak of Him, or exhibit Him, or follow Him, or model Him, or remind anyone of Him in any way, shape, or form. After that, it is not a very big leap that either you, or your children who come after you, will walk away from the Bible entirely and actually stop believing in God at all.

The Peoples of the Book Respond

The Judeo-Christian response to all this is pretty simple. We have two chapters of our own.

Regarding us, PSALM 1:

> *Happy is the man who has not followed the counsel of the wicked, or taken the path of sinners, or joined the company of the insolent; rather, the teaching of Hashem is his delight, and he studies that teaching day and night. He is like a tree planted beside streams of water, which yields its fruit in season, whose foliage never fades, and whatever it produces thrives. Not so the wicked; rather, they are like chaff that wind blows away. Therefore the wicked will not survive judgment, nor will sinners, in the assembly of the righteous. For Hashem cherishes the way of the righteous, but the way of the wicked is doomed.* PSALM 1 (TIB)[2]

Regarding avowed secularists: PSALM 2.

---

[2] Even as Orthodox Jewish husbands sing Proverbs 31 over their wives every Friday evening, so do wives sing Psalm 1 over their husbands! I love it when my wife reads this Psalm over me.

Why do nations assemble, and peoples plot vain things; kings of the earth take their stand, and regents intrigue together against Hashem and against His anointed? … He who is enthroned in heaven laughs; Hashem mocks at them. Then He speaks to them in anger, terrifying them in His rage… Happy are all who take refuge in Him. Portions of PSALM 2 (TIB)

PSALM 2 goes on to tell a fuller story about a king who will reside in Zion, a king for whom Christians and Jews eagerly await even now.

Messiah, come quickly! But while we wait for the Messiah, we must not insulate ourselves in our own religious culture, but find ways to expand our reach into a larger world.

In Christian teaching, one of the most famous paradigms for touching our larger communities is in the seven mountains of influence: media, government, education, economy, religion, family, and celebration/arts.[3] In fact we will discuss the role of the media in the next chapter.

But what is happening like this in the Jewish world? One of the best examples I know is what Orthodox Jew Jonathan Feldstein from Efrat, is doing with his Run for Zion initiative.[4] His organization is adding a Christian flavor to the annual Jerusalem Marathon, which is already a sports/city government/family entertainment event. The marathon, which already attracts athletes from around the world, is becoming a venue for Christian participation through Jonathan. He has created an innovative way for Christians and their families to walk or run in the race, cheer the athletes, and raise money for a number of Jewish charities. The city government of Jerusalem has taken notice, and is fully supportive of an event which opens a whole new kind of tourism to Israel.

And for Christians who are eager to impact the secular world and to be "light in the darkness," I rejoice at your vigor! I also have a bit of news for you. When Orthodox Jews speak of their goals to sanctify the name of Hashem in the secular world, they use the *exact same words*.

Shalom.

---

[3] *The Seven Mountain Prophecy: Unveiling the Coming Elijah Revolution*, by Johnny Enlow.
[4] https://www.runforzion.com/

Asking Gidon

Gidon, many of your fellow Jews, especially those living in the coastal cities, are not "religious." Is the term "secular" or "secularism" ever used to describe that portion of Israeli society that is ardently anti-religious?

Yes, and this is a pet peeve of mine. The media invented (or at least joyfully adopted) the Hebrew terms *Dati* and *Chiloni* to label the religious and the secular, respectively. However, the absolute majority of Israeli Jews are what we call *M'sorati*, traditional. They believe in God and have a good relationship with Him, but would feel uncomfortable being put in the same category as the "religious extremists" of Meah Shearim.[5] So the media paints everyone to the left of Meah Shearim as "secular," but according to the definitions you have laid out in this chapter, barely 3 percent of Israeli Jews are truly "secular." I truly believe that any movement a person makes towards God is worth celebrating, and I don't need a Jew to look and behave like I do before I will celebrate that movement towards God in their life.

I have heard comments from Orthodox Jews that indicate that many secular Jews are turning (or returning) to the roots of their Jewish faith. What might that look like?

People's faith is a very personal thing, and is a journey. But to the extent that it is observable outwardly, it can include changes in dress codes (Kippa skullcap and Tzitzit fringes for men, head coverings for married women and more modest dress for women overall); regular visits to the synagogue for prayer; learning Torah through books, the Internet, or by attending classes; stricter observance of Kashrut rules[6] (it's actually pretty hard not to keep Kosher in Israel given that almost all grocery stores are Kosher and the percentage of Kosher restaurants has increased dramatically, even in Tel Aviv); keeping rules of family purity (such as men and women not touching those of the opposite sex outside of their immediate families); and Shabbat observance, especially refraining from using cars and cellphones. That being said, let me say again that any movement a person makes towards God is worth celebrating, even if it is only observable inwardly.

---

5   https://en.wikipedia.org/wiki/Mea_Shearim
6   http://www.jewfaq.org/kashrut.htm

You live in Judea and you interact with Palestinians on the roads, in businesses and supermarkets. These are people who live in Arab villages, towns and cities, and travel freely within the West Bank. Are there many secular Palestinians? Have you had meaningful conversations with Palestinians personally?

Most Palestinians are Muslim by far. While there is a spectrum of how "religious" a Muslim can be, I would venture that there are very few Palestinians who would identify as secular. I do believe and engage in intercultural dialogue between Israelis and Palestinians (including Muslims), and I hope and believe that the more such dialogue becomes popular with people on both sides, the closer peace and security will be.

CHAPTER 28

The Media's Ten Commandments

I n the spring of 2018, the United States moved its embassy to Jerusalem.[1] Then one year later, Prime Minister Benjamin Netanyahu visited President Donald Trump at the White House. During this 2019 visit, Trump followed up his historic embassy move by announcing that US policy was now going to align with Israel, rather than with the United Nations: the Golan Heights will be considered by the United States to be part of Israel.[2]

Coincidentally, that 2019 visit and the announcement about the Golan coincided with the release of the Mueller Report on whether and how Donald Trump and his campaign colluded with the Russians in the 2016 elections. Upon his departure, Netanyahu spoke very briefly to the media:[3]

> I am now returning from an historic visit to Washington. President Trump's recognition of our sovereignty over the Golan Heights will be remembered for generations.
>
> There is a very important principle in international life — when you start wars of aggression, you lose territory; do not come and claim it afterwards. It belongs to us. We have historic foundations on the Golan Heights. When you dig there, you discover magnificent synagogues which we are restoring.
>
> We have returned to the Golan; the Golan is ours. The Golan is ours by historic right and by right of self-defense, and President Trump recognizes this. That you are not covering this for more than a minute is something you will be called to account for. However, in historical reckoning, this is huge.

Benjamin Netanyahu understands that *what is important* is not necessarily *what*

---

1 https://en.wikipedia.org/wiki/Embassy_of_the_United_States,_Jerusalem
2 https://www.bbc.com/news/world-middle-east-47697717
3 Short link to article at Israel Ministry of Foreign Affairs: https://bit.ly/Bibi-Washington

is reported. How true this is today. But, is the media just *overlooking* that which is historic, or is there something larger going on? Have we underestimated the media?

The Media and its Goal

The essence of "media" is communication. Merriam-Webster defines it as *"a channel or system of communication, information, or entertainment."* The reason we underestimate the media is because it is the arena in which evil has the most control.

As mentioned at the end of the last chapter, Jews were given the charge to be a blessing and a light to the nations thousands of years ago,[4] and so were the disciples of Yeshua.[5] Spreading the knowledge of God to the world is akin to shining light. Our goal is to assist God in fulfilling His promise that:

> *They will neither harm nor destroy on all my holy mountain, for the earth will be filled with the knowledge of the LORD as the waters cover the sea.* ISAIAH 11:9 (NIV)

And we know from many other passages that it is God's desire that this great work happen *through* us.

But evil has a goal as well. The goal of evil is to thwart God's plans to bring light and knowledge of Him to the world. Since "evil' cannot out-power God, it knows that a full-on attack against God is futile. In addition, because mankind has free will, evil cannot intrinsically overpower us and *force* us to commit acts of evil. Instead, evil operates primarily in the field of influence, and it uses *information and knowledge* as a means to influence.

Enter the media.

Media is about the *what*, the *knowing*; and media is about the *how*, how that knowing is *conveyed*. Is it any wonder then, that the "media" is the battleground of light and darkness today?

Where is the Media in the Bible

Let's put on our "media glasses" and go back and take a look at the interaction of Eve, the serpent, and Adam in the Garden of Eden.

---

[4] Genesis 12:3; Isaiah 49:6
[5] Matthew 5:14-16

Before chapter 3 of Genesis, all communication was between God, Adam and Eve. God set the standard for knowledge! He spoke creation into existence, and He began the process of teaching Adam about that creation by the naming of the animals. He also gave mankind its first command.

But by chapter 3, I would contend that an alternative media company had been established. Let us humorously call it the "Serpent Media Corporation," or SMC for short!

Who was the CEO of SMC? Why the serpent of course![6]

Who was the first consumer of SMC information? Eve.

The very first "story" published by Serpent Media began with a question:

> *Now the serpent was the shrewdest of all the wild beasts that Hashem had made. He said to the woman, "Did Hashem really say:You shall not eat of any tree of the garden?"* GENESIS 3:1 (TIB)

As we walk through this dialogue, we can discover some principles that media companies continue to employ. For grins, let us call them the Ten Commandments of the Media, and let's find them on a walk through the Garden of Eden in Genesis chapter 3.

Media Commandment #1. Hook the media consumer (through reading, viewing or listening) with a headline that causes them to want to engage with the story.

Today in the age of the Internet, they call it "clickbait." Back then it was simply an unsolicited question about a topic of interest by a serpent who was watching as Eve happened by.

Media Commandment #2. Publish stories for your *own* purposes.

To the extent that it can get away with it, a shrewd media outlet will choose its stories to advance *its own* objectives, not the objectives of its consumers. You can see this in the entire approach of the serpent. The ultimate objective of the SMC was to foil the good plans of God on earth.

Of course SMC's opening headline — a question — was not consistent with the facts. The Serpent Media Corporation in its error reveals another tried and true

---

[6]   One reviewer remarked that this was the world's first instance of fake news!

media commandment:

Media Commandment #3. Exaggerate the negative.

A shrewd media outlet will raise the possibility of a negative story to the level of something dramatic. We can imagine that if Adam and Eve had had children in the Garden of Eden, with no sins committed yet, perhaps SMC would launch a newspaper called *The Garden Gazette*. In one of its Sunday editions a headline might ask the question:

Will God's Prohibitions Increase?

The article that follows the headline then proposes the *possibility* that God might begin to add new trees to the list of prohibitions. Will there be enough food in such cases? Might the future of mankind be in peril? The chapter defends itself by reminding us that it is not stating facts, only asking questions!

Eve's reaction to the first media story ever recorded in history was to downplay the dramatic negative angle of the questions being asked with some facts of her own.

> *The woman replied to the serpent, "We may eat of the fruit of the other trees of the garden. It is only about the fruit of the tree in the middle of the garden that Hashem said: 'You shall not eat of it or touch it, **lest you die.'"** GENESIS 3:2-3 (TIB, emphasis mine)

Oh Eve! In choosing her facts, she revealed the weakness of her position, for indeed, God had *not* said that if she touches the Tree of Knowledge of Good and Evil she will die! As we discussed in chapter 3, since Eve had no reason to lie, we can assume that it was Adam who told her this in an attempt to make sure that she wouldn't go near the tree. Adam made "the original mistake" by not bringing her into the full knowledge of that which he had received from God.

Did you just notice that Adam was acting in the role of the media? The Latin word 'media' actually means to be in the middle, between. Adam opened his own media company — Dust of the Ground Media (DoGM) — on Oracle Lane even before SMC ever opened its doors on Tree of Knowledge Boulevard.

Now that we are already talking about two media companies, let us stop and say that not every media company today has evil intentions. Dust of the Ground Media (DoGM), was trying to keep the peace and help its customers (his wife). But even a media company with good intentions can produce stories for *its own* interests rather than stories that are completely consistent with the knowledge of God. We all need to understand this! I believe our view of the media is too small if we simply divide media companies into good and bad ones, light and dark ones.

Media Commandment #4. Be sure to serve your own self-interest, because unless you do, you won't be able to help others.

Media companies justify their actions, in part, by the need to keep the doors open and their lights on, to make payroll and to pay their executives bonuses. I suspect that when things aren't going well in the business, then a very strong self-interest combines with the business predicament to birth the most devious of stories. Serpent Media Company had huge self-interest.

Thankfully for SMC, the serpent himself had heard (or perhaps a little bird in the market research department told him) that Eve did not have all the facts.

Media Commandment #5. Know your audience and exploit — oops, *appeal to* — them.

Use knowledge to position stories in a way that will have the most influence. It even happens on local TV news, that you wouldn't think would be so affected. Yet such stations have a saying when picking the order of their stories for each evening: "If it bleeds, it leads."

Certainly, there is nothing wrong with a company knowing its customers, and trying to serve their needs. But Serpent Media did not want to simply inform Eve, it wanted to *exploit* her. Eve never saw that coming. But I believe that God noticed, and had great compassion upon her. I believe this is why God later promised the serpent that the seed of the woman would crush his head.

At this point, Serpent Media shifts from its exaggerated opening question, designed to hook the consumer, and moves to the main point of its story — which it frames as honest-to-goodness NEWS.

> *And the serpent said to the woman, "You are not going to die, but Hashem knows that as soon as you eat of it your eyes will be opened and you will be like divine beings who know good and bad."* Genesis 3:4-5 (TIB)

When hard NEWS is factually wrong, the results can be devastating if believed. And if the media company has sunk so low as to corrupt its own news reporting, the best way to do that is with a mixture of real facts along with lies.

Media Commandment #6. First, gain their trust.

Yes, it is true that Eve was not going to die when she touched the fruit. When she touched the fruit and did not die, she knew SMC was right. Now that SMC had earned her trust, Eve was ready to fall for the lie.

Another commandment we can learn from this passage is how to attack your opponents:

Media Commandment #7. When you can't win with facts, question the motives of your opponents.

God was on the receiving end of the very first media hatchet job in the history of the world! His character and motivations were being questioned. He was holding back an advancement of mankind by restricting that tree!

Media Commandment #8. While attacking others' motives, defend your own motives as pure.

SMC let Eve assume that their intention was simply to inform. Eve was completely unaware that SMC had "a stake" in her decision.

Media Commandment #9. Establish an alternative worldview in your publication, and promise good things will happen if everyone accepts it. SMC's alternative worldview was nothing less than mankind being raised up to a whole new level of existence, being more like God.

> "...you will be like divine beings who know good and bad.." GENESIS 3:5 (TIB)

If you are looking for the place where a globalist agenda might enter these ten commandments, you just found it. It goes back to the Tower of Babel. No, it goes back even further: *to the Garden.*

And finally, the last commandment is:

Media Commandment #10. Ignore all stories that don't reinforce your worldview.

The story that SMC could have rightly published on that day, was the story about how Adam apparently did not reveal the full truth to Eve about God's command regarding the Tree of Knowledge of Good and Evil. That was a valuable story, a scoop worth reporting, which could have changed human history! But SMC smartly ignored that REAL story, and kept completely silent. Instead it launched the alternate story we just read.

And now for the Good News!

What is God's response to these ten commandments of the media? It seems to me that God greatly enjoys defeating the media by launching small stories that eventually change the world. Consider these examples.

- He creates man *out of the dust* of the ground.[7] Really!

- He forms woman *out of the rib* (or side) of a man.[8] In Rivkah Adler's class on Women of the Bible,[9] we learn that Jewish sages say this is the reason women mature faster than men: they grow from flesh, not from dust.

- Moses is drawn up *out of the water* of the Nile and presides over the birth of a new nation and the giving of the Torah at Mount Sinai.[10]

- David is called in from *out in the fields,* shepherding of sheep to be anointed as King;[11] he is a man after God's own heart.[12]

- Yeshua is born *in a manger* in Bethlehem,[13] but has changed the world forever.

- In the 1800s, some Yemenite Jews began to return to the Holy Land, followed by some Jews from Russia.[14] We hardly know their names even today.

- In 1947 the world (through the United Nations) would birth a new nation in a single day.[15]

- Twenty years after that, in 1967, Jerusalem would return to Jewish control,[16] thus returning that land to its original owners, just like the biblical principle of the Jubilee.[17]

- Forty-nine years after that, on April 17, 2016, Prime Minister Benjamin Netanyahu would declare the Golan Heights to be eternally part of Israel.[18] We wrote about this particular story in chapter 17 of our book *Jubilee NOW!*, and called it historic — a "Jewish Jubilee" for land.[19]

- And three years later, in 2019 President Trump aligns the United States

---

[7] Genesis 2:7
[8] Genesis 2:22
[9] https://root-source.com/channels/
[10] Exodus 2-20
[11] 1 Samuel 16:11-13
[12] 1 Samuel 13:14
[13] Luke 2
[14] https://en.wikipedia.org/wiki/First_Aliyah
[15] In fulfillment of the question posed in Isaiah 66:8 *"Who has heard such a thing? Who has seen such things? Can a land be born in one day? Can a nation be brought forth all at once?..."*
https://en.wikipedia.org/wiki/United_Nations_Partition_Plan_for_Palestine
[16] https://en.wikipedia.org/wiki/Six-Day_War
[17] Leviticus 25:8-13
[18] https://www.bbc.com/news/world-middle-east-36067643
[19] http://jubilee-now-book.com/

with Israel's prior declaration regarding the Golan.[20] Someone is blessing Israel *again*! Trump has his faults, but will his faults overshadow and overrule the good things he has done in the eyes of God?

Indeed, it seems to be the pleasure of God Almighty to begin the greatest of stories with the smallest of stories, stories that are overlooked by the powerful. At least at first.

Years from now, when all the distractions and distortions of the present moment blow away like chaff in the wind, we will be left with an eternal reality: **God's stories will prevail.** They will be celebrated and remembered for eternity.

And the best news of all is that He desires that mankind join with Him to write those stories and shine light to the world until *"the earth will be filled with the knowledge of the glory of the LORD as the waters cover the sea."* (HABAKKUK 2:14, NIV).

Every one of us can be a small story in that great big story if we so desire.

Shalom.

Asking Gidon

Gidon, at least when I am with you, you don't rant and rail about "the media" even though I'm sure you feel that the media is not often "on your side." Is it easy to take up a grudge against your own media in Israel?

I don't rant and rail even when we are apart ☺ But I know plenty of people who do. Israel's media, like America's, is perceived as leaning leftward, and many right-leaning media consumers can be frustrated by this.

Where do you get your news of events in Israel?

I get my news from Galei Tzahal (Israel's Army radio), which is much closer to a regular popular station than to something out of the Korean War. I also consult Twitter and Facebook, and sometimes the Times of Israel website.

What do you consider to be the best English-language news outlet, that Christians might be able to access, in terms of reporting the hard facts in the least-biased way?

---

[20] Short link to proclamation at White House: https://bit.ly/Trump-Golan

I don't think that such an outlet exists, but any Israel-based outlet assisted by some trusted friends on social media will give you a pretty good picture. And if you want that friend to be an Orthodox Jew, you are welcome to connect with me on Facebook and Twitter, or by replying to our weekly Root Source newsletter at Root Source.[21]

---

[21] https://root-source.com/free-newsletter

CHAPTER 29

The Battle of the Evening

Darkness had descended and the leaders of the troops gathered in the commander's tent. "Tell your men to prepare themselves. We will attack tomorrow morning at first light."

Those words must have replayed themselves many thousands of times in world history, in most every language and country of the world. While defending a position is best done in the full light of day, an attack is best carried out with as little light as is absolutely necessary. An attack at first light gives the troops just enough light to see where they are going, while minimizing their enemies' ability to see them. In modern times, with the advent of all kinds of electronic technology, it has become possible to carry out large-scale attacks at night. Darkness is the best time to launch surprise attacks designed to engage the enemy earlier than they expect, and catch them unprepared.

First Light in Austin, Texas.

One of the realizations that has dawned on me (pun intended) since undertaking my study of the Jewish roots of our faith,[1] is that our great adversary, the devil, has taken advantage of Christianity's separation from our Jewish roots to launch a sneak attack *on us at night.*

One of the central truths that we have lost in our separation from the Jews is the biblical boundaries of time. We define a "day" from midnight to midnight, a calendar day, whereas God and the devil know that the true boundaries of a day are from sunset to sunset.

And there was evening and there was morning, one day. GENESIS 1:5b

Why it Matters

While God desires to bring His glory and presence into this world, our adversary is always on the lookout for opportunities to bring defilement.

Defilement can take many forms. The Bible describes the defilement of people through demonic presence. While this is widely described in the New Testament, it is not uniquely described there. King Saul, for instance, was troubled by an evil spirit that would leave him when David played the lyre (1 SAMUEL 16:14-16).

The Bible also supports the idea of the defilement of land by the sins that are committed upon it. Moses warned Israel of this.

So let not the land spew you out for defiling it, as it spewed out the nation that came before you. LEVITICUS 18:28 (TIB)

But in the same way that people and land can be defiled, so can *time.* We see this principle laid out clearly in the laws of uncleanliness. A person could become defiled for various reasons for a period of days, or as little as a single day. And those are biblical days, which means that a period of uncleanliness ends — and therefore cleanliness begins — at sundown.

The other side of this coin is the biblical idea of sanctifying time. God commands His people to sanctify the Shabbat day, as He Himself sanctified the seventh day of creation.

---

[1] I am aware that many people prefer to say "Hebrew roots of our faith" or "Hebraic roots of our faith." I am known to use all of these terms, mostly interchangeably. Some prefer to use the word "Hebrew/ Hebraic" over "Jewish" because we are spiritual children of Abraham (Galatians 3:29), who was a Hebrew, a term which itself derives from Eber, who lived six generations before Abraham. However, in this book we are emphasizing those topics which pertain to the interaction and intersection between Jewish understanding and Christian understanding. That is why, in this book, I more often use the term Jewish roots.

Is sanctified time important as compared to land and people? Yes! God in the Bible is shown as sanctifying time (Shabbat) before He sanctified anything else, even land and people![2]

I believe that the adversary has gotten quite good at defiling TIME in our Christian nations today, because he knows that we as Christians don't really get it! *Time* is our weakest of the three objectives of sanctification, because we walked away from God's boundaries regarding time when we walked away from our relationship with the Jews, and the reading of the Torah. Today, we are asking for God's blessings and protections on "days" that begin at midnight rather than sundown. Technically speaking, we have redefined "the day" to be something a bit different from how God originally defined "a day." Said another way, we are not recognizing "a new day" as having started at sundown, but only at midnight. Technically speaking we are not praying in full alignment to God's calendar.

Please don't conclude that I'm suggesting that God won't hear our prayers if we thank God by saying: "Today, Wednesday (from midnight to midnight, or during the daytime) is the day the Lord has made." But what I'm beginning to wonder, is whether our prayers might be *even more effective* and powerful if we align them to God's definition of a day. No, it's not a secret key that opens up for us special revelation (I don't believe that kind of thinking is from God), but rather, might it not actually show a touch of *humility* to align ourselves with God's original definition of a day![3]

An example of where this misalignment between God's definition of a day and our definition might hinder our prayers, relates to Halloween.

The Battle for Halloween Evening!

If you were to ask Americans: "When is Halloween?" They will answer: "*October 31st.*" But, in actuality, Halloween is celebrated *after dark* on October 31st, making it the "eve" of November 1st, which is All Saints Day. Many readers are aware that the word Halloween is actually a shortening of "All Hallows Eve," the hallowed eve of All Saints Day on November 1st.[4]

---

[2] A decade before my five-year journey began, I heard Arthur Burk make that point — a point often overlooked by Christians.

[3] Many books have been written on the biblical calendar: the ending of a week with Shabbat, the biblical months as defined in Exodus, the biblical feast days, and the biblical year in spring corresponding to the first month in Exodus, and the start of the civil or agricultural year in the fall corresponding to the seventh month, Tishri. Introductions to the topics of the calendar and the feasts can be found in *Celebrate the Feasts of the Lord*, by William W. Francis; and *The Feasts of Adonai: Why Christians Should Look at Biblical Feasts*, by Valerie Moody.

[4] All Saints Day commemorates the faithful departed: https://en.wikipedia.org/wiki/All_Saints%27_Day

Do you see what we as Christians have allowed to happen?

By defining a Christian Holiday as November 1st, we have given full access to the powers of darkness to defile that very same day, by celebrating all manner and forms of evil spirits on the night before! They are fighting **The Battle of the Evening**!

We left the door wide open because we have not properly defined "what a day is!" All Saints Day is being defiled by Halloween, because we left the door wide open between sundown and midnight of October 31st! I wonder if the defilement of All Saints Day, occurring the night before, partly explains why All Saints Day is so minimally celebrated in modern times.[5]

We see the same "battle of the evening" principle again playing out in the springtime with the Christian practice of forty days of Lent, which is designed to be a period of cleansing and contemplation beginning on Ash Wednesday. This is preceded by Mardi Gras! Mardi Gras, literally "Fat Tuesday," is a revelry designed to precede Ash Wednesday, whose crescendo is on Tuesday evening, when essentially "anything goes." In God's definition of a day, Fat Tuesday celebrations defile Ash Wednesday![6]

If our adversary can trick people into institutionalizing the committing of sins on the night before an important godly day, he can degrade and defile that entire day. This is a battle strategy of the enemy being practiced under cover of night, by attacking the boundaries of the day that we might desire to sanctify.

Indeed, those who have been caught up in Satanism, when freed from that bondage and brought into the freedom and love of God, have readily shared the extent to which the night of Halloween is the ultimate evening, the very best hours of the year, for Satanists to wage spiritual battle on Satan's behalf.[7]

---

[5] My purpose in mentioning All Saints Day is not meant to be an emphatic endorsement of that day and its history, a day that was never part of my own tradition. It is just a convenient example towards a larger point I am hoping to make in this chapter, which is that when we step away from God's definitions, we might be more vulnerable to a sneak attack. My friend David Pitcher rightly commented during his review that the Battle of the Evening is also a battle against the most vulnerable: our children.

[6] The forty days of Lent is a Christian tradition that is not specifically aligned to God's calendar. Nevertheless, I believe the benefits of forty days of fasting and contemplation have been of great benefit to the Church overall, and I have nothing against that practice. If that tradition encourages you to fast and pray, then I bless you. But, given that this book is about topics related to the intersection of Jewish and Christian understanding, it is important to mention here an historical truth: the week following Lent — the week between Palm Sunday and Easter — has been *the* annual week of terror for European Jewry, as angry Christians stormed out of churches down the streets to the Jewish sections of town. That this could have happened after a period of fasting and contemplation is a grotesque incongruity which is totally inconceivable to me.

[7] Short link to article at the Express: https://bit.ly/Halloween-Satan

Now What

It is for reasons like this that I believe God is leading the Church back to its Jewish roots. I don't presume to know the best strategies to push back against the sins committed during Halloween, whether to see this celebration destroyed, or to find a way to redeem it within God's love, but I do believe that *solving* a problem usually begins with properly *defining* it.

I originally began to draft the words of this chapter in 2018 during the daytime of October 31st, while looking out of my office window in the broad daylight of the noonday sun. In these paragraphs, I have now suggested that part of that proper definition of our Halloween problem begins with seeing Halloween as not only a defilement of an evening, but a defilement of All Saints Day (November 1st) as well.

Looking out the window right now, clouds have moved in. The sun has disappeared. I just checked the weather forecast here in Austin. The forecast says that we will have rain tonight, **beginning at sundown and lasting until 10PM**! The sky will then stay cloudy from 10PM all night, with skies forecast to become bright and sunny once again as of *sunrise* tomorrow morning.[8]

I wonder if this Austin forecast might be a message from God for us all, that as we continually align ourselves more and more towards His purposes, that He is more than happy to bring more and more of His resources to bear into the problems we face.[9]

Indeed, our God truly cares about people, land, *and* time. He wants to guide us in the bright noonday sun, just as much as He wants to guide us in the deep darkness of night.

(Just not necessarily in that order!)

Shalom.

---

https://www.learnreligions.com/is-halloween-satanic-95881

[8] The forecast ended up being correct, right down to the very hour.

[9] Many stories can be found about how God uses weather to thwart, or at least degrade the intensity of certain events that are not supported by those in the city who fear God. Horrific festivals have been completely rained out, for instance. The opposite is also true. Fog and even storms have also been used by God to allow the righteous to flee while escaping detection from their enemies. A famous example is how meteorological phenomena rescued George Washington in 1776, the nation's capital in the War of 1812, and the Union Army in the battle of Gettysburg in 1863. Short link to article at Washington Post: https://bit.ly/Washington1776

Asking Gidon

How pervasive in the Jewish community is the idea that a day begins at sunset? Do you personally look at the sun setting in the West and think, "A new day is coming soon"?

Yes, certainly on Sabbaths and holidays. But, on regular days, I don't see it as being so significant.

People say that the holiday of Purim for Jews is similar to Halloween. What does Purim celebrate, and in what way is Purim similar to, and different from Halloween?

Purim is similar to Halloween in that it is customary to dress up in costume. That's pretty much where the similarity ends. On Halloween, the tradition of Trick or Treat is to collect food gifts, while on Purim we do *"mishloach manot"* — sending gifts of food to our neighbors (see ESTHER 9:22).[10] There are probably other comparable contrasts, but I would say these are the most blatant. Purim celebrates the story of the Book of Esther. For more on Purim, I would recommend reading Esther right now! It doesn't take long in Hebrew: it is just 160 sentences![11]

Do Orthodox Jews celebrate Purim more intensely than their secular Jewish countrymen, and do secular Jews in Israel celebrate Halloween instead?

No one celebrates Halloween in Israel. Regarding the intensity of Orthodox celebration of Purim in contrast to secular celebration, I guess it depends on the person. EVERYONE in Israel lives it up!

---

[10] *"because on those days the Jews rid themselves of their enemies, and it was a month which was turned for them from sorrow into gladness and from mourning into a holiday; that they should make them days of feasting and rejoicing and sending portions of food to one another and gifts to the poor."* Esther 9:22

[11] Seth Young teaches the Hebrew Language on Root Source. https://root-source.com/channels/

CHAPTER 30

Abraham and Gidon, Friendship and Hebron

If you spend much time around Orthodox Jews, it won't take long before you hear some of the stories that have been associated with Abraham for millennia. For instance, Abraham did not just live in a city full of idolatry; his own father was an idol maker! Moreover, his calling from God did not come to him out-of-the-blue, but only *after* Abraham had decided to smash the idols in his father's household.[1] That story adds a bit more context to the call of Abraham, does it not?[2]

One of the most endearing pictures of Abraham that has been passed down is that of Abraham as a man who entertained guests — eagerly and often![3] This picture of Abraham being a man who desired to interact, who desired to be hospitable, is clearly portrayed in GENESIS 18.

> *Now the LORD appeared to him by the oaks of Mamre, while he was sitting at the tent door in the heat of the day. When he lifted up his eyes and looked, behold, three men were standing opposite him; and when he saw them, he ran from the tent door to meet them and bowed himself to the earth, and said, "My Lord, if now I have found favor in Your sight, please do not pass Your servant by. Please let a little water be brought and wash your feet, and rest yourselves under the tree; and I will bring a piece of bread, that you may refresh yourselves; after that you may go on, since you have visited your servant." GENESIS 18:1-5*

In regards to the promised food, Abraham under-promised and over-delivered. He asked Sarah to make cakes, and then he killed a choice calf!

As the story progresses, the men told Abraham that he and Sarah would have a son

---

[1] Midrash Genesis Rabbah 38.

[2] Joshua 24:2 says that Terah served other gods. More generally, the Apostle Peter alludes to a similar history for Christians in 1 Peter 1:12.

[3] This idea was expanded upon by Yose Ben Yoezer, a Jewish sage from the Maccabean Era (about 200 BCE), who exhorts in Pirkei Avot 1:5 that Jews engage in hospitality: https://bit.ly/Avot1-5.

of their own within a year. Then the Lord makes a decision to reveal to Abraham His plan to destroy the cities of Sodom and Gomorrah. That key conversation happens while looking down towards the cities.

> *Then the men rose up from there, and looked down toward Sodom; and Abraham was walking with them to send them off.* GENESIS 18:16

From this verse we know where this meeting must have taken place: near Hebron, a little bit east of the city, where it is possible to view what we call today the Dead Sea.

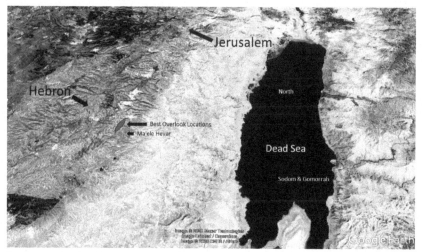

Satellite image of probable overlook locations near Hebron. (Google Earth).

My friend, Orthodox Jew Gidon Ariel lives in Ma'ale Hever, very close to the spot where Abraham had his conversation with the Lord.

Ma'ale Hever, the community in the Judean Desert where Gidon Ariel lives.

The term *Ma'ale Hever* literally means, the ascent to Hevron, or Hebron as it is often called today.[4] Hebron is the place where Abraham would ultimately purchase a cave to bury Sarah after she died. Interestingly, *Hevron* in Hebrew literally means *friendship*. Hevron is the *City of Friendship*! How ironic that Hebron today has become the center of radical Islam within the territories of Judea and Samaria! How ironic that a conflict still rages over the ownership of that burial cave, a conflict within the heart of a city whose name means *friendship*! Gidon, along with other well-known Orthodox Jews such as Hevron Jewish community spokesman Yishai Fleisher, have led many groups into the Cave of the Patriarchs, and are well-versed in the twisted intricacies of this controversy and its history.

All of this background makes the demeanor of Abraham stand out in contrast: the attitude of a man seeking to be friendly and hospitable to *all* who might pass by. The great stories that began near Hevron — the promise of Isaac in a specified time period, Abraham's bold intercession that God save Sodom and Gomorrah — these monumental stories still impact the world today, and they began with acts of *friendship*, close by to the *friendly* city of Hevron.[5]

Bob's Story of Meeting Gidon

I first laid eyes upon Gidon up on the walls of the Old City, just above the Jaffa gate. Christine Darg[6] had gathered our group of about twenty to twenty-five Christians together there, and welcomed Gidon to be part of our activities that day. She told us that as part of that day's prayer focus, Gidon would be helping us learn how to pray for Jerusalem more deeply, and with more insight.

The idea was that after Gidon gave us instruction on the meaning of the relevant Hebrew verses, we Christians would then pray for Jerusalem. I recall one of those instructions was in regards to what it meant to be a *watchman on the wall* standing *guard*. That day, we proclaimed verses primarily from the Old Testament;[7] nevertheless our prayers had a strong Christian flavor. I recall people ending their prayers "in Jesus' name," and I recall certain prophetic prayers and declarations being made. After instruction and prayer at one tower on top of the wall, we

---

[4] The second letter of the Hebrew alphabet, the "bet," is pronounced as a "b" if a dot is inside it, and a "v" if the dot is missing. Because the original biblical Hebrew had no vowels, we often find English speakers saying "Hebron" and "Abraham" while Hebrew speakers in Israel say "Hevron" and "Avraham."

[5] James 2:23 reminds us that Abraham was ultimately given the highest possible designation of friendship, "friend of God."

[6] Gidon first spoke about Christine Darg in the Prologue.

[7] I personally prefer the term *Hebrew Bible*, but this book was not written for my preferences, but to be readily readable by many Christian traditions. Whatever the name used, it is God's Word, and deserves our honor.

walked up to the next tower.[8]

After praying at the first tower north of the Jaffa gate and moving to the second one, I looked on as many Christians ahead of me began whispering to each other and pointing upwards. The skies were changing. Overhead, our bright, sunny winter day had quickly become darker and more ominous.[9] As we reached the second tower in our prayer walk, a new cloud suddenly formed high over us, slightly from the west, as if it had emerged from the sun itself.

I stopped praying and watched as out of the sun came a cloud with swirling white formations — growing and pushing eastward as if to confront the much larger, darker, more sinister formations that had formed directly overhead and were spreading out east of our position, directly over the Old City. The sight was now very notable; thus the whispering and pointing continued during the prayers. Gidon was completely focused on his teaching role in the group, and I do not recall him ever looking towards the sky, but our Jewish tour guide noticed the clouds, and we looked inquisitively at each other. Gidon spoke, and then we prayed some minutes at the second tower, our third prayer stop. When the prayer time ended, Christine asked Gidon if he wanted to make any closing remarks to the group before we continued our walk along the wall.

Gidon said "Yes," he did have something to say. During those wrap-up remarks, I snapped an iPhone photograph of him. And being fascinated by the swirling formations above him, I made sure to include as much sky as possible in the photo. I had no clue as to what he was about to say.

Gidon then spoke to us, saying:

"Now that we have concluded praying, I would like to ask everyone a question: A few days ago in a meeting I had north of Jerusalem, I had an idea, which my wife says is the best idea I have ever had: **How many of you would be interested in studying the Bible with me in an online *yeshiva* for Christians?**"[10]

And when he said this, the crowd gasped, and many quickly said:

---

8   Our first prayer stop was right there above the Jaffa Gate. Then we moved on to the towers along the wall walking north, for a total of three prayer stops.

9   This change, on its own, need not be considered significant. Since Jerusalem sits at the top of the ridge that separates the Mediterranean coastal plain from the Arabian desert, quick weather changes are not uncommon. However, even though I was not yet experienced with Jerusalem weather, the way others who had had years of prayer experience in Jerusalem were reacting, made it stand out strongly.

10   His wife Devra would later confirm she had said exactly this. Years later, she would remark that "saying that" caused her to feel connected to Root Source in a special way. Ultimately, Gidon would invite her to join the Root Source advisory board.

"Yes!"[11]

And right then the Holy Spirit said in my inner ear:

"That's your man!"

Having come to Israel to look for Orthodox Jews to partner with, I interpreted that phrase as meaning:"This is why you came to Israel. Go make him successful!"[12] I heard all of Gidon's words clearly, but to be honest, one of them was a bit of a mystery: the word *yeshiva*. I'd never heard the word! I would soon learn that a yeshiva is a school of learning where Jews come together in a certain manner and style, to study the Hebrew Bible together.Yet, while I didn't know what a *yeshiva* was, the word *online* certainly caught my attention. My prior company *Wintegra* was all about the Internet.

After Gidon finished speaking, I walked over to him and asked if we could meet so that I could hear more about his idea. A date and time for a coffee was set for later that week. Later that evening in my room at the St. George's Guest House, I would finally have time to examine that day's photos. My mouth dropped open when I saw the photograph I took at the moment Gidon was sharing his new idea.

Gidon shares his new Idea.

On the left side above the woman, is a robed figure — looking like a man or an angel — in flowing white robes, with a sword in his right hand, having been

---

[11] Gidon recalls that the first word spoken in response was the word:"Hallelujah!"

[12] It is also true that although I had never met Gidon before, the fact that his wife would say such a thing seemed notable. Moreover, the fact that Gidon would value her opinion enough to include it showed honor and humility, which was also notable. Thus, his own words bolstered my confidence about what I was hearing. The pattern of women, in this case Christine Darg and Devra Ariel, birthing the new works of God as discussed in chapter 4, would take much longer for me to consider.

drawn from its sheath. The man/angel is using the sword to spear the middle of a grotesque head that is facing and hovering right over Gidon. Upon reflection, I believe that the angelic figure holding the sword was an image of "the captain of the host of the LORD," that appeared to Joshua in JOSHUA 5:13-15.[13]

But what was absolutely fascinating about this photo was that the head of this robed figure was missing from the photograph! But wait, I had taken many other photographs! Might it be on one of them?

After examining all of them, it was clear that no head was visible in *any* photograph. The captain's head was missing! Nevertheless, it was fascinating that this robed figure, the part that I could see, had formed as part of the circular cloud that had seemed to grow out of the overhead sun! In other words, that circular cloud that was "pushing out against the darkness" in all directions was much larger than, and yet *comprised* the robed figure. I captured more of that circular cloud in this overhead shot.

Battle in the Heavens directly overhead.[14]

Finally, I looked back to the center of the circular cloud, and the sun was at its center. And lo and behold, a rainbow had now formed in the circular cloud as

[13] For Orthodox Jews, this biblical personage is an angel. For Christians, this biblical personage is an early appearance of Christ.

[14] This photo does not do justice to what it truly looked like to the group, that ominous feeling which came over all who looked up at the clouds.

seen below.

Looking back at the sun, hidden behind the tower.

Why these Clouds?

After I reviewed all the photos, it seemed to me that these clouds were a sign that something *good and important* was happening on the walls of Jerusalem at that moment. Gidon had done something important. And whatever had been hindering that work in the past, that hindrance was now removed. The sword of the captain of the host of the Lord had done its work, striking a blow on the head of the chief adversary of this work.

I could not resist sharing this photo with Gidon two days later at the Aroma Cafe coffee shop on Emek Refaim St.[15] Gidon seemed intrigued. I was quick to tell him that I believed there was no face in the clouds *for a reason.*[16]

Why then, might God have taken such an interest in Gidon's yeshiva idea?

---

[15] Emek Refaim street literally means the "valley of the giants," the location where David defeated the Philistines when they approached Jerusalem from the southwest in 2 Samuel 5:17-22. That cafe would become a convenient meeting place for us in the years to come.

[16] The night before meeting Gidon for coffee, God had strongly warned me to "treat him as a peer." I took that message to mean that I must never let Gidon's opinion on Jesus have any bearing on anything: our relationship, our projects, our plans, etc. After hearing that, I asked God for New Testament verses that would confirm these instructions. Those verses were later submitted to the men in Austin, to whom I held myself accountable, before accepting Gidon's invitation to be more than his consultant — to be his partner and co-founder. Christian men must base major decisions on the Word of God, not just messages from God, and must allow themselves to be advised by other godly men.

The reason Gidon's idea was novel is that there has been an unwritten rule within the Jewish world for hundreds, if not 2,000 years, that Jews should only be teaching other Jews. Throughout history, whenever Jews have taught Christians, Christians have turned around and used what they learned in disputations with the Jews. That always ended badly for the Jews, especially if the Jewish debating skills proved superior to that of the Christians![17] So in the years before Root Source, if Christians wanted to learn from Jews online, they would quietly join an English-based Jewish online class, such as those from Aish HaTorah.[18] The Christians would keep their heads down, and try not to ask any questions that gave their identity away. Jewish instructors were *not unaware* this was happening. Gidon called it the "don't ask, don't tell" rule among Jewish educators.

Therefore, among Orthodox Jews, the attitude for centuries had been that Jews were better off keeping to themselves. When Jews interacted with Christians, eventually they had to either *move*, or *die*. Gidon once told me about a Jewish saying he was taught when he was young: "In Europe, the grave of a Jewish grandson will rarely be found next to the grave of his grandfather."

Gidon's primary motivation, as I have come to observe it, was that he believed that the love expressed by Christians towards Israel is now genuine, and that "love demands a response." In the Orthodox Jewish world, next to inviting someone to come stay in your home, the highest form of relationship comes through an offer to study the Bible together. Therefore Gidon's response, the idea he expressed on the walls of the Old City of Jerusalem, was to reverse the traditional animosity and create an online website that would bring him into continuous, *overt relationship with Christians*, teaching them about the Hebrew Bible, Jewish ideas and thought, by using the modern invention of the Internet.

In fact, I remember where we were in the car in early 2015, driving in Jerusalem, when we both hit upon the key idea: "*Root Source is about relationship!*"

Abraham and Relationship

Why then, might God have taken such an interest in Gidon's idea for *relationship*? Because of Abraham!

---

[17] Disputations between Christians and Jews during the Middle Ages were connected with burnings of the Talmud and violence against the Jews. For two of the more well-known examples, refer to the following. The Disputation of Barcelona in Aragon, Spain, 1263:
Montgomery, Ray & O'Dell, Bob, *The LIST: Persecution of Jews by Christians Throughout History*, (Jerusalem, Israel: Root Source Press, 2019), 180.
Disputation of Tortosa, Spain, in 1413-14: Ibid, 235.
[18] https://www.aish.com/

I believe that Gidon carries within himself nothing less than a modern-day embodiment of that wonderful characteristic of Abraham, a man who eagerly sought out relationships with those who might pass by.

It has been said that the best ideas are often the simplest ones.

Speaking of *relationship*, I must also thank Dr. Marvin Wilson for making a comment to me that inspired this chapter. He remarked about the resemblance between Gidon and Abraham.[19] In all these years, I had never "seen it" myself. Yes, Gidon lives near where Abraham lived, but I had never made the connection between Abraham "welcoming strangers," and Gidon "welcoming relationships with Christians" — until Dr. Wilson's insight.[20]

Friendship and Hebron

In early 2018, four years into my work with Gidon, with Root Source having been launched for three years and many relationships built, I began to feel uneasy. Something was slightly off center. I began to feel pressure to step back a bit and encourage Gidon to take on more Christian partners. Nothing was wrong with our friendship!

Gidon began visiting Texas in 2018, especially the Dallas area, and he began making — and building — more and deeper relationships in Texas. Then, on the 9th of Av in 2018, I finally saw a verse that explained where that internal pressure was coming from:

> Thus says the LORD of hosts, 'In those days ten men from all the nations will grasp the garment of a Jew, saying, "Let us go with you, for we have heard that God is with you." ZECHARIAH 8:23

I began to laugh at myself.

You see, when I first came to Jerusalem in January 2014, my idea was that I might be able to consult for *ten* different Orthodox Jewish organizations. (I didn't learn the ZECHARIAH 8:23 scripture until later; *ten* was just a round number.) But when

---

[19] The Apostle Paul writes that this resemblance need not be limited to the physical seed of Abraham, like Gidon. Dr. Wilson of course, agrees that Christians are Abraham's descendants spiritually (Galatians 3:29), a theme so important to him was the title of his groundbreaking book, *Our Father Abraham*.

[20] He made that remark while reviewing this book, during a phone call when I was seeking his advice on a few theological points. When he said it, I immediately knew that this chapter would need to be written. Before now, I had never shared those photographs publicly. People should not need swirling clouds to decide whether they are interested in Root Source. But here, I felt the clouds demonstrated that God was taking notice of what would be birthed, and therefore, that they should not be omitted.

I saw Gidon, God had told me: "That's your man!"

Over time I began to take notice that God had *not* said, "That's your first man!" In the coming months, I realized that helping Gidon start Root Source was going to be almost a full-time job for months, if not years!

So, first God gently and lovingly corrected my thinking from focusing on *ten* Orthodox Jewish ideas, to just *one*! And now he was lovingly correcting me again towards the idea that Gidon should not have *one* Christian partner, but *ten*.[21]

This verse implies that in God's model, for every Jewish idea, there should be ten others who look at the idea and come to their own conclusion that "God is with him," and be willing to walk alongside him. Every person has something to offer. Yes, money can and should be part of that for those who have such means, but the most important gift you can give is *yourself*, whatever talents, skills, time and resources you can make available for the work. I do not see this verse in any way demanding that Christians should only work with Jews. But, I believe the great and high calling of Christians in these latter days, and perhaps one of the reasons why clouds might form in the sky above Gidon, is to see this verse fulfilled. Nothing prevents it!

By the end of 2018 Gidon had at least five Christians on his advisory board, and by the end of 2019 he had about ten such *go-alongers*. That term is mine: Gidon just calls them advisors!

The city of Hebron is the city of friendship. Friendship is what I see happening today within Gidon's advisory board. This is how a city of friendship might be built.

Eleven Men

One day, when Gidon and I were talking about ZECHARIAH 8:23 and the "ten men" walking with a Jew, I remarked to him that ten plus one makes only eleven! Smiling, I asked:

"Gidon, given that there are *twelve* tribes of Israel, why do *you* think God wrote ZECHARIAH 8:23 so that the total number of people walking together was only

---

[21] I do not see this scripture as excluding women. I believe that the verse says *men* to model the kind of relationship God envisions, that of peer-to-peer relationship. If the verse had said *men and women*, then we might wrongly interpret the verse as describing two different kinds of relationship within the group. Thus the word "women" is best not included; but neither is it excluded.

eleven, and not twelve?"

He thought for a moment. Then he replied:

"All eleven still need a leader. For Christians that leader will certainly be Yeshua. For us, I suppose, it is Joshua. But in any case, we are going to have to walk together in a bit of mystery, are we not?"

Yes, Gidon. Yes we are.

Shalom.

Asking Gidon

Is there a character trait of Abraham, or a story of Abraham that stands out for you, personally?

Of the hundreds of people mentioned in the Bible, only a few are national — and even universal — heroes. Of these, it seems that all have serious character flaws. Only Abraham, while human and with the foibles of a human, is called beloved by God, and whose memory is brought up again and again by God as the one with whom He made a covenant, and with whom He will always honor subsequent covenants because of the Abrahamic covenant.

One story that stands out is the story in Genesis 13, in which Abraham encourages his nephew Lot to choose another area to settle and graze his flocks in, in order to minimize friction between his shepherds and Abraham's. Ultimately, Lot chooses Sodom and Gemora, which at the time is a lush green area, before it was destroyed by God as recorded in Genesis 19. At the end of Genesis 13, just before Abraham returns to Hebron, God appears to Abraham and promises him the entire land that would be known as Israel, and progeny as abundant as the grains of sand of the earth. Since this chapter's story takes place between Sodom and Hebron, which is exactly where I live in Ma'ale Hever, I claim that it actually takes place in my backyard.[22]

How do you react to the idea I presented in this chapter, that the work of Root Source is a work that follows in the example of Abraham? Had you ever thought about this comparison before now?

---

[22] This wonderful video shows his amazing backyard: https://root-source.com/lessons/special-broadcast-archive-20141020/

Well, that is quite humbling; Abraham's are very large shoes to fill. But it is an example which I feel is the right one for a Jew and any other follower of Abraham to make an effort to follow.

You had worked to build relationships with Christians for many years before having the idea to create an online yeshiva for Christians. What did it mean to you when you heard your wife say that she thought this was "the best idea you ever had"?

That is a compliment of the highest order, as Devra had heard many ideas from me since we'd met ☺

CHAPTER 31

Many More than Four Fathers

Over the last five years in my work in Israel and with Orthodox Jews, none of my viewpoints has changed more dramatically than with respect to Jewish forefathers.

Honor your father and your mother, that you may long endure on the land that Hashem your God is assigning to you. EXODUS 20:12 (TIB)

I had always thought about this verse with respect to my own father and mother. But as I worked with Gidon I began to see that the Jewish people have a much larger view on this verse than I knew. Here are a few quotes that I began to pick up from Gidon and his friends:

"The sages tell us…"

Excuse me, but who else even uses the word *sages* anyway? But there it was being used over and over regarding the collective set of rabbis and teachers and elders and those who have said things that have stood the test of time.

Then there was the time Gidon said this to a group of Christians:

"I am privileged to be part of an unbroken chain of relationship to rabbis back to Moses."

Here is what he meant. Orthodox Jews have a responsibility to be connected to a rabbi who can help them answer questions about the finer details of following the *halacha* (or the way) of living. This rabbi is not necessarily the rabbi of the synagogue they attend. They can choose any rabbi they like, as long as that rabbi agrees, of course. And the rabbi they choose has a rabbi with whom he is in relationship as well, and so on and so forth all the way back to Moses.

Excuse me, but who else talks like that? As we consider our Western independent mindset, who do you even know who says such things about their Christian heritage except perhaps the Pope? About the closest I ever heard of that sentiment was when Dr John D. Garr[1] introduced himself to a room full of Christians as:

> *"I am a preacher, and son of a preacher, my father; and the grandson of a preacher, his father; and the great grandson of a preacher, his father; and the great-great grandson of a preacher."*

That sounds like a man who knows and appreciates his forefathers! He has *four generations* of forefathers who are preachers. I cannot even imagine what it would be like to have such a pedigree. But the Jews have *many more than four forefathers*.

I remember also hearing Christian theologian Dr. Marvin Wilson talk about being a young man sitting in a classroom looking upon his Jewish professor (a rabbi), who was speaking specifically of *his forefather Moses*. It brought home for Marvin that he was looking at a man who felt completely connected to his forefathers. All of a sudden the faith of the Jews became so real to Marvin, so personal, and so present in the room.[2]

So What?

What is the impact of this reality for the Jewish people? Are they elitists who rest on the laurels of the accomplishments of others? Do they hold back from pushing on the boundaries of thought because it has already been covered by others? Somehow I don't think that trait comes up very often in the Jewish gene pool![3]

I wonder if it is just the opposite. Jews comprise less than 0.2 percent of the world's population,[4] yet they have received more than 22.5 percent of all Nobel prizes ever awarded.[5] Perhaps part of the reason they have excelled in innovation,

---

[1] Dr. Garr is one of a rare group of men I know who have been studying and writing about our Hebraic heritage for fifty years. Two others are Dr. Brad Young and Dr. Marvin Wilson. Dr. Garr's works includes the prodigious volume *God and Israel*, https://amzn.to/2XGVBGN, and he can be reached at https://www.hebraiccommunity.org/. Online courses from all three men may be found at Dr. Garr's Hebraic Heritage Christian College, https://www.hebraiccollege.org/.

[2] In 2 Timothy 1:3 we can see that Paul also honored his ancestors. In chapter 2:2 he honors those who are faithful and take the time to teach the next generation.

[3] *Tikkun olam* (literally: repairing the world) is an idea which is pervasive among all Jews, not just the Orthodox: the drive to make a difference in the world for good. I have heard Rabbi Ken Spiro say it this way, "Not all activists are Jews, but all Jews are activists." Rabbi Tuly Weisz says it as, "The drive to make a difference in the world by Jews is very strong. Therefore if they are not doing it in a way aligned with the Bible, they will do it in a way aligned with a progressive agenda. This explains why so many Jews in America have historically leaned left, and why for instance left-leaning Jews comprise a surprising percentage of the U.S. Supreme Court justices in 2019." Currently, three of the nine justices, or 33 percent, are Jewish: Ruth Bader Ginsburg, Stephen Breyer, and Elena Kagan.
Short link to article at Wikipedia: https://bit.ly/Jewish-justices

[4] https://www.ynetnews.com/articles/0,7340,L-4291987,00.html

[5] https://www.jewishpress.com/indepth/columns/the-22-5-test/2019/09/20/
https://en.wikipedia.org/wiki/List_of_Jewish_Nobel_laureates

is that they have had great appreciation for those who came before them. Perhaps they have heaped upon themselves a generational blessing.

Overall, it seems to me that what is happening is that historically, Jews are both *progressive* and *conservative* at the same time.

Judge Not

A majority of Bible-believing Christians today are politically conservative. They appreciate the consistent values of the Bible and the fact that God does not change. When it comes to the founding of the United States, for instance, they appreciate the founding fathers of the nation, their faith, and their Judeo-Christian values. They recall to mind verses about the ancient paths being the right ones:

> *This is what the LORD says: "Stand at the crossroads and look; ask for the ancient paths, ask where the good way is, and walk in it, and you will find rest for your souls.* JEREMIAH 6:16 (NIV)

Such Christians often feel judged by those who are less conservative. Conservative Christians are considered to be out of touch, unreasonable, and legalistic in the face of a changing national culture. Much hurt is spread between those who hold different views. Judgment abounds.

And yet, when it comes to the Jews, *conservative Christians* can fall prey to the same judgment! They can see religious Jews as being out of touch, unreasonable and legalistic in the face of the massive spread of Christian culture around the world. Christians who are judged by those who are less conservative, turn around and judge Orthodox Jews who are *even more conservative* than they, who are preserving the value of their forefathers from *thousands* of years ago, not just *hundreds* of years ago.

I believe the temptation to rush to judgment can only be broken in the context of relationship. It is SO much harder to criticize, compartmentalize, impugn and judge the motives of those with whom you have a relationship. I am more empathetic now to those whose views are different from my own.

Conclusion

The verse about honoring your father and mother is the *fifth* of ten commandments.

> *Honor your father and your mother, that you may long endure on the land that Hashem your God is assigning to you.* EXODUS 20:12 (TIB)

That is interesting because the first five commandments, including the commandment above, are considered by Jews to be those commandments that reach upward to God, while the second five commandments are considered to be those that reach outward to humanity! Why do they include honoring parents with the upward commandments? Because, the Jewish view is that honoring one's father and mother is akin to honoring God. In other words, the Jewish view is that God treats the honoring of one's parents, when it happens, as if God was being directly honored as well.

Does that insight not help our understanding of why the Orthodox Jews might honor their forefathers more than we do?

Honoring those who have gone before isn't easy, especially when we know about their sins, limitations and failures.[6] But perhaps a lot more honoring of our forefathers would honor God as well. It is not that we in the Christian world never honor our forefathers, but our "honoring muscle" seems to be too weak, and needs to be flexed and strengthened in order to *prepare the way of the Lord*.

And if we do so then we, and our children and the entire world, will be blessed.

Shalom.

Asking Gidon

Gidon, who is "your rabbi," and how long has he been your rabbi?

For most issues that are not self-evident, I consult with Rabbi Gedalia Meyer, who students of Root Source might remember as the teacher of *God: the Jewish Image*.[7] Soon after I met him, probably about fifteen years ago, I "adopted" him as my rabbi.

Is this rabbi the rabbi of the synagogue which you attend in Ma'ale Hever in Judea? If not, where is he located? How did you meet him?

Rabbi Meyer is not the rabbi of the synagogue of Ma'ale Hever. In fact, he lives in my previous place of residence, Ma'ale Adumim. We moved to Ma'ale Hever from Ma'ale Adumim in 2012, and I felt attached to Rabbi Meyer

---

[6] But the decision is not really optional is it? It is necessary, and prophesied in Malachi 4:4-6.
[7] https://root-source.com/channels/

before that move. We had been neighbors in Ma'ale Adumim for possibly a decade or more.

How often do you see your rabbi face-to-face in a month or year, and about how often in a month or year might you reach out to him for advice on a particular matter regarding *halacha*?

In my case, we see each other once or twice a year or so. I make an effort to drop by his home when I visit Ma'ale Adumim. We ask him questions by phone when they arise, often while preparing for holidays, a few times a year.

Does the rabbi get compensated by you for the help he offers to you, and for being available?

No. Ours is a friendship, not a business.

This last question is meant generally, not about your specific rabbi. Do most rabbis do counseling and deal with specific issues, or do they refer to specialists?

It really depends on the rabbi. Pastoring or counseling is not necessarily a traditional task of a rabbi, but in the 20th century it has become so for sure. Rabbis who want to pursue this side of their position should (and I would guess do) pursue further pastoral training. There are many rabbis who are licensed psychologists and mental and emotional health specialists already. Those who come across cases that are too big for them certainly refer to specialists.

CHAPTER 32

From Minor to Major

One of the minor prophets, Zechariah, makes a major-league promise in his eighth chapter when he declares that all four major fast days of the Jewish people will one day be turned into joy, gladness and cheerful feast days, in the last days:

> *Thus said the LORD of Hosts: The fast of the fourth month, the fast of the fifth month, the fast of the seventh month, and the fast of the tenth month shall become occasions for joy and gladness, happy festivals for the House of Yehuda; but you must love honesty and integrity.* ZECHARIAH 8:19 (TIB)

This promise comes as part of God's answer to the question that was asked by some of the returned exiles from Babylon soon after they had rebuilt the Temple. They wanted to know if they should continue to fast on the day that the Temple was destroyed, now that a new Temple was built.

> *In the fourth year of King Darius, on the fourth day of the ninth month, Kislev, the word of Hashem came to Zecharya—when Beit El-sharezer and Regem-melech and his men sent to entreat the favor of Hashem, [and] to address this inquiry to the Kohanim of the House of Hashem and to the Neviim: "Shall I weep and practice abstinence in the fifth month, as I have been doing all these years?"* ZECHARIAH 7:1-3 (TIB)

The fast of the fifth month is commonly referred to as the **9ᵗʰ of Av**, which in Hebrew is called **Tisha B'Av**. It is the ninth day of the fifth month (Av).[1] God's

---

[1] In God's original introduction of His calendar, the first month was called Aviv, because of the barley that must be ripened before it begins. After Babylonian exile, the Jews brought back some of the Babylonian names for those same lunar months, often named after Babylonian gods. The first month became Nissan. And yet, if God was offended at this change, then why did He allow some of these Babylonian names to end up in the canon of Scripture? **I believe God works within our past, and eventually redeems it.** Any Christian who is offended by the Jews adopting *month names* of Babylonian gods, in order to be consistent, must also reject all seven days of the week today, which are all named after Greco-Roman and

answer in the rest of that chapter was not an easy answer nor a simple answer, and it left no doubt that they should continue to fast. But God's word to them ended with an amazing promise that one day, this day of fasting (along with some other days of fasting) would become an amazing source of joy!

Since that answer from God, the Jews have not stopped fasting on the 9th of Av every year. Then, after more than 2,400 years of fasting, in 1948 Israel became recognized as a Nation again.

Fast forward another seventy years to 2018. Now that seventy years have elapsed since the modern rebirth of the Nation of Israel, many Jews of Israel have begun to wonder if it might be time for Israel to begin to transition from fasting on the 9th of Av, to joyous feasting.

In chapter 6 we discussed Christian revival. In this chapter we shall take up the topic of what might happen to music in a Jewish one. Let us suppose that the days of fasting are transformed into days of feasting. *What would happen to the music of Israel?*

That is an impossibly difficult question, so let us ask a simpler one:

> *As the State of Israel transitions from its first generation since rebirth (seventy years ago) into its second generation (of rebirth), how might its music begin to change as well?*

This question came upon me, not as a flash of light from the sky, but as a note from the air. One of the most interesting rabbis in Israel is Rabbi Yitzchak Ginsburgh, who is a pillar in the Chabad movement and in Israel at large. His teachings are deep *and* wide. His lectures will touch on physics as often as the inner workings of the human soul. This I have known for years. What I did not know was that he is a musician as well!

Soon after it was published in late January 2018, an email reached me from Ginsburgh's Gal Einai Institute, featuring a newly released piano melody from Ginsburgh.[2]

It is primarily a minor melody that recalls for me — I don't claim to be a musical expert — a feeling of Ashkenazi melodies of Eastern Europe. It is quite beautiful. But what captured my attention upon first hearing it, was the sudden and surprising allusion to joy in the midst of the piece, where there is a shift from

---

Norse gods.
[2] https://youtu.be/vZD154IscpA

the minor chords to a brief sequence of major chords. But that transition is fleeting. Almost as quickly as it comes, it is gone, and we return to the minor key.

The first time it happens in the piece is for only five seconds at 0:48, and then for ten seconds at 1:10. And then in the second half, the strongest and most noticeable departure to a major key occurs at 3:48 for ten seconds, followed at 5:02 for five seconds.

A pianist's hands are shown with their mirror image reflection.

While this piece is beautiful, it would not have inspired an entire chapter. But four months later in May 2018, a second piece was published on the same piano, by the same pianist, and by the same composer: Rabbi Ginsburgh.[3]

This time, the composition was entirely different! And just like any good movie description doesn't describe the second half of the movie, neither will I describe this second piece of music.

If you listen to this piece, be sure to listen to what happens at the 2:23 minute mark! I suggest you listen to both pieces in sequence and compare them.

Can you hear them as two interconnected parables? Can you see them as two prophetic stories? Continue reading for my answer.

The next line provides the answer.

Just as these two pieces stand in isolation from each other, but in transition from one story to the other, they reveal what must happen in the days to come for the music of Israel, and for Israel itself. The first piece of music is primarily in a minor key, but it transitions to a major key, but only briefly for a few seconds. The second piece of music begins in a *major* key. It has transitioned to joy! Nevertheless, for a few seconds at the 2:23 mark it drifts back into minor, as if to recall a memory of the past.

This is the transition that I see happening in Israel. We are somewhere between the first piece of music and the second. The restoration of Israel is underway.

---

[3] https://youtu.be/L2nIIYlooSA

Major events have taken place in Israel that cause the world to now look upon Israel with newfound respect. Perhaps not entirely coincidentally, the publishing of the second piece of music occurred after the United States moved its embassy to Jerusalem. Tourism is breaking records in Israel with over 3.6 million visitors in 2017,[4] 4 million in 2018,[5] and 4.55 million in 2019.[6] A September 2018 survey in Israel cited that 89 percent of *all* Israelis (not just Jews) were satisfied or very satisfied with life in Israel.[7]

I find it quite appropriate that the first name of the composer of these two pieces is *Yitzchak (Isaac)*, which was a name chosen not by man, but by God. Isaac means *laughter*. That same word *laughter* is found here.

> When the LORD brought back the captive ones of Zion, we were like those who dream. Then our mouth was filled with laughter and our tongue with joyful shouting; then they said among the nations, "The LORD has done great things for them." PSALM 126:1–2

Indeed, the transition from exile to return, and the transition from fasting to feasting, are indeed *major* changes in every sense of the word.

Shalom.

Asking Gidon

This chapter is about instrumental music, but the Torah itself contains two songs with words: the song of deliverance from Egypt in EXODUS 15, and the Song of Moses in DEUTERONOMY 32. How do the Jewish people relate to those songs today? Are either of them sung during the year by the Jews? If so, how and when?

The Song of the Sea in Exodus is sung every morning as the culmination of the *Pesukei Dezimra* (the verses of song), which are recited before the *Shema* and its blessings, and after the *Shemonah Esreh* main silent prayer. The song of Moses in Deuteronomy is recited joyously every year on the eighth day of Sukkot (Feast of Tabernacles). That day is referred to specifically as *Simchat Torah*, which is the celebration of the culmination of the annual weekly Torah reading cycle, and the song of Moses is recited over and over until every male

---

4   Short link to article at Times of Israel: https://bit.ly/Israel2017tourism
5   Short link to article at Times of Israel: https://bit.ly/Israel2018tourism
6   Short link to article at Jerusalem Post: https://bit.ly/Israel2019tourism
7   Short link to article at Behold Israel: https://bit.ly/Israelis89

member of the congregation gets a chance to read along with some of it.

What is your perception from inside Israel? Are things overall getting better in recent years?

This is a rhetorical question! Yes, things are getting better and better, faster and faster in Israel. I have been here for forty years, and I still find myself breathless when I see some new things here.

What metric of improvement and/or growth of Israel affects you the most personally?

This is almost like asking which of your children do you love most! I cannot think of an aspect of my life that is not impacted considerably by the growth of Israel. As an example, I just generated a random word(!) and found the word "population." The size of Israel is now approaching nine million, as opposed to barely three and a half million when I moved to Israel in 1978. Because of this greater critical mass, Israel is a viable market for many more things than it was then. In spite of our being an "island economy," that is, not able to include adjoining states in our economy, we already have enough people quantitatively, and a great mix of qualities, to have a quality of life that challenges that of most western countries.[8] See the book *Start Up Nation* by Dan Senor and Saul Singer.[9]

Do people talk openly about things getting better, or do the troubles of the day, week and month tend to dominate the conversations instead?

I think it depends on who you hang out with. One of my favorite Israeli journalists is Gil Hoffman,[10] chief political correspondent and analyst for the Jerusalem Post, who proudly quotes Israel Television, which called him "the most optimistic man in Israel." As you mentioned in this chapter yourself, 89 percent of Israelis would challenge him for that title. I am sure that any tourist who interacts with any locals for more than a few seconds will see this!

---

[8] *"In 2006, Israel was rated as having the 23rd-highest quality of life in the world by the United Nations Human Development Index. In 2010, Israel was ranked 15th in quality of life. In 2011, Bank of Israel Governor Stanley Fischer said that Israel had a standard of living two-thirds as high as that of the United States...*
The country ranks 11th in the World Happiness Report of 2017 with a rating of 7.213, landing it between Sweden and Costa Rica...
According to a 2014 OECD survey, Israel is the fourth most educated country in the world."
See this wikipedia article for more details and scores: https://en.wikipedia.org/wiki/Standard_of_living_in_Israel

[9] https://amzn.to/3gHBlNn

[10] https://www.jpost.com/author/gil-hoffman

CHAPTER 33

A View Too Small: Prophecy

We continue with our discussion on our view of things in the Christian world. I have long felt that something is amiss in the Christian world in regards to our view of end-times prophecy.

Before launching into what may be amiss, I want to begin by commending two aspects of end-times prophecy.

First, many pastors and preachers avoid talk of end-times prophecy like the plague (Zechariah and Revelation puns intended). So those who are willing to venture into this field deserve respect. In fact, the New Testament book of Revelation is the only book that explicitly promises a blessing just for reading it.[1] Perhaps the Apostle John knew something about how the Church was likely to steer clear of this book.

Second, the good thing about a study of prophecy is that it forces the student to consider **every verse** in the entire Bible simultaneously. Because if we believe that the entire Bible is true, then we have to consider that God will not contradict Himself, and so every verse is used to help in the interpretation of every other one. Therefore any student who delves into end-times prophecy is forced to dig deep and wide and learn the entire Bible.

A View Too Small

Nevertheless, despite these benefits, I am troubled by much of what I see today in the world of Christian end-times prophecy.

In one sense I speak not as an outsider, but an insider. Gidon Ariel and I have

---

[1] Revelation 1:3

published two books that some might put in the end-times genre: *Israel FIRST!* and *Jubilee NOW!* Yet in another sense I am truly an outsider, because my views would not please many leaders in the end-times arena.

First, for a very long time I have been uncomfortable with the business model of the prophetic industry. It simply requires *too much money* to sustain itself. As was mentioned in chapter 28, *The Media's Ten Commandments*, it is human nature to try to increase the revenue of an organization and to extend its reach. The need for money precipitates self-interest, and self-interest forces sales plans and pledge drives. I simply don't see that kind of prophetic activity appearing in Scripture: not in the New Testament and not in the Old Testament either. The prophets in the Bible usually worked outside of normal life, maintained an extremely modest lifestyle, were usually outcasts, and never raised funds for their work. The biblical model seems a whole lot safer to me, a whole lot less susceptible to bias based on self-interest.

Second, since prophetic products today are often *sold*, business principles come into play. People only spend money when they have a felt need for a product. Marketers (I was one for twenty-five years) know that future negative events generate a greater perceived need than future positive events. **In other words, threats are more emotionally powerful than opportunities.** In particular, fear is an extremely strong emotion that encourages people to spend money. All this has made the prophecy industry too *negative* for my taste. This is exactly the same criticism I made of the media. The biblical reality is that God's kingdom is advancing and growing every day.[2] God does not lose any ground. God does not lose any round. We do not limp into the future.[3]

Third, while various prophetic predictions of the future are regularly given publicly to the Church at large, to all who will listen, I find this practice incomplete.

---

[2] No Root Source teacher covers this better than David Haivri. One of his favorite prophecies fulfilled by the modern state of Israel is: *"Again you will plant vineyards on the hills of Samaria; the planters will plant and will enjoy them."* (Jeremiah 31:5). Against the advice of Israeli agricultural experts, the local farmers planted vineyards anyway, and local wineries such as Tura Winery are winning top awards in Europe: https://turawinery.com
David's channel is Israel and the Nations: https://root-source.com/channels/

[3] Even though, as Gidon mentioned in the Q&A in chapter 1, *"Jews focus more on what we are supposed to do, than on what God is 'supposed' to do,"* I have found that Orthodox Jews are very respectful of the prophetic declarations made in the Hebrew Bible. However, beyond the Gog/Magog war in Ezekiel 38 & 39 and the continual war with Amalek in Exodus 17:16, I find they do not focus their energies on the still unfulfilled *negative* prophecies of the Bible nearly as often as do Christians. Rather they focus on the *positive* prophecies, especially those that specifically relate to Israel. My explanation for this difference is based on how I see that they categorize prophecy into the positive and the negative. Their view is that all positive prophecy is guaranteed, but that negative prophecy is not, because it is conditional and may be later changed by acts of God or repentance of man. (The story of Jonah is often cited as an example.) Therefore, the Orthodox would rather focus on that which is ultimately guaranteed.

Where and how are such leaders holding themselves publicly accountable to such words during the waiting period after the word is given? Who is apologizing for being wrong after the word does not happen as predicted? How many leaders are offering to submit their prophetic words in advance to other major leaders, so that they can be vetted and confirmed, before they are delivered to the public? It seems that often those best positioned to shepherd the industry are unwilling; some because they are making their living from that very industry.

We held ourselves fully accountable in our book *Israel FIRST!* We listed our predictions and proclaimed our hits and misses.[4] The experience was simultaneously satisfying[5] and humbling.[6]

Fourth, I perceive that we spend a lot of time coming up with an end-times model and then fitting current events into that model. What model do I prefer, do you ask? **I have a suspicion that none of these current models are big enough, grand enough, and magnificent enough to give God the freedom to wind up history in the way He deserves.** I am reminded of the Sadducees who asked Jesus a no-win question regarding their "model" of what they thought the resurrection might look like (MARK 12:18-27). In their question they offered Him *seven* different options to choose from! Instead, Jesus completely reframed their argument and concluded: "God is the God of the living, not the dead." He told them that they were misguided because they did not know the Scriptures (well enough) nor did they understand the power of God. Do we Christians think we can read such an interaction and *not* allow that interaction to apply to us? Are we who study end-times prophecy free from small thinking? Hardly.

Fifth, I perceive that many predictions are too short-term in nature, as if they are designed to fit within the predictor's lifetime. The Bible is a story of many generations, of a patient God who will not rest until He brings forth fullness in everything He cares about, but not by overriding man's free will. Our New Testament quotes Jesus as saying "I am coming soon", but He has not returned in almost two thousand years. Is this some sneaky marketing tactic, as if it were designed to elicit urgent behavior? No! We are to walk forward, holding in divine tension the Messiah's imminent coming (without falling prey to escapism), yet also working as if our torch must be passed along to multiple future generations before the Messiah comes.

---

4   To be fair to ourselves, we were proposing certain possibilities and predictions through the interpretation of Scripture, not making prophetic predictions as though we were receiving them directly as words from God.

5   https://root-source.com/blog/category/prediction-updates/

6   https://root-source.com/blog/prediction-update-did-god-press-the-pause-button/

Sixth and lastly, I perceive that many verses are already claimed to have been fulfilled, and yet miss the point of an ever-greater fulfillment yet to come. What is greatly needed is the perspective of the Word of God as both living and enduring.[7] If we truly believe that the Bible is living, then *no verse should ever be discarded* when it is fulfilled, but it should rather be seen as having been strengthened, and remaining in play for another, even more glorious fulfillment. My friend Ray Montgomery has said of this idea, "Alas, so many divisions have been created on prophecy interpretation — when many times they have all been correct."[8]

A Prophecy Gathering I Dream About

How different today's prophetic activity would look if we were first trying to understand and grow in our understanding of God's ways and heart. If the Word of God is living and enduring, then nothing in it is ever to be discarded and nothing in it ever dies. Imagine gathering to investigate how every truth spoken from the mouth of God *was always* true, *is* true at this very moment, and *will always* be living and enduring in the future. If we were to feast in this way upon the magnificent beauty and power of God's Word, our Christian prophetic activity, indeed our own prophets, would be transformed. Then, the world will be drawn towards us, our faith and our humility.

This is the kind of prophetic activity — a brighter, hopeful, uplifting prophetic activity — to which many more people might start looking *forward*.

Shalom.

---

[7] 1 Peter 1:23; Isaiah 40:8
[8] My friend Ray, with whom I am co-author of *The LIST*, believes the following:
Unraveling prophecy in Scripture is like peeling back the layers of an onion — the more layers you peel off, the more there is to discover. Many prophecies have multiple fulfillments, such as:
   1.   being fulfilled in the lifetime of the prophet;
   2.   being fulfilled in the life of Christ;
   3.   being fulfilled in the early Church;
   4.   being fulfilled in the Church age historically;
   5.   they are to be fulfilled in the life of the believer;
   6.   they are to be fulfilled in the End Times;
   7.   they are to be fulfilled at Christ's second coming.

Asking Gidon

Gidon, in the Hebrew Bible, the most recently written book was written about 400 BCE. Is it understood by Jews that we already have enough prophetic insight (prophecy) to last until the Messiah comes? In other words, is everything we need to know already "covered"?

A famous teaching from the Talmud says that since the destruction of the [first] Temple, prophecy was taken (withheld) from prophets and given to children and mentally unstable individuals (Baba Batra 12b).[9] However, we also understand that any prophecy recorded in the Bible is recorded for generations (Megillah 14a).[10] I understand this to mean that the way to hear God's message for today is to read the Bible and listen to how to apply its messages to our day.

Bible prophecy experts like the late Chuck Missler have pointed out that concerning the book of Revelation, after its opening and the seven letters to the seven churches, practically everything in Revelation is prophesied elsewhere, in various books in the Hebrew Bible. How do you react to that?

I have never read the entire book of Revelation so I cannot comment. But definitely the entire New Testament reads as a Jewish document. Its authors were Jews. It is written in a Hebraic style. It is quoting the Hebrew Bible quite often. Overall I would say that there is no question that even though it was written in Greek, the New Testament is a Jewish document, from alpha to omega.

Can you please explain how the six days of creation relates to the Jewish view of the Messiah, and based on the Jewish calendar, how close are we to the End of Days?

The psalmist says in PSALM 90:4: *"A thousand years in Your eyes are like a single day that passed."* The sages in the Talmud (Avoda Zara 9a)[11] connected this to the concept that the Sabbath is considered "a hint, a taste of the World to Come," and taught that world [history] is [to be] six thousand years long: two thousand *tohu* (confusion); two thousand *Torah*; and two thousand *Mashiach*.

---

9 https://bit.ly/BavaBatra12b
10 https://bit.ly/Megillah14a
11 https://bit.ly/Zarah9a

So some people believe that since we are currently in the year 5780, we are about 220 years before the deadline of Messiah's arrival. I personally think we are much closer than that.[12]

---

[12] Nobody covers this more frequently than my friend Eliyahu Berkowitz. Born Jewish, this former French chef and hippie from New York came to Israel, and amazingly became an Orthodox Jew living in the Golan region. Today he has become an end-times writer-extraordinaire. Eliyahu (Hebrew for *Elijah*) told me a priceless story about studying in an Israeli yeshiva, having had the head of the yeshiva pair him with the smartest student in the class. This story is so wonderful that if you don't watch any other video in this whole book, I beg you to watch this video starting at the 39-minute mark: https://youtu.be/Cpg127jklvc This simple 6-minute clip teaches more about my friend, about yeshivas and about the heart of torah study, than a world full of books could ever do. My one regret in recommending this clip is that he compliments me in it, but with regard to him calling me his friend, I shall not regret that as long as I live.

CHAPTER 34

A View Too Small: Punishment

I grew up in an environment where I was taught to fear the Lord, His righteousness, and His judgment of the world — in short, His ability to punish the wicked. It wasn't that any of that was wrong, but since knowing Gidon, and since spending more time studying the Jewish roots of our faith, I realized my view was a bit too small. To that end, I would like to share three examples of a larger view.

Example #1. Gidon Speaks of God's Restraint

I remember hearing one of Gidon's teachings about the morning prayers. He was covering the prayers of praise, *Pesukei Dezimra,* which is based on PSALMS 145-150. In one of his lessons[1] he translates the Jewish prayer written about PSALM 145:8 as saying:

> *And He is compassionate, will atone for sin and not destroy, and very much restrains His anger, and will not awaken all of His rage.* (From Pesukei Dezimra, translated by Gidon.)

Gidon went on to say that God's ability to refrain from all the anger that is justified, is evidence of God's power and might! When God has the ability and the right to do something, and He restrains Himself from doing it, it shows His power because He is able to restrain Himself!

This can actually be frustrating for the righteous. Solomon declares it:

> *In my own brief span of life, I have seen both these things: sometimes a good man perishes in spite of his goodness, and sometimes a wicked one endures in spite of his wickedness.* ECCLESIASTES 7:15 (TIB)

---

[1] https://root-source.com/lessons/jewish-prayer-036/

It seems to me that in His restraint, God is giving time for the wicked to repent, and ultimately laying the groundwork for a righteous judgment in which the wicked, having been given every advantage in this life, will be without excuse in judgment.

Example #2. The Torah Punishes us Harshly?

But interestingly, the Torah commands quick punishment in certain cases.

> You shall keep the Shabbat, for it is holy for you. He who profanes it shall be put to death: whoever does work on it, that person shall be cut off from among his kin. EXODUS 31:13 (TIB)

Then there's the story in NUMBERS 15:32-36, which tells the story of a man found gathering wood on the Shabbat. The Lord told Moses that he was to be put to death by having the entire congregation stone him with stones. Indeed there are other death penalties listed in the Torah, such as:

> If anyone insults his father or his mother, he shall be put to death; he has insulted his father and his mother—his bloodguilt is upon him. LEVITICUS 20:9 (TIB)

First, let me hasten to say that according to Jewish tradition, and unbeknownst to most Christians, *there simply is no record of the Jewish people inflicting any Torah-prescribed death penalties on anyone in the years following Sinai.*[2] I mention this because many Christians have assigned to the Jews a desire for handing out severe punishments. The long historical record of the Jews speaks to an opposite conclusion.[3]

Nevertheless, the man who gathered wood on the Shabbat was stoned by people. Why did God tell Moses to do it? Why did God require it? Where is God's restraint?! Where is His compassion? Is this an example of the God of the Old Testament acting in judgment while the God of the New Testament acts in mercy? NO, NO!

The answer came to me during my year of reading all the footnotes and commentaries in the ArtScroll Torah. After looking at all the commands and seeing everything together, I suddenly saw a fascinating possibility!

What if the man who is put to death in such a case, is not intended to be shamed

---

[2] Gidon made this comment in an answer at the end of chapter 13.

[3] On the other hand God absolutely carried out such penalties directly and creatively, for instance in Korah's rebellion in Numbers 16 and the unusual case of Uzzah touching the ark in 1 Samuel 6:7. It is precisely for God's direct intervention in the Tanakh, that many Jewish commentaries suggest that the carrying out of such death penalties is to be placed in the hands of God.

and sent to hell? What if God's intention is that he repent and *accept* his punishment before God as an example to everyone else? In such a case, would not that man's *work* on earth continue on even after his death? Would not the God of compassion assign to his eternal credit every instance in which *his death inspires* an Israelite to *keep and safeguard* the Shabbat?

An example of this idea is found in the New Testament as well, in the case of Ananias and Sapphira who both died for lying in ACTS 5:1-11. Their case taught a powerful lesson to those who came after.

> *And great fear came over the whole church, and over all who heard of these things.*
> ACTS 5:11

Neither Ananias nor Sapphira were given any chance to apologize before God took their lives. It might be that this case is even harsher than the man who was stoned for gathering wood,[4] but it definitely is not harsher than the case of the sons of Aaron who died immediately and without warning for offering "strange fire" before the Lord.[5] But this harsh treatment brought the fear of God into the church, and kept many from sinning afterwards. Perhaps we need to remember all these cases with appreciation and humility rather than pointing fingers!

Example #3. Edom is Punished?

We Christians do not think too kindly about Esau and his kingdom of Edom, do we? Starting with their harsh refusal to let the Children of Israel pass through their land, continuing with the prophet Malachi, requoted by Paul in Romans 9:13, reminding us that God says, *"Esau I have hated,"* and ending with the still-to-be-fulfilled sweeping judgments pronounced by the prophet Obadiah over all Edom, we would like to keep Edom far, far away from us.[6]

On the very day that I first met Gidon, after he shared his new idea and as we walked along the wall of the Old City together, I asked him my first question of thousands to come:

"Who do the Jews consider to be their primary biblical enemy?"

Expecting him to say Ishmael, I then received my very first surprising answer

---

[4] His punishment was not instantaneous as was Ananias'; he would have had some time to speak out his repentance at least towards God, if not everyone.

[5] Leviticus 10:1-2

[6] That is a tip of the hat to my favorite line from *Fiddler on the Roof*, spoken by a rabbi who was asked if he would like to speak a blessing on the Russian Czar. His response: "God bless and keep the Czar — far away from us."

of thousands. He said that the sages of old say the number one enemy of the Jews is Edom (i.e. Esau), because there is no struggle greater than brother against brother. But later I learned that Jewish sages see the Roman Empire, and therefore Christianity — through the Roman Catholic Church — as coming from Edom![7]

Jewish sages saw Rome as Edom because Rome acted with the same kind of "personality" as Edom: strong, brutal, and living by the sword. But the second part of that idea, of connecting Rome/Edom to Christianity, easily riles up Christians. The Bible clearly proclaims that Edom will be punished! Let's be honest. We as Christians want nothing to do with a connection to Edom, because we know God hates Esau, right?[8]

But what if I were to tell you that the Bible also gives great honor to Edom?

Edom Receives Honor

Don't believe it? OK, you are right in this sense: God does not give great honor to *all* of Edom, but He gives an honor to a *remnant* of Edom. And even more than that, the honor was completely deserved because of two amazing stories of two men from Rome in the New Testament. Care to guess who? One of them already got his own chapter in this book. If you need a clue for the other one: he was also a centurion.

1. In MATTHEW 8, Jesus praises a centurion in Capernaum, who had more faith for the healing of his paralyzed servant than anyone Jesus had met in all of Israel. Jesus then exclaims to all: *"I say to you that many will come from east and west, and recline at the table with Abraham, Isaac, and Jacob in the kingdom of heaven"* (MATTHEW 8:11).

2. Then in ACTS 10, we see the second praiseworthy centurion: Cornelius, who feared God, gave alms and prayed, and was even *"well spoken of by the entire nation of the Jews"* (ACTS 10:22). As already discussed in chapter 10,

---

[7]   One claim is that Rome was founded by one of the sons of Edom. See Midrash Esther Rabbah 3:5 https://www.sefaria.org/Esther_Rabbah?lang=bi and Ken Spiro's Islam course on Root Source: https://root-source.com/lessons/history-israel-ishmael-4/
The founding myth of Rome is of two brothers, raised by wolves, where one brother eventually rose up and killed the other. This was Esau's situation: he was not close to his mother, being essentially close to his father only. He spent much time outdoors. He wanted to kill his brother Jacob, but delayed because of his father. And this last part is my own addition: God raised up Hadad from the royal line of Edom to harass the Kingdom of Solomon after he sinned with foreign wives. That chief was repulsed, and fled to Egypt and then went out from Egypt to go to "his own country." Note, the passage does not say he wanted to "go back to his own country." Might he have taken his Egyptian wife and moved northwestward? His descendants would have been ripe to begin a whole new country, which begins with a city, which might have been Rome (1 Kings 11:14-22).

[8]   I would remind readers of the lessons of chapter 18, *Unoffendable*.

he would become the first Gentile follower of Jesus.

Both of these men were well-honored by God with supernatural miracles at the time, and they both deserve our respect even today. However, there is still one last piece to the puzzle.

In Acts 15, in the famous Council at Jerusalem where the requirements of new Gentile Christians were determined, after hearing all the evidence (including retelling the specific story of Cornelius in verse 8), James, in verse 16 takes his justification from the prophet Amos:

> On that day I will raise up the fallen booth of David, and wall up its breaches; I will also raise up its ruins and rebuild it as in the days of old; Amos 9:11

But don't stop there! Continue reading the very next verse in Amos:

> That they may possess the remnant of Edom, and all the nations who are called by my name. Amos 9:12[9]

In other words, the remnant of Edom is the very first of all the nations to come into the rebuilt Tabernacle of David! A remnant of Edom, descendants of Esau whom "God hated," is honored by God as the first nation who "gets in!"

And one last point. If you consider the fact that Esau's kingdom was primarily *east* of Israel, and that Rome was *west* of Israel, the east/west comment by Jesus makes even more sense: *"I say to you that many will come from east and west, and recline at the table with Abraham, Isaac, and Jacob in the kingdom of heaven."* (Matthew 8:11). The *remnant* of Edom is in fact coming from not just the east, but the west as well.[10]

Summary

In closing, I am wondering if our view of God's punishment is still too small.

1. We do not give God enough credit for His *restraint* in punishing the wicked.
2. We do not give the *punished* enough credit for restraining sin in the righteous.

---

[9] In Acts 15:17 Stephen translates *Edom* as *all mankind*. This meaning is also true, and is completely appropriate for the situation faced by the church in Acts 15, but it does not invalidate the more specific meaning of *Edom*. Because Stephen does not stop at verse Amos 9:11, but also quotes verse 12, the word *Edom* must also be applicable, albeit in a more hidden sense, which is *exactly the point we are making: that the remnant of Edom was the first of all mankind to join in the new work of God.*

[10] Edom also finds itself mentioned in Lamentations. One of the best lectures I ever heard on Edom from a Jew is from Rabbi Chaim Eisen. It has lessons for both Jews and Christians. https://youtu.be/4qYuSGZRL6k

3.   We do not look hard enough to find the *beautiful remnants* in the horrific stories of a nation that will be punished.

In all these things, and many more, may God give us eyes to see a larger view of Him, and a larger view of His plans and purposes on the Earth.
Shalom.

Asking Gidon

What lessons do Jews take from some of the examples of harsh punishments established by God in the Torah?

These issues, perspectives and concepts are not usually dealt with frequently by Jews today. We focus more on what we need to do according to modern Jewish law books, and less on inapplicable punishments (inapplicable because they must be meted out by a Sanhedrin that does not exist today). But they certainly teach about what God sees as wrong behavior!

Why do you think God prescribed the ultimate penalty — death — for such things as cursing your parents and breaking the Sabbath?

If we go against these things, which attest to the most important values in God's world, then we are not deserving to be in that world.

If ultra-Orthodox rabbis in Israel (the Meah Shearim group you mentioned in chapter 27) had control over the judicial system, would these biblical directives for stoning and such become the "law of the land" in Israel?

I highly doubt it, and much would have to happen before those rabbis would have control over Israel's judicial system. That being said, the relationship between modern law and Torah law is a fascinating subject about which much has been written. The reviving of Torah law with the advent of the State of Israel, like the revival of the Hebrew language, fired up and continues to fire the imagination of numerous scholars, including Israel Supreme Court Justice Menachem Elon, Nachum Rackover, Michael Baris, and many, many more.

Many Christians, including me, believe that God has every right to punish the United States for the millions of unborn souls we have allowed to be killed through legalized abortion. How do Orthodox Jews interpret the Torah's view on abortion. Does the Torah forbid it? Some Christians criticize Orthodox Jews for not doing enough to stop abortion in Israel, whose democracy allows it, and whose government pays for it at least in certain

cases. Is such criticism fair?

I am not as well versed in this topic as you seem to think. While the abortion debate seems to be on the top of the issues in United States politics, in Israel it holds a much lower priority. I suggest reading the Wikipedia article about Jewish perspectives on abortion https://en.wikipedia.org/wiki/Judaism_and_abortion and perhaps this twenty-year-old article at Slate: https://bit.ly/Orthodox-abortion

CHAPTER 35

A View too Small: First Steps

When I first moved to Austin in 1983, I rode a bus each day from south Austin, up the interstate highway. The bus would exit and then turn left on Martin Luther King Jr. Blvd, crossing a big concrete bridge over the interstate highway to attend classes at the University of Texas. The master's degree I earned in Computer Science allowed me to stay in Austin, meet my future wife, meet Israeli Jews in 1988, start a company with one of them in 2000, and leave that company in 2013 with the freedom to choose any path.

With time on my hands, I studied the Blood Moons, and soon realized I would need to learn Jewish history as well, which exposed me to the history of Jewish persecution. Stirred to make a difference, I came to Jerusalem in January 2014 looking for Orthodox Jews to help with their business ideas. There I met Gidon on the walls of Jerusalem and we started Root Source. Over the next five years I walked alongside Gidon and many Orthodox Jews, some of whom you are still to meet in the pages yet to come. In 2018, that fifth year of working with Orthodox Jews, I marked my 50th lifetime visit to Israel. Upon my return to Austin, I proposed to Gidon a series of columns that would eventually become this book.

Those are the steps of my life, and this is the final chapter that touches upon the things about which our Christian view is too small. But this chapter is less about teaching, and more about stories that *celebrate first steps*!

In the matter of first steps, we all get it! We have all looked back at our *first steps* and seen that our initial view is way too small, compared to what happened in the days and years that followed. God agrees. In fact, God even poses it as a question:

> *For who has despised the day of small things?* ZECHARIAH 4:10

The answer? **Everybody.**

All *first steps* are viewed too small — whether they be the first steps of a one-year-old child, or the first steps of an adult who takes on a new path late in life. It even applies to the first steps of a nation like Israel. It is the looking back that brings forth the wonder. It is the looking back that engenders the awe. And it must be for this reason that God commands us to *remember*, so very often.[1]

Unseen First Steps

In chapter 30, I told you all about my first meeting with Gidon. In chapter 16, I told you all about my *hearing the sound of aliyah* that enabled that first meeting to happen. But in this chapter, I would like to share my favorite *first steps* story of all. It began with that bus ride I took every day in 1983, when I first moved to Austin. But like most good first-step stories, the significance of those first steps would be forgotten for a time — in this case a full twenty-seven years!

Twenty-seven years later, in 2010, my wife and I attended a fund-raising dinner for the Austin House of Prayer. There I heard from the main speaker, my friend Thomas Cogdell, a story that got me both excited and angry. Here is what I learned:

> In 1975, eight years before I first set foot in Austin, a debate raged in the city council about renaming one of the larger streets, 19th Street, after civil rights leader Rev. Martin Luther King Jr. who was assassinated in 1968. 19th Street ran east-west from the University and the prosperous white side of town, into the heart of east Austin, the predominantly black part of town.
>
> When a group of young black students in east Austin approached the city council with the idea to rename 19th Street to honor the black hero of the civil rights movement, the council approved the change. But quickly the downtown businessmen heard about it, and resisted. The strongest pushback was from business owners on the western portion of 19th Street, saying that it would be costly to their businesses, and problematic. It was then discovered that renaming a major street that crosses over an interstate highway would require replacing a number of exit signs, and would cost the city $55,000. In an effort to compromise, the idea was proposed by the city council to rename 19th Street after Martin Luther King Jr., but only the *eastern stretch* of the road, the part that traversed the black part of town.
>
> The original idea of the black students was now scrapped. The city council voted to start the discussion over from the beginning, at a future date, and to investigate new street-naming options that would not incur any unplanned expense. Upon concluding this vote, a man in the audience raised his hand. The former pastor

---

[1] For example, Deuteronomy 8:2, or 32:7.

and president-emeritus of the historically black Huston-Tillotson College in east Austin, J.J. Seabrook, raised his hand to speak. J.J. Seabrook had been advising the black students for months, mostly behind-the-scenes.

While the allotted time for public comment was over, knowing *who* had just raised his hand, the mayor moved to permit him to speak. All eyes, including those of the all-white city council, watched as he walked towards the podium, disgusted to say the least.[2] There he spoke, and made an impassioned plea for the council to favorably reconsider the original proposal of the young black college students, reminding them they had previously approved it! With passion and force of speech, the usually quiet man declared that the proposal of the black students was the only right proposal. He also reminded them that renaming 19th Street only in east Austin would go against everything Martin Luther King Jr. believed in: unity, and the bringing together of people regardless of the color of their skin. While speaking, and before he could take his first steps back to his seat, he faltered and fell. Many people rushed forward. One council member broke with the cultural norms of that period: a white woman gave a black man mouth-to-mouth resuscitation. An ambulance quickly arrived, but J.J. Seabrook would be pronounced dead upon arrival at the nearby hospital. At age 76, J.J. Seabrook had died from a massive heart attack.

The council meeting was immediately adjourned on that day, May 1st 1975. But upon its next convening, 19th Street would be quickly renamed Martin Luther King Jr. Boulevard — over its entire span across the city.

I was excited to hear such a powerful story. But I was angry that I had lived in Austin for twenty-seven years and had never heard it! I began asking myself, "Why?" In the days that followed I checked with friends, and nobody else I knew had heard the story either! Then I phoned Thomas Cogdell, who had told the story, and I asked him:

"What has been done to honor the memory of J.J. Seabrook?"

Thomas replied, "Very little has been done, and nothing specifically relating to the circumstances of his death."

"Has west Austin done anything?" I asked.

"No."

We checked our calendars. May 1st 2010, the 35th anniversary of the death of J.J.

---

[2] While Austin's first African-American city council member was elected in 1971, the makeup was white by the spring of 1975. But the year 1975 would ultimately become a turning point for black and hispanic representation.

Seabrook, was exactly six weeks away.

The next six weeks were a blur. Somehow, even though Thomas and I were working full time, we managed to pull together a team.[3] It was one of those rare moments in life where everything falls into place at high speed. Six weeks later we held a commemorative public event with all the following elements:

- Our commemorative program was based on consultation with current black city leaders, such as state representative Wilhelmina Delco, Pastor Joseph Parker, and city council member Sheryl Cole, after gaining their perspectives on what steps might be appropriate.

- We rented an event hall whose address was on the western stretch of Martin Luther King Jr. Blvd., where the business persons had originally rejected the proposal of the young black students.

- We found some of those former students, and invited them to attend and speak.

- We found J.J. Seabrook's niece, a surviving closest family member, given that Dr. Seabrook and his wife had left no children, and invited her to share memories of her uncle.

- We brought in local black pastors, the current President of Huston-Tillotson University, and invited city council member Sheryl Cole to speak.

- City Council member Cole awarded the niece with a certificate that designated May 1st 2010, as *J.J. Seabrook Day*.

- Media coverage of the event was excellent.

- We recruited about a dozen west Austin business persons to establish a new scholarship at Huston-Tillotson University in the amount of $55,000.

- Sheryl Cole agreed to bring to the City Council the idea to rename the bridge over the interstate highway, the bridge connecting east and west Austin, as the *J.J. Seabrook Bridge*.

Twelve days later, on May 13th, 2010, the renaming proposal would be passed unanimously.

Why this story?

This story would not be included in this book, except for a phone call that my

---

[3] We brought on Frank Costenbader as a consultant, which eventually led to the work on Isa Dreams as discussed in chapter 16.

friend Thomas Cogdell made to *his* friend Greg Burnett on May 13th, 2010. It went something like this:

> Thomas: "Hi Greg! You'll never believe what just happened. Do you remember telling me about the connection between MLK Blvd and J.J. Seabrook back in 2004? The city council just voted to name the MLK bridge the *J.J. Seabrook Bridge!*"

> Greg: "Wow! That is great news!"

> Thomas: "It seems as though your words way back then have come true, when you told us that *'God will bless the Austin House of Prayer because it is close to Martin Luther King Jr. Blvd., and because of the death of J.J. Seabrook.'*"

> Greg: "Yes, I definitely did say that. But did I ever tell you how I became aware of the importance of Dr. Seabrook?"

> Thomas: "No, you didn't. Please tell!"

> Greg: "It was in a dream that I had a couple of years prior to making that statement to you. I only shared this dream with my wife."

> Thomas: "Wow! I really want to hear this!"

> Greg: "Around about the year 2000, I had a dream in which I was looking down on the city of Austin from high above. It was like I was seeing it in Google Earth, except that Google Earth hadn't been invented yet. The dream was also unusual because we had not lived in Austin for many years, although we still had great fondness for the city. Anyway, as I gazed down at the city from high above I saw the river, and downtown, and the University, and I-35, and so forth. Then suddenly while I was looking down on Austin, a massive foot came down on the bridge!"

> Thomas: "You mean the J.J. Seabrook bridge?"

> Greg: "Yes, that bridge! A giant leg and foot came down with great force. The foot was so big that it was blocking all the lanes. The toes were pointing northwest towards the University of Texas. Then as I'm watching, I heard a thundering voice, clear and powerful. It was definitely the voice of God."

J.J. Seabrook Bridge.

Thomas: "What did God say?"

Greg: "He said,'**I will bring East and West together**.'"

Truth is stranger than fiction. If I had known that these were Greg's exact words to Thomas all the way back in 2010, it could have changed my path. I would have connected this message of bringing east and west together, as being *first steps* toward a larger worldwide move of God to bring Orthodox Jews together in relationship to Christians.[4] However, not knowing those exact words, I would not make any connection between the J.J. Seabrook story and my Israel story until several years into my relationship with Orthodox Jews.[5]

Giant Footprints in Israel

Almost ten years after the bridge was named, and having spent more than five years with Orthodox Jews, I was excited to finally meet Greg Burnett in Austin, Texas. Driving to the restaurant, I could hardly wait to ask him if he, the man who had seen God put His foot down in Austin, had ever heard about the giant footprints in Israel. "No!" he said, "Please do tell!" This is what I told him.

"When the Children of Israel came into the Promised Land, they were given clear instructions by God to build an altar on Mount Ebal. However, since the 1800s, when some of the biblical sites were first explored by modern archaeologists, no such site had been found. In 1967, after The Six-Day War, and with Judea and Samaria now under Israeli control, teams of Israeli archaeologists rushed in to examine the land for new possible sites. Mount Ebal in Samaria was both hard to reach and huge, spanning eighteen square kilometers.[6] The searches on it were very difficult.

"It would take until the early 1980s for an unusual structure to be found

---

[4] Besides being older, Hebrew culture is an eastern culture, whereas Christianity, having massive Greek and Roman influences, became a western culture. Because Root Source lessons are offered in English, it favors the connection of the Jews to western cultures. Persons in the Hebrew Roots movement correctly note that a person's journey is not just a journey to gain knowledge of Hebraic roots, but to also shift one's mindset, one's way of thinking, from a Greek mindset to a Hebraic one.

[5] For reasons nobody can explain, what Thomas heard from Greg was more of an interpretation than a quotation. He heard Greg say God's words to be: "I am taking my stand in the city of Austin, and I have permission to do so at this point because of the death of my servant J.J. Seabrook." Thomas's recollection was documented in a wonderful video he made soon after those events, which can be viewed here: https://youtu.be/5svhE6SD20U. When I finally met Greg myself in 2019, I asked Greg to tell me his dream word-for-word. Greg said God's message was exactly and only: "I will bring East and West together." Those seven words he heard God speak were still as vivid and powerful as the very night he had the dream; he could not have possibly forgotten them.

[6] About seven square miles.

on Mount Ebal by a team working under Adam Zertal.[7] Zertal, an Israeli Jew, was wounded in the Yom Kippur war in 1973. Now with a permanent disability, barely able to walk, he was forced to take some first steps into a new area of study. He chose to become an archaeologist. Adam Zertal was also an atheist, and like many of his academic peers, he doubted that the Exodus ever happened. Mount Ebal was remote, not fully explored, and might, he thought, contain something on which he could write his doctoral dissertation. While he was looking for interesting archaeology, he was not looking for Joshua's altar.[8] The structure his team uncovered on the northeast side of Mount Ebal around 1980 was unlike any known structure in use by any of the surrounding cultures, like the Canaanites. It would take two years to dig the new structure.

"One day in the fall of 1983, about three years after the initial site discovery, the team sat in a meeting room at their college, drinking Turkish coffee. They were speaking once again about this unknown structure they had found, when an Orthodox Jew named Zvi,[9] whom Zertal knew from another archaeological project, happened to walk by. As he took a few steps into the room he glanced over at the drawing of the structure that Adam Zertal held in his hands. Adam Zertal describes what happened next in his own words in his book, *A Nation Born:*"

> *When Zvi Kenigsberg saw it, he jumped as though he'd seen a ghost. I can't remember ever seeing a man turn so white so fast. He froze, staring and speechless, and began to turn red in the face. Then he dashed out of the room, only to return a few minutes later holding a small brown book. This was one of the six orders of the Mishna.[10] He sat down, huffing and puffing, and opened the book to the Order of Kodashim (rituals). This was the third chapter that dealt with the rules of the altar in the Second Temple in Jerusalem... Together with this description there was an illustration of the grand altar for burnt offerings in the Second Temple. Apart from a few details, the diagram was a dead ringer for the sketch that I had drawn a few minutes earlier.[11]*

---

[7] He eventually wrote *A Nation Born*, which is available at the following link: https://amzn.to/3dtMqzp

[8] All archaeologists in Israel are at least somewhat familiar with the biblical stories, even if they are not openly discussed or believed. Zertal had certainly read the passages mentioning Mount Ebal.

[9] Zvi Koenigsberg

[10] The Mishna is that part of the Talmud that records additional explanations of how to keep the commands as written in the Torah. It is part of the Oral Law.

[11] Zertal, Adam, *A Nation Born*, (Haifa, Israel: The Samaria and Jordan Rift Valley Survey Association, 2017), 51-52.

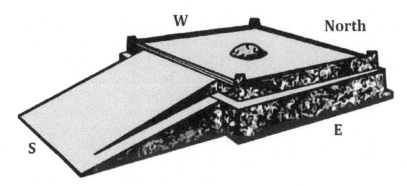

Diagram of the Altar from the Second Temple Period.

Joshua's Altar reconstruction similar to the diagram Adam Zertal had held in his hands.

Joshua's Altar today, being visited by a tour group.

The site of Joshua's altar not only looked generally like altars of the Second Temple period, but in their exploration Zertal's team uncovered only the bones of *kosher animals*! Other artifacts were found that put the altar in the right time frame, the early conquest of Canaan.

But when Adam Zertal's team examined the entire site around the altar, they discovered the altar was surrounded by an ancient man-made wall that had a similarity to that of a giant footprint, many hundreds of yards long.

Giant Footprint on the side of Mount Ebal with Joshua's Altar inside.

In the years that followed, Adam Zertal and his teams would discover at least seven large footprints in Israel, all dating to the 13th to 11th centuries BCE, which is well before the period of the First Temple. The most well-preserved of all of these footprints in Israel is the Argaman Footprint near the Jordan River, shown below.

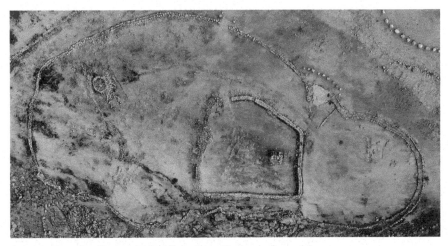

Argaman Footprint. Also a right-foot footprint in the shape of a sandal.

I, like many people, have been fascinated with these giant footprints since I first learned of them. I first heard about them from Avi Lipkin, in Jerusalem in the fall of 2016. Avi Lipkin is an Israeli Jew who has been speaking in churches since the 1990s, and is an author of many books regarding Islam.[12] Avi mentioned the giant footprints at one of Christine Darg's conferences, and said he had brought along a few DVDs that would be available for sale. Avi sold out of those DVDs before I could even reach his products table.

The producer of those DVDs was Avi's son, Aaron Lipkin, who is the most knowledgeable person that I know regarding the footprints of Israel, especially now that Adam Zertal has died. Over time, Adam Zertal had eventually written that the biblical Joshua's Altar *had been found*. As Aaron likes to tell the story, Adam Zertal's announcement about Joshua's altar prompted a powerful response within the worldwide academic community.

It was the sound of *complete* silence!

But Adam Zertal was going to move even further away from the views of the academics. The implication he began to wrestle with was that if Joshua's Altar was real, then the Exodus was also real, and if the Exodus was real, then perhaps the Bible is not just fairy tales after all. While Adam Zertal never spoke openly about his new-found faith, Aaron Lipkin was convinced that Adam Zertal had indeed changed. Aaron once quipped in a small meeting that Adam Zertal had become a "born-again archaeologist." Everyone laughed. Zertal also laughed, and then looked down at his notes.

By 2015, as Adam Zertal was getting older, Aaron remembers pressuring Adam over the phone to do more to get the word out about his discoveries — discoveries that clearly show the Bible is true. After Aaron said that, he recalls a long silence on the other end of the line. Finally the silence was broken when Adam confessed, "I'm just a professor. I don't know how to do these things. Please help me!"

Those would be the last words Aaron would ever hear Adam say. He died two weeks later. Aaron eventually decided that he would dedicate himself to try to fulfill Adam Zertal's last request, and Aaron began to take his first steps towards

---

[12] Avi Lipkin teaches a class on Islam at Root Source: https://root-source.com/channels/. He famously began predicting a 9/11-type event was coming to America for many years before it happened, although he credits his wife Rachel, who heard those threats on Arabic television. In giving credit he often says, "I am not a prophet, I just listen to my wife!" His prediction appears on p. 266 of his first book, *Is Fanatic Islam a Global Threat?*, published in 1997 under a pen name, Victor Mordecai, (and incorrectly listed on Amazon as June 2003): https://www.avilipkin.net/product-page/is-fanatic-islam-a-global-threat.

what is now a wonderful series of DVDs on the archaeological sites in Samaria.[13] In addition, Aaron Lipkin has a Biblical Archaeology series on Root Source.[14]

Why the Footprints?

Why did the early Israelites lay down stones to create these footprints? Many theories abound, and Aaron Lipkin covers them in his DVD series, but their orientation offers one answer. Every footprint is built on the side of a hillside where it would be possible for many people to come and sit and view, and even hear, the events going on within the footprint. Aaron refers to it as a natural amphitheater.

Argaman footprint with amphitheater viewing area behind.

Some footprints like the Argaman footprint also have a double wall that can be seen around most of the circumference. This double wall is large enough for people to walk between, seemingly in some sort of procession. Aaron refers to this structure as the procession road. At the Argaman footprint, that procession road around the heel of the footprint seems to lead to the natural path up the hillside. There the seating area is large enough to allow 100,000 people to sit and view the footprint! So the footprint is *absolutely* a large meeting place.

---

[13] Short link to the Lipkin Tours (English): https://bit.ly/LipkinTours
[14] https://root-source.com/channels/

But this doesn't answer why the shape should be that of a footprint. The shape of the footprint allows the site to be not only a meeting place, but a place of remembrance!

Consider this. From the site of the Argaman footprint can be seen the path that Abraham took down the Jabbok River to the Jordan River, where he first stepped over into the Promised Land. This same Argaman footprint stands beside the great Tirza valley that the Israelites ascended when they went up to Mount Ebal to build Joshua's Altar near Shechem, in Samaria.

But what of the shape of the footprint being that of a sandal? Imagine being gathered with the people of Israel on the other side of the Jordan River, about twenty miles to the south, preparing to enter the Promised Land. Imagine listening to Moses when he told them:

> *"Every place on which the sole of your foot treads shall be yours"* DEUTERONOMY 11:24a

And shortly after that, imagine hearing about the words that God spoke directly to Joshua after Moses had died:

> *"Every place on which the sole of your foot treads, I have given it to you, just as I spoke to Moses."* JOSHUA 1:3

The footprints in Israel mark *the first steps of the nation of Israel* into the *land of Israel*. They are a place of meeting and a place of remembrance, and since the Israelites didn't walk on their bare feet, they are shaped like a sandal!

Finally, the footsteps are huge! They are big not only because God's promises are big, but because the journey is not walked alone; it is done in teams, in groups, in families, among young and old, and in nations. God's plan for Israel was NOT for their steps into the Promised Land to be steps that *step* on or *vanquish* the entire world, but for those first steps to be a *model* for the entire world. Their steps would be not just for their own sakes, but for the sake of the great work that God wanted to showcase before the world. He had not chosen Israel for elitism; He had chosen them for light in a dark, dark world. God's great plan was that He would ultimately bring the entire world — from the east and the west — together to be His sons and daughters. And He had chosen a people, Israel, and a location, Israel, from which to accomplish this.

Final Steps

The work to bring east and west together is costly. It began with an out-of-the-way trip to build Joshua's Altar with uncut stones. Then six tribes would stand on Mount Gerizim and six would stand on Mount Ebal, with the Levites in the valley below. Those standing on Mount Ebal would say "Amen!" and accept curses onto the entire nation when certain key commandments from the Torah were disobeyed.[15] The work to build an altar of uncut stones is costly. It takes time. And then animals must be sacrificed in burnt offerings and peace offerings. Death is near. The final steps those kosher animals ever took were to walk towards the altar.

The final steps that a good man, J.J. Seabrook, took, were towards a podium. But the final steps of some enable the first steps of others.

J.J. Seabrook's last steps to the podium would lead to the first steps of a team who worked to bring east and west Austin just a little closer together.

Adam Zertal's last steps to the hospital would lead to the first steps of Aaron Lipkin to lead many others into the wonder and awe of the Bible, through biblical archaeology.

Moses' last steps towards Mount Nebo on the other side of the Jordan would lead to the first steps of Joshua, who would lead all Israel into the Promised Land, and to quickly go and build Joshua's altar, and then separate into two groups on two mountains, as a testimony to the whole world.

But in every case we need to remember! We need to remember those first steps! Because everyone's view of *first steps* is just way too small — even in Israel, where the footprints are just as big as they can possibly be.

Shalom.

Asking Gidon

Gidon, as you well know, the Argaman footprint is not only where Abraham entered the Land, it is the place where Jacob re-entered the Land. When we first met Aaron at the Argaman footprint and interviewed him, you made an interesting impromptu connection between the word *Jacob* and the footprint. Will you please share this?[16]

---

[15] Deuteronomy 27:14-26
[16] https://root-source.com/blog/root-source-tours-giant-footprints-in-israel-part-1/
https://root-source.com/blog/root-source-tours-giant-footprints-in-israel-part-2/
https://root-source.com/blog/root-source-tours-giant-footprints-in-israel-part-3/

I was listening to Aaron's explanation of the footprint, and I recalled that even before Moses mentioned the place where the sole of the foot shall touch, we have our forefather Israel, also known as Jacob. So I told him, "The name Jacob (or Ya'aqov) means to grab someone by the foot. But the last portion of the word Jacob (Ya'aqov) is "*aqov*," which sounds like "*aqev*" and means footprint, or "*eqvot*," which is footprints. Therefore, the name Jacob could be said to mean, *you will make a footprint!* And if you think about it, the whole goal of the Israelites, the Jewish people, is to make an impact or imprint on the Land of Israel, and in the entire world, and throughout history."

Gidon, your first step toward Christians was clearly the step you took towards the International Christian Embassy in Jerusalem. But your first steps of success on the Internet was a Facebook page that you started well before Root Source. What was that Facebook page called, and what were you trying to accomplish?

That page is "Jews Who Love Christians Who Love Jews (And The Christians Who Love Them)."[17] I was thinking of creating a space for the few Jews like myself who had stepped into the world of engaging with Christians, but thought that it would be improper to throw a party and not invite the guest of honor, so I opened the group up to those Christians who love Jews as well. It wasn't long before there were over 6,000 Christians in that group!

---

[17] https://www.facebook.com/groups/432075225332/

CHAPTER 36

Where are the Children?

It has happened too many times to count. Our family would be on vacation somewhere and our daughters, Kristen and Allison had wandered out of sight. Suddenly my wife asks:

"Where are the children?"

That question breaks me out of 'wherever I was at the moment' and brings three thoughts to mind in quick succession.

1. Why is it always *Marisa* who is the first to ask this question and never me!

2. My wife's first motivation in asking it is to make sure they're *safe*!

3. I hope the kids are also *discovering* something!

The Argaman Footprint

In the last chapter you learned about the giant footprints in Israel that were built by the Israelites before Jerusalem became the capital city. You learned that the footprint at Argaman could seat 100,000 people. In this chapter we will attempt to answer the question: *where were the children?*

The best time of year to visit the Argaman footprint would be in the spring or fall, perhaps during the week-long holidays of Passover or Sukkot. But whenever they gathered, a visit to the Argaman footprint would have been a multi-day experience. This meant families needed to pitch camp nearby.

In the story that follows, you will hear about how Aaron Lipkin and I discovered evidence that the Argaman footprint was *more* than just a footprint. Maybe much, much more.

We believe the Argaman footprint may have included right next to it, an educational center for the children.

Now that sounds a bit formal, so let's say it this way. The Argaman site may have been so much fun for kids, that from their perspective, visiting the footprint might be as exciting as visiting *an ancient theme park*! And the biggest attraction of that theme park is....drum roll please...

A "tour of the Exodus!"

Would it be so surprising to learn that the ancient Israelites loved their children, and valued education, just like Jews do today? Hardly! The Argaman site seems to be a place that offered families a hands-on walking tour in which children were taught their own history of the Exodus in a fun and exciting way! This would be critically important for the multiple generations of children who were born in the land of Israel — they would have no memory of the forty-year stay in the wilderness. And it was critically important for the parents, who were *commanded* to help their children remember those amazing events.[1]

Let us begin our story.

Go Google Maps

After filming Gidon's interview of Aaron Lipkin at the Argaman footprint in early 2017, I flew back home to Austin to edit the footage. Early into the editing I wondered: could I find the Argaman footprint on Google maps? Yes I could, but it was *much* harder than I thought. I circled it in the picture below, but you, like me, may have trouble spotting it.

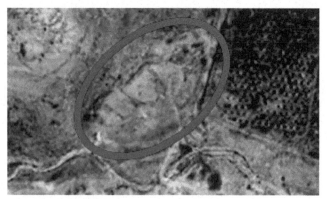

Argaman Footprint. The Sandal is pointing to the upper right.

---

[1] Deuteronomy 6:7; 11:19, and Joel 1:3.

But while the sandal was difficult to find, something else was not. In fact, it was the first thing I saw when I started looking for the footprint on google maps. I saw something that looked like a bird; specifically, a bit like an eagle. The eagle, pictured below, is viewed from above, as if you were flying over it, looking down on it while it is flying beneath you.

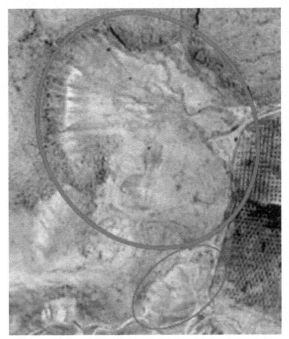

Argaman Eagle. Tailfeathers to the left, wing at the top, head to the right.

The next time I visited Israel, Aaron and I met at the site and started investigating all the land around the footprint, both on the ground and using his drone. The eagle was not man-made; it was a natural feature of the valley. If you walked to the middle of the eagle's back, between the wings, you could see at least one of the wings and the head and the tail feathers. That area of Israel is very hot in the summer; it is below sea level, and gets very little rain, meaning that the landscape would not have changed significantly over time. This natural eagle-like feature could possibly have been noticed for thousands of years, but that doesn't *prove* that it was ever noticed by the ancient Israelites. I had found it on Google maps, a tool they did not have.

From the middle of the eagle, we next walked up the tall hills behind the footprint until we stood directly behind the "eagle's tail feathers." From there we looked down upon the "eagle," which is where I took the photograph below.

View from behind the eagle shows four unusual rocks in a line, equally spaced.

The photograph shows four big rocks in a straight line. However, this line of rocks did not stand out at the time, only later when I carefully examined Aaron's drone footage. He had photographed the "eagle" from high above. Now back in Austin, I saw four large boulders in a straight line on drone footage, pretty close to being equally spaced apart. What are the chances that those four rocks had naturally rolled down the hillside and stopped in a straight line like that? Not very high, but still that didn't *prove* it wasn't just coincidence. It would take another trip to Israel to inspect further.

On the next visit to Israel I inspected all four rocks, and saw something! Some of the boulders had been propped up from behind with smaller rocks! The boulders clearly did not roll there! They had definitely been moved and positioned there by *people*! But that still didn't prove that they were moved and positioned by the *ancient Israelites*.

Stone Circles

Besides investigating around the "eagle," Aaron and I had also walked south of the footprint too. We started seeing stone circles. We found patterns of stone circles all over the valley, hundreds of them, but only in areas where the ground was relatively flat. On first impression, the stone circles seemed to be marking ancient campsites. Really? We investigated further.

The stone circles never appeared inside the footprint, or right next to the footprint (even though the ground was flat there), but only a short walking distance away from the footprint. This makes sense if the footprint was part of a religious site; you would camp a respectful distance away. There were also no stone circles in

Stone Circles were found all over the valley, going all the way back to the peak shown to the south, and to an area almost that wide as well.

the entire area up above and behind the footprint! This was odd, as there were definitely many good, flat places up there, and the view is excellent.

The stone circles seemed to be consistent with the idea of campsites for the visitors to the footprint! But why not use the area above the footprint for camping, since that was both flat, and a respectful distance away? Perhaps the answer is because the area behind the footprint was used for another purpose.

A Children's Theme Park and the "Walking Tour" Theory

If the adults were sitting in the amphitheater area, their kids would naturally get restless. Where would they be allowed to go? Certainly not down onto the footprint itself. However, parents would naturally allow the kids to go up behind them, up above the footprint, to an area which was fairly flat, safe and protected. It would be a perfect place for children to play or learn.

So, putting it all together, here is my theory about this site, a theory that I never got to propose to Adam Zertal, because it only came to light about two years after he died.

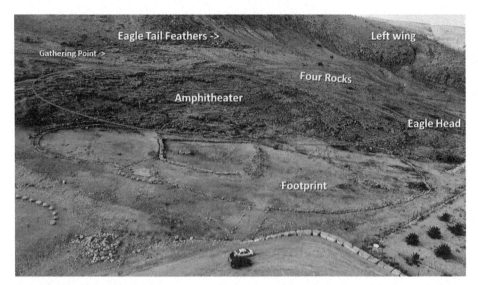

Argaman Theme Park Site Map.

The kids go up from the amphitheater and meet at the gathering point as shown, which is a cleared circular area with a big rock in the center, where a speaker could stand.[2]

From that gathering place you can see across the Jordan River to where Abraham and Jacob came down and crossed over into the land of Israel! The leaders and teachers probably told the children the stories of the patriarchs from that very point. But when the teachers got to the point in the story where they tell about the Exodus, groups of children would leave the gathering area to begin a walking tour.

I have examined this site a number of times, and I have seen things that cause me to propose an even more detailed theory of the "hands-on walking tour" visit.

1. The first stop from the gathering area is a small-scale site model of the Israelite dwellings in Egypt. There they would speak about the Passover meal, and the preparations for the Exodus. In this area is a series of rocks that looks like they could have been a place to create a small model of a city.

2. Next, there is a place in that area that might possibly allude to the burial place of Joseph. The kids would be reminded that Joseph asked for his bones to be buried in the land of Israel when they left on the Exodus.

---

[2] We will not include all photos in this chapter.

3. The group now walks many meters towards two giant boulders. The boulders were placed there, propped up by man; they were not natural. (We have not gotten to the four big rocks yet.) At the big boulders they would stop and talk about how the Israelites gathered at the Red Sea with the Egyptians in pursuit. Perhaps the two rocks are a gateway the children walk through, or perhaps one rock is a marker and the other is representing the pillar of fire that prevented the Egyptians from catching them?

4. In any case, when the children leave these two giant boulders, they walk for many meters — first going down slightly, then up again. Perhaps with some additional fabric on either side of them, it would be easy to construct something that allowed the kids to feel that they were walking down through the Red Sea with water piled up on either side, as they went down and up. This is the only place on the walking tour that goes down and then up again, so it would be the perfect place to help them envision the Red Sea.[3]

5. After coming back up from the Red Sea, the children begin their stops at the sequence of four big rocks. The first of these rocks has been positioned in such a way that water can run off it. Perhaps this was a prop for the waters of Marah turning from bitter to sweet? Please note that this rock was propped up from behind, or else the water would not flow over it when it rains as it does today. If the rock was designed to "catch water" it need not have been propped up at all, but instead it seemed to have been positioned for water to run off it easily. Over the years, water has discolored it where it flowed.

The Marah Rock? The rock is propped up in the back allowing the water to flow off it.

---

[3] This experiencing of the Exodus is not optional for Jews, but is a part of the Passover Seder even today. The Mishnah in Pesachim 10:5 states that in every generation a man must consider himself as having personally come forth out of Egypt: https://bit.ly/Pesachim10-5.

6. Another rock could have been a place where they talked about God giving manna in the wilderness.[4]

The Manna Rock? This boulder might have been the stop where they discussed the manna in the wilderness.

7. Another of the four rocks is smaller and I do not feel confident enough to suggest its possible use.

8. But the final rock in the "line of four" is the most exciting of all. It seems to be the grand finale of the tour.

The Grand Finale

The final rock looks like this. Notice the gap down the middle. This one is the tallest of all the rocks, and is at least ten feet tall. It can be seen from a great distance away.

The Fourth Rock at Argaman. The tour grand finale.

---

[4] The principle of using stones to remember key events was not uncommon in Israel. See verses like Exodus 24:4, Joshua 4:5, 22:28, and 1 Samuel 7:12.

This rock is not just a rock that weathered over thousands of years and then split in two. No, it is two different rocks propped up side-by-side. In addition, unlike the other rocks, it seems that one of the rocks has been chiseled down from its original size. Many stone shavings appear below the rock, which give the ground around this rock a look unlike any of the other rocks in the area. Why would it have been chiseled?

I believe this is a small scale model of the split rock of Rephidim, where Moses stood before the rock and spoke to it, and the rock split in two and the water came out (EXODUS 17:1). The rock was chiseled to make sure that the rock looked like a split rock, where you can easily look through it and see the split. But when I saw this rock for the first time, it reminded me of something I had once seen in a photograph.

Before showing that photograph, I need to tell you something.

I am inclined to believe that the real Mount Sinai is in Saudi Arabia, rather than in the Sinai Peninsula.[5] The pioneering work of Jim and Penny Caldwell in the 1990s,[6] all the way up through the recent, excellent work by Joel Richardson[7] and his colleagues, is building up evidence that seems to "check the boxes" on all the features, including the Exodus path that the Israelites took to get there.[8] For dozens of reasons now, it seems very likely that Mount Jebel el Lawz[9] in Saudi Arabia is the right location. Now let's be clear. Our discussion about Argaman in no way *requires* Jebel el Lawz to be the right site. It will take many years — even decades — for general opinion to swing around strongly to the Saudi Arabian option. It might be sooner if Saudi Arabia fully opens up the area for tourism.[10] For now, the traditional site of Mount Sinai has over a thousand years of momentum behind it.[11]

---

[5] The Apostle Paul says it is in Arabia in Galatians 4:25, although many still argue for the traditional site of Mount Sinai in the Sinai Peninsula. Indeed, that one verse would not be proof that modern Saudi Arabia is exactly what Paul meant when he wrote *Arabia*.

[6] For more information please contact Split Rock Research at https://splitrockresearch.org/

[7] For his DVD and book *Mount Sinai in Arabia*, see here: https://store.joelstrumpet.com/collections/bundles

[8] For maps, videos, and extensive information about the Exodus route and Jebel el Lawz, these are good places to start:
http://realmountsinai.com/
https://www.arkdiscovery.com/mt__sinai_found.htm
https://www.arkdiscovery.com/red_sea_crossing.htm
An interesting travelogue video of the Exodus route and examination of evidence can be seen here:
https://youtu.be/8y-uiccliSY

[9] Also Jabal al-Lawz.

[10] Tourism in Saudi Arabia is continuing to get easier, even though Jebel el Lawz is not fully opened yet.
https://www.bbc.com/news/business-49848068

[11] Opinions of archaeologists are very deeply held, and once an archaeologist makes a decision on an

Comparison of Argaman Split Rock, and Saudi Arabian Split Rock.

So while you don't need to believe in Saudi Arabia as the site of Mount Sinai to accept the idea that the Argaman site might be laid out something like an educational center, if you *do believe* that Saudi Arabia is the site of Mount Sinai you are really going to like this next photo.

The picture on the left shows the Argaman split rock, which is about ten feet tall. The picture on the right shows the 60-foot high split rock in Saudi Arabia atop a 300-foot high hill, truly a massive structure. Notice that not only is the Argaman "rock" formed by two rocks side-by-side, but the right-hand rock has a piece sticking out in front, just like the split rock in Saudi Arabia. I admit that the left-side rocks are a bit different: the left-side rock at Argaman is not as wide as the split rock in Saudi Arabia. But then look again! A large piece has broken off the Argaman left-side rock and fallen over to the left. If we were to compare these two rocks before they had broken off, the two rocks would have been almost identical!

If I were the leader of the walking tour here is what I would do. After telling the kids this story about the split rock of Rephidim, I would say:

"Don't move, children!"

Then I would add:

"*When our forefathers came to Mount Sinai, the Lord told us: "You have seen what I did to the Egyptians, how I bore you on eagles' wings and brought you to Me."* (Exodus 19:4, TIB).

Then I would tell them:

---

historical narrative behind their work, they never seem to change their minds.

"Look all around you. Can you see it? We are all standing on the back of a giant eagle's wings right now!"

The children then delight in picking out the tail feathers behind them, the wings to the left and right, and the head of the eagle up ahead. Their whole walking tour has been transformed. They now find that they are standing on the back of an eagle, an eagle that is taking them to Sinai, just as God told their forefathers!

Why do I think this theory is plausible?

- **Because the split rock of Rephidim as described in Exodus is the last stop before Sinai, and the mentioning of the eagle by God.**

- **Because the split rock of Argaman seems to have been placed on the exact center of the back of the eagle's wings.**

- **And because the split rock of Argaman is placed at the only location on that massive hillside where a person can turn around in all directions and see the whole eagle from the ground!**

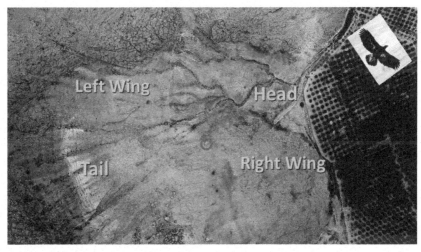

The Eagle from above.

I am not an archeologist, and I'm not making a decision; I'm just proposing a theory. But something unusual is going on at this site that needs to be explored. The site is open and available to inspection — no fence, no gate, no admission fee. Anyone can walk the site at any time, and I would be happy to provide a photo guide-book and directions to the footprint to anyone who emails me.

Final Thoughts

We love our children.[12]

We want the best for our children.[13]

We enjoy it when our children get excited about the stories of the Bible, and remember them. To that very point, I will never forget my first visit to Shiloh Israel Children's Fund to meet Orthodox Jew David Rubin. After touring his non-profit center we happened upon some young children at the Shiloh Elementary School next door singing loudly out in a courtyard, preparing for a performance for their parents that very evening.

"What are they singing?" I asked him.

"The Torah," he replied.

"What do you mean *the Torah*?"

He paused, listened and said, "It sounds like they are in Numbers right now."

"What do you mean *right now*?," I asked.

He smiled, turned to me and said loudly, so that I could hear him speaking over the singing: "Over the course of their schooling they will all memorize all five books of the Torah, word-for-word."

I stood in stunned silence, realizing that a foretaste of ISAIAH 11:9[14] was coming alive before my very eyes.

How might the ancient Israelite teachers have compared to these teachers in the hills of Shiloh? How much effort might the ancient teachers have expended to help their kids remember, and to experience the Exodus for themselves?

---

[12] My friend, Orthodox Jew Ruth Guggenheim, has allowed me to do a lot of personal due diligence on her organization, World Emunah: https://www.worldemunah.org/. Started by Orthodox Jewish women in the 1920s, it is now the largest faith-based organization in Israel that helps its children. Rabbi Yechiel Eckstein, who founded the International Fellowship of Christians and Jews, https://www.ifcj.org — the largest Israeli philanthropic organization of them all and now led by his daughter Yael Eckstein, is a big donor to the work of Emunah. I have tremendous respect for both organizations.

[13] On a smaller scale, David Rubin, former mayor of Shiloh, founded the Shiloh Israel Children's Fund: https://www.shilohisraelchildren.org/. They do great work helping kids deal with the trauma of terrorism. Some of the most creative giving opportunities I have ever seen come from my free subscription to the https://www.israel365.com/ mailing list run by my good friend, Rabbi Tuly Weisz.

[14] *They will not hurt or destroy in all My holy mountain, For the earth will be full of the knowledge of the LORD As*

So it is time to answer the question: *where were the children* at the Argaman footprint? My theory is that they were close to their parents, having a lot of fun, in a protected area right behind the amphitheater, learning about this history in a hands-on way that made their history come alive.

Suddenly, being a child in the ancient world seems a lot more fun than before.

That is the theory. It may be right, or it may not be right. But one thing is for certain: No parent then or now could ever love their children more than our Father God. And He loves it when kids *enjoy* learning about Him!

Shalom.

Asking Gidon

Gidon, this chapter is about children. Do you want to say anything about yours?

Devra and I are blessed with five children, plus three children-in-law and two grandchildren as of this writing. Our oldest, Ellie, lives in Jerusalem and is studying to be a bookkeeper. Akiva is studying Human Resources and Sociology at Ariel University in Samaria within the framework of the "Shiluvim" project, combining advanced academic studies with Yeshiva Torah studies. He lives in Har Bracha, overlooking Joseph's tomb in Shechem with his wife Rivka and their son Netanel Baruch, whose name means "God has given us a blessing." After Akiva comes Shira Rina who is studying education in Jerusalem and lives near us in our community of Ma'ale Hever with her husband Ori and our grandson Nachman Simcha, who is named for the famous Rabbi Nachman of Breslov.[15] Our next son, Chayim Zvi, recently got married to Liel. They live in Tzfat in the north of Israel. Chayim Zvi is in the army, serving as a Chaplaincy Services Specialist. Rounding out our five is Moriyah, who is in tenth grade in an all girls sleepaway school in Dimona, about an hour south of us. All of our children are inquisitive and independent, just the way I like it! ☺

---

the waters cover the sea.

[15] Rabbi Nachman from Breslov, Lithuania was known for living a life full of joy. https://en.wikipedia.org/wiki/Nachman_of_Breslov. The word *simcha* means joy, and forms part of the most common holiday greeting used for all the feast days: "Chag Sameach," which literally means "Joyful Holiday."

How likely do you think it would be that the ancient Israelites would make the efforts to create a "kids program" and/or "educational adventure" for their children at the place where they are gathering at a footprint for many days?

This is a fascinating theory, though anachronistic to the extreme. I would guess every generation, certainly ours, tries to see history through their own modern (whatever that means) glasses. Wikipedia traces the history of modern amusement parks to the 1100s or the 1500s and then jumps to the 1860s. To call what you propose the Israelites created some 3,000 years ago a "prehistoric Theme Park" sounds a little too Flintstones for me ☺ But I admit that your discoveries of arguably man-made artifacts demands some sort of theory, and yours is a challenge to archeologists — professional or amateur — to respond to. Kudos!

Regarding what ancient Israelites might have done to pique the curiosity of their children, the Mishna (committed to writing 1,800 years ago, based on oral traditions hundreds, and maybe thousands of years older) does mention more family focused games and amusements; the Passover Seder night comes to mind. And archeologists have found marbles and tic-tac-toe boards dated 3000 and 5000 BCE. But to invest in moving massive rocks so tens of thousands of children can keep out of trouble and learn experientially what they would be required to know textually by heart... let's answer with "not extremely likely in my opinion." But I will proudly eat my hat Bob when you get the Nobel Prize for Archeology![16]

---

[16] I think the work being done to place the real Mount Sinai in Saudi Arabia is monumentally important, because it puts so many other archaeological conflicts on a better path towards resolution. If the split rock at Argaman helps bolster the case for Mount Sinai, even tangentially, then that's enough of a reward for me.

CHAPTER 37

A New Look at the Prodigal Son

Oneof the most beautiful and thought-provoking stories in the New Testament is that of the prodigal son. It is also one of the most taught. And yet, one day a thought struck me that caught me off guard. It was an insight into this well-worn tale that I had never previously considered.

Prodigal Son Story

Since it is fairly short, let us begin with the whole story from LUKE 15:11-32 (NIV).

> *Jesus continued: "There was a man who had two sons. The younger one said to his father, 'Father, give me my share of the estate.' So he divided his property between them.*
>
> *"Not long after that, the younger son got together all he had, set off for a distant country and there squandered his wealth in wild living. After he had spent everything, there was a severe famine in that whole country, and he began to be in need. So he went and hired himself out to a citizen of that country, who sent him to his fields to feed pigs. He longed to fill his stomach with the pods that the pigs were eating, but no one gave him anything.*
>
> *"When he came to his senses, he said, 'How many of my father's hired servants have food to spare, and here I am starving to death! I will set out and go back to my father and say to him: Father, I have sinned against heaven and against you. I am no longer worthy to be called your son; make me like one of your hired servants.' So he got up and went to his father.*
>
> *"But while he was still a long way off, his father saw him and was filled with compassion for him; he ran to his son, threw his arms around him and kissed him.*
>
> *"The son said to him, 'Father, I have sinned against heaven and against you. I am no longer worthy to be called your son.'*
>
> *"But the father said to his servants, 'Quick! Bring the best robe and put it on him. Put a ring on his finger and sandals on his feet. Bring the fattened calf and kill it.*

Let's have a feast and celebrate. For this son of mine was dead and is alive again; he was lost and is found.' So they began to celebrate.

"Meanwhile, the older son was in the field. When he came near the house, he heard music and dancing. So he called one of the servants and asked him what was going on. 'Your brother has come,' he replied, 'and your father has killed the fattened calf because he has him back safe and sound.'

"The older brother became angry and refused to go in. So his father went out and pleaded with him. But he answered his father, 'Look! All these years I've been slaving for you and never disobeyed your orders. Yet you never gave me even a young goat so I could celebrate with my friends. But when this son of yours who has squandered your property with prostitutes comes home, you kill the fattened calf for him!'

"'My son,' the father said, 'you are always with me, and everything I have is yours. But we had to celebrate and be glad, because this brother of yours was dead and is alive again; he was lost and is found.'"

The Standard View

The way this story is typically taught is to reveal the love of God the Father, embodied in the father of the story, towards those who wander off or squander time, money, and their life's purpose in the pursuit of the pleasures of this world. The picture of a father that saw him a long way off, and did not wait for the son to reach him, but instead *ran* to the son, is a compelling image. I have personally witnessed this story soften the hearts of people who are far from the love of God, or at least feel like they are.

One of the most interesting comments I ever heard about this story, told in the traditional manner, was by an unnamed preacher who once said:

> *In that distant country, the prodigal son lost* **everything he owned** *except......*
> *his* **memories of home**.

Indeed it is hard to bring a new thought to such a well-worn story, but that preacher did.[1]

The Hebrew Roots Movement View

Now let's switch gears and look at the story differently.

---

[1]   I don't know the original preacher, but I heard this story quoted by Arthur Burk.

Those people involved in Hebrew or Jewish Roots ministries, Messianic congregations, and pro-Israel Christian churches might consider that this story can also be applied to the relationship between Christians and Jews. But in that case, who is the *younger* brother? I could also ask that question with a stronger emphasis: "Who *gets to be* the younger brother?" You see, one of the inconvenient aspects of this story is that the *older brother* doesn't look very good in this story, does he? Yes, the older brother is faithful to his father, not squandering his possessions like the younger son, but he refuses to join in the celebrations, and is clearly upset about the sudden celebration underway for his younger brother!

As I have considered how this story is applied to the relationship between Christians and Jews, the thing I have often noticed is that:

Everyone wants to be the younger brother!

Indeed, I'm ashamed to say it, but in this context, we who do care about the Jewish roots of our faith *tend to see ourselves* as the younger brother "coming back from the pagan influences in Christianity." Or if you will, "coming back to an appreciation of the Torah," and relishing the celebration of the feasts and the renewed intimacy with God — in the form of the Father, or through Yeshua HaMashiach.[2] But then are we not relegating our Jewish colleagues to the role of the older brother, who not very coincidentally reminds us of the Pharisees?

Yet, in the Hebrew Roots perspective, and when considering the rejoining of the two sticks of Ephraim and Judah in Ezekiel 37, Christians are in fact correct to claim that the brother Ephraim is *younger* than Judah. In addition, it was the northern kingdom of Israel that wandered away from their Jewish roots first, also paralleling the story of the Prodigal Son.

About this desire to be the younger brother, I have several strongly-held points to make.

1. First, all of us need to assume that we *simultaneously* have some of the attitudes of *both brothers* inside us! We should recognize that there are some aspects of our lives in which we are more prone to "run away from God," and others where we are more prone to "think we stand faithfully with Him," when perhaps we are not as aligned with the Father's heart as we might imagine.

2. Regarding the perspective Christians should have towards Jews, I very much like the approach taken by Canon Andrew White, in his book *Older*

---

[2] Literally Yeshua the Anointed One, His formal name in Hebrew.

Younger Brother.[3] Andrew White was one of our very first interviews back in 2015.[4] His book acknowledges that our relationship with the Jews is complex and rightly contains elements of both older and younger brother simultaneously.

3. The story of Dean Braxton is fascinating. Dean, a former social worker living in the Northwestern United States, had a near death experience, spending one hour and forty-five minutes in heaven. Dean was a typical Christian; as in, not particularly interested in Jews, his Jewish roots, or Israel. His book *In Heaven!*,[5] is one of the best of its class, because Dean found in Scripture everything he saw in heaven! Not only did he see God sitting on His Throne, but he also had three separate encounters with Jesus in that single experience. One story (not found in the book) was told to Jonathan Bernis.[6] In it, Dean relates that Jesus told him that "The Prodigal Son Story is not about wayward Christians, but it is a Jewish story, and the Jews are like the younger son — they are coming home." In that one encounter, Jesus completely overturned Dean's world view of the Jews, by placing them into a story of great hope, return, and future celebration; and then Jesus went on to place Christians in the less enviable role of the older brother!

For any Orthodox Jewish readers of this chapter I would hasten to point out two things about Dean's story.[7] First, please note that "coming home" can mean many things, including returning to the land of Israel! Second, I do *not* see this story as a teaching moment for all Jews, but rather a teaching moment for Christians who have grown up with Dean's prior outlook: namely that God is finished with the Jews. I also find it fascinating that later on in that same video Dean speaks of how his experience in heaven taught him that...drumroll please... *the culture of heaven is actually Jewish*! Dean then states that after his experience in heaven, he began to *seek out* and learn about Jewish culture himself.

What then was New?

Everything I have just written above, I have known, and been contemplating for at least a few years.

---

3 https://www.jerusalemmerit.org/product-category/books/
4 https://root-source.com/lessons/special-broadcast-arch-20150110/
5 https://amzn.to/2ABEGwB
6 You can hear this starting at 14:00 on this YouTube video: https://youtu.be/-RPB_THcYiA
7 Gidon gave his impressions of this story in an interview. See the questions at the end of this chapter for more details.

But I began this chapter by saying that something caught me off guard. Yes, I just saw something in this story that I had never seen before! Are you ready for it?

Neither of the two men in the story felt as if they had a brother!

Both brothers lived their lives focused only on *themselves* and their relationship with *their father*! Neither of the brothers made *any of their decisions* in the context of having a relationship with their brother. Neither brother showed any sentiment or feelings for the other!

Yet, through this story, the father reveals that not only has each of his sons misjudged the heart of their father, but the father tries to awaken in the older brother a new desire for brother-to-brother relationship. In so doing, the father reveals His inner desire that *the brothers begin to act like the brothers they truly are*.

The story concludes without an answer.

Summary

The purpose of this book has been exactly that. To encourage us as Christians to think differently about our relationship with our brothers, the Jews. It is well past noon, and while the sun still shines, the brightness of the day is beginning to wane. The day of pretending that we Christians can perfect our relationship with God the Father by playing in *our sandbox alone*, as if we are God's only sons — that day is darkening as the sun sinks minute-by-minute towards the Western horizon.[8]

We need to wake up and realize that there is a celebration going on in the land of Israel. The Father is rejoicing, and it's time to accept that a party has been thrown for somebody who is very different from us.

We are going to have to learn all over again how to interact respectfully. Gidon often says to groups, "I learned in kindergarten to play nicely with the other children." Yes, I think a kindergarten level of friendship is a great place to begin. And to the extent that Jesus' statement to Dean Braxton applies to the Jews, how wonderful it is, how surprising it is, that God puts it on the heart of some of the sons of Israel, like Gidon Ariel, to be willing to open the door to that ongoing

---

[8]   One reviewer added the following comment: *"In technology, a sandbox is a place of isolation, a place where you can try things out without causing potential harm or undesired results to your system, but a sandbox can also limit the potential for meaningful change."* His comment deserves mention and application. The father in the story did not rebuke his sons for their lack of interaction with their brother *in the past*. He gave them time in their own sandbox. But, the father's will *in the present* was now clear. He revealed his heart's desire for the brother's relationship to take the first step towards meaningful change.

celebration in Israel, and *invite us in.*

Gidon makes it easy for us. We don't even have to knock at *his* door. He knocks at *ours.*

Does that remind you of anyone?

Shalom.

Asking Gidon

Gidon, you reacted to the three parables of Luke 15 in an interview I did with you: The Parable of the Lost Sheep, the Parable of the Lost Coin, and the Story of the Prodigal Son. That was the first time you had ever heard those, and commented on them.[9]

In that interview, regarding the Parable of the Lost Sheep where a man left the ninety-nine sheep to go after the one, you connected the parable to a story passed down by the Jews regarding Moses. Would you mind telling the readers about that here?

Here is an authoritative translation of the source of that story in the Great Midrash (Midrash Rabbah):[10]

> … *Our teachers have said: Once, while Moses our Teacher was tending [his father-in-law] Yitro's sheep, one of the sheep ran away. Moses ran after it until it reached a small, shaded place. There, the lamb came across a pool and began to drink. As Moses approached the lamb, he said, "I did not know you ran away because you were thirsty. You are so exhausted!" He then put the lamb on his shoulders and carried it back. The Holy One said, "Since you tend the sheep of human beings with such overwhelming love — by your life, I swear you shall be the shepherd of My sheep, Israel."*

Regarding the Prodigal Son story, if you were to place Jews and Christians into the role of the brothers in that story, which of the two brothers would you say is "coming home" and which of the two brothers "never left."

I think you could look at it from both sides. Jews naturally believe that their belief system is the correct one, and so anyone distant from that system is the

---

9   The full interview is at https://youtu.be/x7cdYgNtcTA
10   https://bit.ly/Rabbah2-2

one that needs to "come home." So that would cast the Christians in the part of the returning son. Of course, Christians are the younger son, having come on the scene thousands of years after Jews. On the other hand, as you wrote in this chapter, Jews are returning home to Israel in our day, and clearly being shined upon by God for doing this (or by His bringing them back). Christians who felt that they were God's chosen ones while Jews were distant, in other words followers of Replacement Theology, might be indignant of this turn of events, like the older son in our story.

These three parables were largely unfamiliar to you until you read them in our interview. Have you read any particular portions of the New Testament?

I probably read through much of the New Testament for the first time some ten or twenty years ago. But it did not impress me as much as the Jewish Bible (the Old Testament) and especially the Talmud and the Midrash, with which I had much more familiarity and identity. Today, I enjoy reading portions of the New Testament with Christian friends for both of us to discover their Jewish perspective. I think many Christians are fascinated to hear from a "Christianly-uninitiated" Jewish perspective about these texts, which were composed at about the same historical time and by the same Jewish people who composed the Talmud, and so am I!

CHAPTER 38

The Greatest Love Story You've Never Heard!

I f you grew up in Christian circles, you probably never heard the wonderful love story in Genesis about Joseph and Asenath. I only discovered it once I started reading the ArtScroll Torah along with the Jewish commentaries.

The story we tell herein has nothing to do with the apocryphal work *Joseph and Asenath*,[1] most likely written by Christians perhaps as late as the sixth century. Rather, we go directly to the Torah and then weave our way back into the aspects of that story that are filled in by the Jewish Midrash.[2]

We begin our story by reasoning from the text, using the sequence and style put forward in a video I recently discovered which had been published by El Shaddai Ministries, featuring Orthodox Jewish speaker David Nekrutman.[3] I will summarize David's main points as I introduce you to the greatest biblical love story you've probably never heard![4]

The Problem in This Story

David Nekrutman says that the purpose of the Midrash, or Drash as he calls it, is to try to answer the questions that we *should have asked* when we read the text.

---

[1] https://en.wikipedia.org/wiki/Joseph_and_Aseneth
Full text here: http://markgoodacre.org/aseneth/translat.htm
[2] A *midrash* is a collection of rabbinic investigations of the books of the bible, usually a verse-by-verse exegesis. It comes from the word *drash*, meaning to interpret.
[3] David is the first Orthodox Jew to attain a Master's degree in Christian Studies at Oral Roberts University. His supervising professor was Dr. Brad Young. My interview of David was one of the most enjoyable interviews I ever did: https://root-source.com/blog/david-nekrutman-full-interview-with-root-source/. David is the director of the Center for Jewish-Christian Understanding and Cooperation. You can reach him at http://cjcuc.org
[4] His presentation can be seen here: https://youtu.be/NK-S8obXEtk

Not one, not two, but three times does the Torah explicitly tell us that Joseph married "Asenath, the daughter of Potiphera, the priest of On." Let us read all three:

> Pharoah then gave Yosef the name Zaphenath-paneah; and he gave him for a wife Asenath daughter of Poti-phera, priest of On. GENESIS 41:45 (TIB)

> Before the years of famine came, Yosef became the father of two sons, whom Asenath, daughter of Poti-phera, priest of On, bore to him. GENESIS 41:50 (TIB)

> To Yosef were born in the land of Egypt Menashe and Efraim, whom Asenath daughter of Poti-phera priest of On bore to him. GENESIS 46:20 (TIB)

Why is every mention of Asenath in the entire Bible also accompanied by the declaration that she was "daughter of Potiphera, priest of On"? David remarks, "For a Bible in which nothing is without purpose, this emphasis is quite notable, is it not?"

More than that, the very idea that Joseph would have married a woman who was a daughter of the Egyptian priesthood that routinely practiced divination and sorcery, is bothersome as well. Imagine what such practices might do to Joseph's future family heritage and bloodlines if he were to marry such a woman? Why then *three* explicit mentions?

Another question, a potentially much more *Jewish-centric* question that David poses, is even more striking. David asks, why did Joseph voluntarily disobey his family heritage and "marry outside of the family?" David in his video reveals the pattern of *three other verses* in Genesis that show how serious an offense it would be for Joseph to do so! Abraham made Eliezer swear to an oath:

> But you will go to my country and to my relatives, and take a wife for my son Isaac. GENESIS 24:4

And Isaac charged Jacob to do the same:

> Rebekah said to Isaac, "I am tired of living because of the daughters of Heth; if Jacob takes a wife from the daughter of Heth, like these, from the daughters of the land, what good will my life be to me." So Isaac called Jacob and blessed him and charged him, and said to him "You shall not take a wife from the daughters of Canaan." GENESIS 27:46–28:1

And in the case of Esau we see how much his choice affected both Isaac and Rebekah:

> When Esau was forty years old he married Judith the daughter of Beeri the Hittite, and Basemath the daughter of Elon the Hittite; and they brought grief to

Isaac and Rebekah. GENESIS 26:34–35

David Nekrutman mentions here how "brought grief" (*morat haruach* in Hebrew) can be translated as "brought bitterness to their spirit." But even more so, David says this act, as rendered in the Hebrew, was nothing less than "spiritual rebellion!" Therefore, Jews read these passages and ask themselves, "How could righteous Joseph do such a thing?"

And if Joseph's decision to marry Asenath was in fact *unrighteous*, then the sons issuing from that union should be negative as well. How then can Jacob bless Joseph's sons with such fervor and intensity and prophesy that all Israel will pronounce the blessing upon their sons by which he blesses them (GENESIS 48:20)? It makes no sense! And to top it all off, Jacob then *adopted* Joseph's sons as his own, and gave Joseph a double portion of land in Israel!

So we have three verses that explicitly call out Asenath as a daughter of a priest of Egypt, and then three verses that reveal that if Joseph married such a woman, then he would be breaking the commandment of his fathers and would be acting in spiritual rebellion!

How do we resolve it?

Could it be possible that Asenath renounced her allegiance to the gods of Egypt and took on the faith of Joseph? This would go a long way to resolving the problem, would it not?

One verse we read above actually makes such an inference in Jewish interpretation.

> *Before the years of famine came, Yosef became the father of two sons, whom Asenath daughter of Poti-phera, priest of On, bore* **TO HIM**. GENESIS 41:50 (TIB, emphasis mine)

Notice the fact that the sons were born TO HIM! And here it is again:

> *To Yosef were born in the land of Egypt Menashe and Efraim, whom Asenath daughter of Poti-phera priest of On bore* **TO HIM**. GENESIS 46:20 (TIB, emphasis mine)

Jewish interpretation states that these verses imply that the two sons were born **TO JOSEPH'S FAITH**.

This is as far as we can get with the verses themselves.

Enter the Midrash.

The Midrash offers tantalizing possibilities, each of which allows us to step into what could have been a monumental love story that we have never heard.

First, what if Potiphera (the priest) was the same person as Potiphar, to whom Joseph was sold into slavery? This is *exactly* what the Midrash says.

This idea immediately opens a window into a long-running love story between Joseph and Asenath. They had known each other for years! Consider the possibility of the story of a woman, a daughter of Potiphar, who had been admiring the slave Joseph for years. She, probably younger than he was, had admired him at first for his wonderful physical attributes, and then later as a competent manager of all of Potiphar's affairs, even more competent than her father! She must have learned something of his faith and his God, even in those early days.

Later, as a growing young girl perhaps nearing womanhood herself, she must have watched with horror as her own mother took it upon herself to seduce Joseph. She knew it couldn't be true — her heartthrob would never have turned against everything he believed and allowed himself to be entrapped in an affair with her mother. With Joseph's life in peril, she pleaded with her father not to have Joseph *killed*, the standard punishment for "rape by a slave." Suddenly we see mercy in the idea that Joseph was simply thrown in prison, and not killed.

Asenath mourned and ached for years as she grew up into a beautiful woman herself, and watched the beloved slave Joseph hemmed in by prison with no escape possible. It seemed hopeless. Until, when she had all but given up hope and all but agreed to her father's demands for her to marry someone else, Pharaoh had a dream. When Joseph was raised to power, it was Pharaoh who asked Joseph "whom do you want to marry?" That Joseph would be allowed to marry the daughter of Potiphar's wife showed the world, finally, how righteous he really was all along. Potiphar's acceptance was rewarded. He was quickly promoted to be the Chief of the priests of On, with Joseph's blessing. The marriage was now a marriage of great rank and stature. Everyone got something.

But, wait! There is more!

The Midrash offers an even more tantalizing addition to the story that nobody sees coming. It is the kind of secret that is revealed only towards the end of a great story. A piece of information that changes the entire complexion and purpose and meaning of the story.

What if Asenath was not actually *the daughter of Potiphar's wife*?

What if instead, Asenath *was actually the daughter of Dinah*, the daughter of Jacob, about whom we know almost nothing in Scripture! What if Asenath was birthed *after and because of the rape of Dinah by Shechem*, the son of a Canaanite prince?[5] What if Asenath's story was complicated, and she somehow found herself sold into slavery, eventually being placed into the household of Potiphar?

Was it possible that Asenath and Joseph were *both* slaves, both from the household of Jacob in the first place? Did Joseph essentially marry his niece (which was allowed in past practice)? If this is the case, the story takes on another amazing dimension because not only did Asenath get married, she was officially *adopted by Potiphar* as his own daughter! If that is so, she was legally Egyptian, but at the same time ethnically Hebrew! In this story, everything is preserved! The lineage of Asenath's mother, Dinah is also redeemed, because Dinah becomes the grandmother of Menashe and Ephraim! And Joseph has in Asenath a soulmate in whom he can truly confide, someone who would never reject him for his Hebrew heritage, because she is a Hebrew herself!

Is it possible to write a more beautiful love story from this Jewish perspective than this? A woman who was reviled for her heritage can now be celebrated for her fidelity, her steadfastness, her faith and hope, when the man she loved suffered for twelve years for a crime he didn't commit. She is eventually adopted and raised to prominence! This is not just a "rags to riches story;" this is a "rags-rags to riches-riches story" that is full of faith and hope in the redemptive God of Israel.

As David Nekrutman says, "I can't prove this is what happened, but I can tell you that this story has been passed down through the ages within the collective consciousness of the Jewish people for over 2,000 years."[6]

Indeed, it is a love story that no man could write. Only God could write such a story. Only in God could such a story be true.

These are the kind of "jewels" that are available to us as Christians, when we humble ourselves a bit, and are willing to listen to and learn from the Jews who work hard not only to resolve the tension in verses, but to look for redemption in them as well. Three verses say one thing; three verses say the opposite. How can

---

[5] Genesis 34
[6] Sometimes the most interesting evidence for a claim comes from what is missing. Have you considered this? If Asenath was *not* a Hebrew — in other words, if she were fully (genetically) Egyptian — would not some of the tribes, at least in a conflict when they opposed the actions of Ephraim and Menashe, have made reference to those tribes' genetic roots as coming from Egypt? And yet the negative association of Ephraim and Menashe with Egypt, with Egyptian values and ideas, is completely missing from the Hebrew Bible! It seems that the true and undivided loyalty to the family of Jacob was completely beyond question. How would this have been possible otherwise?

these two worlds collide and both be true all at once?

Yes, Joseph and Asenath is a great love story, a strange love story, but it is a story no less great and no less strange than the great story we are all privileged to embark upon together as we learn to lovingly interact as Christians and Jews.

God is love.

Shalom.

Asking Gidon

Gidon, this chapter is based around a story that has been passed down over the centuries by the Jewish people. In chapter 37, you told us about Moses turning aside to find a lamb that had strayed, as a precursor to noticing the burning bush. How much emphasis do these background stories get when rabbis speak to their congregations? Are they repeated often?

This phenomenon is both exciting and fascinating, and bothersome at the same time. Certainly these teachings are interesting and help understand issues in Scripture, and introduce their readers to great traditions. On the other hand, some of them are taught hand-in-hand with the scriptures themselves, as if they are written explicitly in the Bible! I personally find this troublesome. I believe that God made a point in including certain things in the written Bible (sometimes cryptic), and other things in the oral Bible — and all are true, just different levels of true.

I mentioned that I first heard about the background story for Joseph and Asenath in the commentary notes on the Torah, published by ArtScroll. How might Christians be able to hear more of these stories in English?

That site is one good source for them.[7] Two other good compilations are "The Midrash Says"[8] and "The Little Midrash Says."[9] Much success in your learnings!

---

[7] https://www.artscroll.com/8
[8] https://amzn.to/2ycwJxg
[9] https://amzn.to/2SnsbuG

Can you give an example of such a background story that was memorable to you as a kid?

It seems to be a national pastime to teach such "background stories" as you call them to schoolchildren, sometimes even before they know how to read. I found a source sheet of a sampling of such teachings, all of which are well known. Enjoy! https://bit.ly/NotTorah

My favorite story that I remember as an older child, probably age fourteen, was about the midrash that Abraham observed the entire Torah, even before it was actually given some five hundred years after he lived (this is based on the verse in GENESIS 26:5 (KJV): *"…Abraham obeyed my voice, and kept my charge, my commandments, my statutes, and my laws."*). At summer camp, my group put on a skit about Abraham, naturally irreverently funny, which included the funniest boy in the bunk playing Sarah. The scene I remember depicts Abraham and Sarah going down to Egypt and being stopped at the border by a customs agent. (This is also a midrash that I won't go into here for fear that this comment is growing to the length of a book itself.) The customs agent searches through Abraham's suitcase, and finds his *tefillin* (or phylacteries — boxes containing copies of the four passages in the books of Exodus and Deuteronomy that describe them — that are donned during morning prayer). Abraham tells him, "Those are my tefillin." The agent responds "What's that?" And Abraham delivers the line that keeps me laughing until today: "I have no idea, but the Midrash says I wore them, so there they are."

CHAPTER 39

The Future of Israel

We only have two more chapters to go!

I only have two last chances to inspire and encourage you to think bigger, wider and deeper than you ever have about the purposes of God in Jewish and Christian relations. I'm sure there are better writers out there, better thinkers who could reveal these things — and many more — to you and me. Yet, if you got to this chapter in sequence, not simply jumping ahead because of its enticing title, I'm grateful.

More than seventy years have passed since the re-establishment of Israel in 1948. Most people reading these words are not old enough to remember those early days. In the 1970s, a theory began to make the rounds in Christian circles that the end of the age will happen within forty years of the re-establishment of Israel, in other words before 1988.[1] When 1988 came and went, many Christians had to acknowledge that their view of the future of Israel was too small.

Meanwhile, since I first visited Israel in 1990, I have watched as the people of Israel themselves have grown in confidence and strength regarding their own future. I didn't notice a change on each and every visit, just like we don't see our kids growing every time we look at them, but over time the change in Israel has been unmistakable.

In this chapter we will look at two massive changes underway in Israel, that we

---

[1] This was a misreading of Matthew 24:34, quoting Jesus in the parable of the fig tree as saying "This generation shall not pass away until all these things take place." The two errors made were (a) defining a generation as precisely forty years, when there are at least five definitions of generation: 20, 40, 70, 80 and 120 years; and secondly, (b) the word "generation" (Greek: *genea*) can be just as easily translated "race" or "family". In other words, the Jewish people will not pass away until all these things take place. I see this verse as an emphatic statement by God, as stated in Amos 9:14-15, that the Jewish people will never be uprooted from Israel again.

Christians are not necessarily noticing: one secular and one spiritual.

The Big Secular Change

For a nation's population to remain stable without immigration the birth rate must be at least 2.1, meaning 2.1 children are born for every woman in the nation. *Israel has the highest birth rate of any Western nation,* at 3.1 in 2017 according to the World Bank.[2]

But the critical statistic about which most Christians are unaware, is that the birth rate within the Orthodox community is likely 3.5, which means that the non-Orthodox community averages less than 3.0. And since the Orthodox community is more conservative — i.e. it votes for more conservative parties, like Likud — this means that the Nation of Israel is getting more conservative over time! *This situation is unlike any western nation!*[3]

And even more amazing, in the series of 2019 and 2020 national elections, the young voters were the most conservative of all![4] *This again is unlike any western nation!*

Work sectors — such as high-tech — are also changing, as the number of Orthodox workers joining the workforce is rising. I have personally watched high-tech electronics (as its percentage of Orthodox Jewish workers) rise from roughly one out of every ten workers in the year 2000 to perhaps one out of three today. One Orthodox friend told me that inside his company all food is now kosher, and they have a *mezuzah*[5] on the doorframe of every room. "Things are changing," he said. *This trend is unlike any western nation!*

What this also means is that Israel is getting more religious over time, not less. The percentage of people in Israel who say they believe in God is growing. It was about 80 percent ten years ago[6] (which was the same as America at that time), but it is growing, and may be close to 90 percent today (while belief in God in America has declined). *This increase in Israel is unlike any western nation!*

Thus, given enough time, even a fully democratic nation like Israel should be able

---

[2] Short link to article at The World Bank: https://bit.ly/Israel-birthrate
[3] If you want to learn more about Israel's political system, Gidon suggests you begin here: https://rootsource.com/israel-politics-overview/
[4] Short link to article at the Times of Israel: https://bit.ly/kids-rightwing
[5] A *mezuzah* is a small enclosure that contains the verses of the *shema* (Deuteronomy 6:4-5) rolled up as a tiny scroll, and is attached to the door frame [in Hebrew: *mezuzah*], as part of the commandment: "You shall write them on the doorposts of your house and on your gates." Deuteronomy 6:9.
[6] https://en.wikipedia.org/wiki/Religion_in_Israel

to fend off the push for legalizing activities that the Orthodox oppose, such as same-sex marriage. Perhaps one day, even abortion will be illegal.

Another interesting outcome of this trend will be *more Jewish immigration* to Israel. I marvel when I see God get two opposing groups (Israeli liberals and Israeli conservatives) come into agreement with His will, for completely different reasons! Conservative, religious Jews want all Jews to return because the Bible prophesies it, and because "it is the right thing for Jews to do." Liberal Jews want more Jewish immigration to keep the conservative leanings of their own country in check!

The future-Israel is a more God-fearing Israel than we realize, an Israel that will come into better-and-better alignment with the Bible, the Torah, and a righteous worldview naturally over time.

This brings me to a pet peeve that I will stop and address. Christians who point fingers at Israel's legalized abortion laws and warn that "*God will judge the Jews*" for allowing abortion in Israel, are not giving credit to the Orthodox for following God's command to be fruitful, multiply and fill the Earth. The Orthodox are obeying that command, while we Christians do not. Most Christians today practice careful birth control and limit children, and then we watch as our overall population declines into immorality. Meanwhile, both Israel and other Christian nations legalize abortions. Which nation do you think is going to be rewarded as being the one that has taken the talents given to it, and is increasing them the most?[7]

The Big Spiritual Change

During my many visits to Israel in the last few years, I began to pick up on something that I didn't quite understand at first. Judaism in Israel is not fixed, but is going to change in the coming years.

Now wait, you say! Isn't Judaism more steeped in tradition than any other religion in the world? Isn't the respect for past practices in Judaism such that changes are almost impossible? And while the Reform and Conservative movements do change a bit over time, isn't the fact that Israel's religious Jews are almost completely Orthodox, making for even less potential change rather than more? While all that is true, there is one wildcard that is going to overturn everything else!

---

[7] That sentence is a reference to the parable of the talents in Matthew 25:14-30. By the way, we raised our family in the age of birth control, perhaps just like you did. Apparently there is no rewind button on that tape. All many of us can do now is to encourage younger married couples to have more children than we did — and to trust that God will provide for them, even as they have the faith that their own quivers might be full of children (Psalm 127:3-5).

That wildcard is "the Land of Israel!"

You see, Judaism since the destruction of the Temple in 70 CE has been developing around the exile. With the Temple destroyed, the power shifted away from the centralized authority of the Sanhedrin, and shifted to the local rabbi. That rabbi *had* to exert more authority within the Jewish communities, or else the Jews would have drifted away from each other in their practice of Judaism.

This is called Rabbinic Judaism.

It was necessary. It was a matter of survival. Therefore, the focus of Rabbinic Judaism was on those things that were universal to Jews, those things that could keep them distinctive as a people!

But now, as more Jews are returning to Israel (as compared to the number of Jews in the rest of the world), those commandments associated with the Land of Israel (and there are many of them), are going to rise in importance. Even more so, hundreds of additional commands would become activated if a Temple were built. Since the oral traditions for matters regarding the Land of Israel are few, the landscape is wide open for change. The Jews of Israel will have to consult the Torah, and come together to figure out how they are going to fulfill such matters. The focus will swing away from the local rabbi and towards the Torah itself! Not that rabbis will be demoted, but such decisions cannot be made at the rabbinical level; they have to be made at a national level.[8]

An Example that Involves Us!

Let me offer you one example of the changes in Judaism that are underway.

Rabbi Yitzchak Ginsburgh put out an article entitled: *The Fourth Revolution in Torah Learning.*[9] In it he explained that every once-in-a-while, Jews **need to transgress** the Torah. To clarify, when Ginsburgh was talking about transgressing the Torah, he means to go against certain prior rulings in the *oral* Torah, not the *written* Torah.

His first example of the need every-once-in-a-while to transgress the oral Torah

---

[8] I am not aware of many resources in English for Christians to learn more about this. Occasionally, some of the podcasts by Eve Harow from Land of Israel Network (http://thelandofisrael.com/author/Eve/) tackle these topics. Another English resource for Torah-related articles is: https://www.zomet.org.il/eng/?pg=sitemap&CategoryID=169

[9] The full text of the article is here in this short link: https://bit.ly/4th-revolution
Why this article is so important is discussed here at this short link to Israel National News: https://bit.ly/4th-revolution-2

was Rabbi Yehudah HaNasi who determined that in order to save Judaism in the exile, it was going to be necessary to "write down the Oral law."

After giving two other examples in the centuries that followed, the Rabbi then proclaims it is time for a fourth revolution of the Torah:

"We are being called to begin offering Torah to non-Jews…"

Many Orthodox Jews noted the importance of Ginsburgh's article after it was first published. Rivkah Adler of Israel365 News wrote an article about it,[10] and Gidon commented to me about it as well.

Rabbi Ginsburgh has great foresight to take this stand. I remember with fondness meeting him in 2014. We previously discussed his musical compositions in chapter 32. But I believe his writing on the fourth revolution in Torah learning is his very best *composition* yet!

The Future of Israel

Israel is already unlike any other western nation. Its conservative population is growing, and the strength of its base is in its younger generation.

And spiritually, Israel is in a transformation from Rabbinic Judaism to Torah-based Judaism, driven by the return of Jews to the Land of Israel again.

If this world had ended in 1988, it would have been a very different Israel that would have limped into the Millennium. Now, less than forty years since, Israel has seen many profound changes, and still more profound changes are coming.

The "future of Israel" is now much bigger than what could have been envisioned forty years ago. And suppose the Messiah tarries another forty years hence, then what? What will the future of Israel look like forty years from now?

I would suggest that the future "future of Israel" will again seem incomparable to the future we envision today.

I suspect it will *always* be that way, because our God who loves to think about the *future*, wouldn't dream of having it any other way.

Shalom.

---

[10] Short link to article at Israel365 News: https://bit.ly/Gentiles-Torah

Asking Gidon

Gidon, is the fact that Israel is getting more conservative over time often discussed in the media? For those who are not pleased with this trend, what do they propose in response?

The (mainstream) media is liberal, and I have found that they tend to bury their heads in the sand about this. They try to promote policies that counter the conservative-leaning trend, like encouraging nonreligious immigration, but there is really nothing they can do about it.

One of the strongest criticisms of the Orthodox by other Israelis is their desire to study Torah instead of serving in the military. As one who has studied the Torah and served in the military, is it frustrating to be lumped into the category of Orthodox, when the actual conflict is only with the ultra-Orthodox?

No, it is frustrating that well-meaning people divide Jews at all. By now, most Israelis recognize that the ultra–Orthodox conscription issue must be and will be dealt with through negotiation, and the minority who want to turn this into a matter of friction will continue to do so no matter what.

With regard to the land of Israel bringing change to the Orthodox world, what aspect of Rabbinic Judaism would you most like to see change now that the Jews have returned?

The answer to your question is not what I would like to see, but what will change. The answer of course is the construction and reinstatement of the Holy Temple. May we see it speedily in our days![11]

---

[11] No Root Source rabbi has been more closely associated with the Holy Temple and the Temple Mount than Rabbi Yehudah Glick. Gidon and I first interviewed him in early 2015 after his miraculous recovery from an assassination attempt: https://root-source.com/blog/rabbi-yehuda-glick-discusses-miracles/ and many times since. Yehudah Glick is the only Root Source teacher to become a member of the Knesset. Upon leaving the Knesset he started the Shalom Jerusalem Foundation: https://www.facebook.com/ShalomJerusalemYehudahGlick/ Root Source carries his insightful teachings on the books of Joshua, Judges, Samuel and Lamentations on his Holy Temple channel: https://root-source.com/channels/

CHAPTER 40

Where Does it End?

This book has now reached its final chapter. We have attempted to explore many different aspects of the relationship between Christians and Jews.

The discipline of writing these things down has forced me to take a large number of swirling thoughts about various topics and attempt to give them language. When ideas are written down, they become transportable! I am indebted to Gidon Ariel for reading each of these essays, and helping me to articulate my ideas about the Jewish world without ever asking me to alter them. I also appreciate his patience with my Christian mindset. But I had to express these ideas or else I felt I would burst. I think I now understand a tiny bit of what Jeremiah felt:

> I thought, "I will not mention Him, No more will I speak in His name"—But [His word] was like a raging fire in my heart, Shut up in my bones; I could not hold it in, I was helpless. JEREMIAH 20:9 (TIB)

We have one major topic left: Where is the relationship between Jews and Christians heading?

Where does it end?

I now look back at somebody and laugh. How silly he was! How cartoonish he was! How shallow he was! That person was me.

The "end" of the relationship between Christians and Jews, I used to think, would occur when we were homogenized together, as if red wine and white wine were going to be poured into a carafe to create a new Rosé blend. And the chief issue that had to be resolved for that to happen, in my mind, was the Jewish understanding of the identity of the Messiah.

This focus on the identity of the Messiah by us as Christians is quite common. It is characterized quite well in many different ways. For instance, take the joke that is often told when loving Christians and Jews are in the same room together.

Somebody, either a Christian or Jew, says, "When the Messiah comes we will ask Him if this is His first or second visit!" It always gets a laugh.

I have also enjoyed hearing a few different spins on the identity of the Messiah by some Jewish friends. Rabbi Ken Spiro[1] often ends his talks to Christian audiences by saying, "If the Messiah turns out to be Jesus, I'll be the first in line to let you baptize me." Nehemia Gordon has ended some of his talks to Christian audiences by allowing Christians to pray that God would reveal to him who the Messiah really is.[2] Gidon Ariel suggests to audiences that Christians should not try to convince him through their words about the knowledge of "a revelation" about Jesus that *they* received directly from God; in other words Gidon suggests to Christians "to let God do the revealing."

But let's move on from that topic to a larger one. A larger approach is to consider what shall be the *reaction of the two groups* at the "coming of the Messiah." We Christians tend to assume that the Jews will be the "most surprised group" when the Messiah arrives. That's where I personally began my journey. Yet, almost a full year before meeting Gidon, I had an unexpected question suddenly occur to me:

> *What if Christians were as surprised by the "Second Coming" as the Jews were surprised by the "First Coming"?*

Then, over the years, I had heard this general idea also expressed by a few well-known Christians, and at least one well-known Jew. When Rabbi Shlomo Riskin once famously suggested at a major Christian conference that *Christians will be asked by the Jewish Messiah* to "convert" to Jewish practices,[3] he said the hall was filled with "absolute silence."

But I would like to end this section with two more comments: one from a Christian and one from a Jew.

A Christian I knew once told a story about a dream he had had. Jesus had arrived on earth and was going to hold His first press conference. The room was set up like the White House press briefing room, while people packed the room with anticipation. Everyone, including that Christian, had questions that they had carried for years, if not their entire lives: all those "why questions!" Jesus was coming, and so were the answers! Finally He arrived and walked into the room and stood there at the podium smiling, to the cheers of those in the room. And

---

1   Rabbi Ken Spiro teaches *Jewish History, Jewish Future* on Root Source: https://root-source.com/channels/
2   Nehemia justifies that request from Psalm 119:18 where David, who already has the Spirit of God upon him, is yet asking God to "open his eyes." Nehemia's site is: https://www.nehemiaswall.com/
3   Short link to article at Religion & Politics: https://bit.ly/Riskin-CUFI

just as suddenly, what this Christian described was that all his questions no longer mattered to him any more, and neither did anyone else's. Jesus, looking around the room, seeing that there were no questions to be asked after all, then invited everyone to leave the room with Him. Apparently there was work to be done!

That story I first heard many years ago. But this second comment from a Jew is new to me, spoken by Rabbi Chaim Eisen, who has been interviewed on Root Source.[4] I heard Rabbi Eisen say this recently to a Christian audience:

> *"When the Messiah arrives we are all in for some shocks!"*

I believe Rabbi Eisen's view is my favorite. It is both wise and humble. Possibly the very best predisposition among both groups is the attitude that neither group has a full read on the situation.

Where's it heading?

But none of these stories so far exactly explains where this trend is heading — this journey of God's call for Christians and Jews to come together. Where does it end?

I will now offer you *my best guesses* based on everything I've seen in my *five years with Orthodox Jews*.

No Rosé

First, don't expect Rosé wine. Don't expect that Christians and Jews will be blended into any form in which there is *less* diversity, where Christians simply become more "Jewish" and Jews become more "Christian." Then how will such diversity be expressed? The expressions of that diversity are not revealed by simple study; they require a revelation from God. Paul prayed for Christians that,

> *"the eyes of your heart might be enlightened, so that you will know what is the hope of His calling, what are the riches of the glory of His inheritance in the saints [holy ones]."* EPHESIANS 1:18

Paul knew that it was not possible for Christians to understand the magnificence of the diversity of the heritage of God without supernatural revelation. My mother, of blessed memory, prayed this prayer for me every day for years when I was a child. At the time I found this prayer confusing and largely uninteresting! I think I would have easily settled for her to pray for good grades at school! Half a century later it is beginning to dawn on me just how amazing her prayer really was. We

---

4   The interview can be found here at this short link: https://bit.ly/Eisen-interview

focus so much on who God is and how amazing He is, and yet this verse is about His people, His creation.

Utter Completion

Second, do expect complete, total, utter, nothing-left-behind redemption![5] That which was lost *will* be found. The time that has been eaten by locusts *will* be redeemed. That which is dead *will* rise. That which is impossible with man *will* be possible with God. This is not a football game where God makes some plays, the devil makes some plays, but ultimately God wins the game. No, we are talking about complete, utter *vanquishing of the enemy*. Every square centimeter of ground will be taken. Every cubic centimeter of the oceans will be taken and conformed into God's Kingdom until,

> In all of My sacred mount nothing evil or vile shall be done; For the land shall be filled with devotion to Hashem as water covers the sea. ISAIAH 11:9 (TIB)

No Disrespect

Third, don't expect any degradation of the Torah. In the future, the view and valuation and appreciation of the Torah will never be lower in the nations of the world, than it is *right now*. In other words, its appreciation will only *increase*.

> "Do not think that I came to abolish the Law or the Prophets; I did not come to abolish but to fulfill. For truly I say to you, until heaven and earth pass away, not the smallest letter or stroke shall pass from the Law until all is accomplished. Whoever then annuls one of the least of these commandments, and teaches others to do the same, shall be called least in the kingdom of heaven; but whoever keeps and teaches them, he shall be called great in the kingdom of heaven." MATTHEW 5:17-19

Moses Honored

Fourth, don't expect any degradation of Moses. We can see this amazingly in the book of Revelation where the holy ones join together to sing: *The Song of Moses and the Lamb*, which interestingly has neither the words *Moses* nor *lamb* contained within its words!

> Great and marvelous are Your works,
>
> O Lord God, the Almighty;
>
> Righteous and true are Your ways,

---

[5] Acts 3:21

King of the nations!

Who will not fear, O Lord, and glorify Your name?

For You alone are holy;

For "ALL THE NATIONS WILL COME AND WORSHIP BEFORE YOU,

FOR YOUR RIGHTEOUS ACTS HAVE BEEN REVEALED."

Even though this song is recorded in the book of Revelation,[6] nothing in it is uniquely sourced from the New Testament. It is all consistent with the Hebrew Bible. Following this song is a mysterious phrase that encapsulates the concepts of *The Temple, The Tabernacle,* and *The Testimony.* It seems so beyond understanding that I won't even venture to guess about it![7]

David Honored

Fifth, even though the Messiah will be King, don't expect any degradation of King David or man's role in ruling. In the second to last recorded sentence spoken by Yeshua in the New Testament, He ties Himself to David by saying,

"I am the root and the descendant of David..." REVELATION 22:16b

But there is one more observation that I would like to make — my very last one to leave with you! It only came to me in the latter stages of this writing project, and it would have been worth writing them all in a cave, if only to see this one thing.

The Blessing of Unity

Let us quote PSALM 133 from The Israel Bible.

A song of ascents. Of David. How good and how pleasant it is that brothers dwell together. It is like fine oil on the head running down onto the beard, the beard of Aharon, that comes down over the collar of his robe; like the dew of Hermon (★)[8] that falls upon the mountains of Tzion. There Hashem ordained blessing, everlasting life. PSALM 133 (TIB)

This is the second-to-last song of ascents. You may recall a prior discussion about the Prodigal Son in chapter 37, how the sons were focused on themselves, and their relationship with their Father. For each of them, their brother hardly existed.

---

[6] Revelation 15:3-4. Capitalization by the author.
[7] Revelation 15:5
[8] This asterisk is explained in the following paragraphs.

This PSALM 133 answers the question of "what it would look like if they truly loved and cared for each other, and dwelt together in unity."

> *How good and how pleasant it is that brothers dwell together. It is like fine oil on the head running down onto the beard, the beard of Aharon, that comes down over the collar of his robe;*

Something good is here. Something pleasant. Something as precious as the special recipe of anointing oil that was created by God to be poured upon the high priest,[9] an event that is so rare it only occurs once in that high priest's lifetime, yet with immense and lasting impact.

> *like the dew*

Next in PSALM 133, the dew is mentioned. Here is what The Israel Bible commentary has to say about that:

> *(*) Tal (טל), 'dew,' is a common biblical symbol of Hashem's bountiful blessings. Rain is another sign of God's love for mankind. What is the difference between rain and dew? According to Jewish mysticism, rain is a sign of God showering His abundant blessings freely from above. Dew, which forms below from condensation of atmospheric water vapor, is related to the divine blessings which are a result of man's own efforts and achievements. This psalm teaches that Hashem's blessing from above allows for the flowering of man's work below.*

Do you see the implication of this comment upon the divine interaction between Christians and Jews? We now look at where the dew comes from, and where it falls.

> *like the dew of Hermon that falls upon the mountains of Tzion.*

The dew is *from* Mount Hermon, which resides at the northern border of Israel and on the other side of the Jordan River from Jerusalem. But somehow this dew from Hermon is transported to, and falls upon the mountains of Jerusalem. How does the dew of Hermon become rain that falls on Jerusalem? It is a mystery.

The psalm concludes with the phrase:

> *There Hashem ordained blessing, everlasting life.*

I had always read this verse in terms of one's personal experience of having "everlasting life." But recently, I was looking at the many stories in the Bible involving people "coming together." I was looking for patterns and principles, looking to discover "what is on God's heart" in this idea of people "coming

---

[9] Exodus 30:30

together." One thing I discovered shocked me.

In almost every case, when people "come together in God's design," something brand new is birthed. Something unexpected. Something that is more than the sum of the parts.

Let's take an example. Consider the oneness of marriage between man and woman. God's design was that a man leave his father and mother and become one with his wife. To what end? Was it just for children? Was it God's plan that Adam and Eve should fill the Earth with many exact copies of Adam and Eve, exact replications? No! By the end of the beginning, which is to say, by the end of the book of Genesis, we find the makings of a nation being formed. A nation about which God will promise hundreds of years later that, "I will take you for My people, and I will be your God."[10] Something much more majestic would derive from the fruitfulness of Adam and Eve, the complicated history of their children, and God's loving intervention in human history.

Then what of PSALM 133? What of the unity among brothers? What does it mean to have the blessing of "everlasting life?" The Hebrew is rendered as:

life even to forevermore
Chayyim ad ha-olam

Remember that Adam called his wife Eve [*Chavvah*], because she was the "mother of all living." The word *life* in PSALM 133 recalls her name to us! Eve is about *life*!

Here is what I believe.

Something greater is here. Something in this final phrase of PSALM 133 takes us to another dimension of life. It is so much greater than "be fruitful and multiply" that we cannot even contain it! We cannot understand it!

Yet somehow, the dwelling together of brothers creates not just new life, but a guarantee that new life will never stop coming, never stop being birthed. It is more than having discovered the proverbial fountain of youth. Rather, it is like having discovered the means to birth an *infinite number of individual fountains of life*, in ever-increasing numbers, manners and forms, without ceasing, forevermore, without end, and with the blessing of the One True God.

I have no idea what that last sentence means! But I believe that my *spirit* knows

---

[10] Exodus 6:7

what it means, and so does yours. It is probably the reason that you have read to the end of this book. Something is drawing your spirit towards something *very good*.[11] For this "*good*", you push aside the cares of the day long enough to touch base with the God of Abraham, Isaac and Jacob. Something calls you onward, and you don't know why.

This is why:

It's not a wound to be healed.

It's not a pain to be comforted.

It is a call for "life even to forevermore."

We all want it.

May we all be willing to walk any walk, hope every hope, and pay whatever price to obtain it. It must be something that burns inside the heart of the Messiah. It is the calling for the Jewish World and All Nations of the World to come together. To paraphrase the words of JEREMIAH 20:9:

"Try as we may to shut it up within our bones, we simply cannot hold it in."

It will come to pass.

Shalom.

Thanking Gidon

Bob to Gidon:

Thank you to Gidon.

Thank you Gidon for reading all these thoughts when they were written as columns, and for the suggestion to publish them in a book. Thank you for moving beyond your surprise when, after praying about this project, I asked you if you would be willing to add your own commentary and answer questions. I think the readers would agree that your words have made this book a whole lot more interesting.

Gidon to Bob:

You're welcome ☺

---

[11] Genesis 1:31

Twelve Baskets Full

Congratulations. You finished the book! You are hereby commended and released, with no further obligation to read anything more!

But for all of you who just couldn't get enough of what this book had to offer to you — or as the self-deprecating joke goes: to both of you who couldn't get enough — Appendix A is for you!

As writers, we bring to God what we have brought from home in our little lunch basket — our five loaves and two fishes — and then look to see what He does with them. I wonder what that little boy felt like when he saw twelve baskets full of leftovers at the end? The leftovers alone were many times more than what he had originally brought! *My guess is: he got overwhelmed with the awe of God!*

This appendix is about being in awe of God! It describes *more awe moments* I had, but which didn't fit into a chapter of their own. In fact, only one of them has ever been published before.[1] So as a last hurrah, I will now introduce twelve more insights, but limit myself to just *one paragraph* per topic. You don't have to agree with all these, but please look for the awe of God in them!

Smarter writers than me would have held back some great ideas for a sequel, but I felt a prompting from the Lord to hold nothing back. And even if I did hold back, what might a sequel to this book be called anyway: *Ten Years with Orthodox Jews?* Now there's a rousing title... said *nobody ever!*

Thomas Wolfe said, "you can't go home again." And I will never be able to "go to Israel again" in a way that recreates that feeling of wonder and awe during those first five years. Going to Israel now is like... well, to do a complete reversal on the

---

[1] Basket #7

last quotation... it feels like going home.

So here goes! Twelve topics that engender the awe of God. Ready? Set? Go!

Basket #1. Where was the Garden of Eden?

Please forget all you've ever heard about the Garden of Eden being in Turkey or Iraq. The Garden of Eden was in Israel. And the very center of the garden was a place you may have heard of: Jerusalem! If everything in the Bible *ends* in Jerusalem, why wouldn't everything *start* there? Jews believe this too. From scripture they reason that the foundation stone on which the Temple stood, was the very first dry land (rock) formed on the third day. It has also been passed down to them since the time of Moses that Adam and Eve are buried in the Cave of the Patriarchs in Hebron.[2] Regarding Jerusalem, I believe the Tree of Life grew where the Ark of the Covenant would eventually be placed in the Holy Temple, and the Tree of Knowledge of Good and Evil grew where Christ died on the Cross! Doesn't that also make perfect sense that Jesus goes back to the place of the original sin to offer himself? Many Bible experts, after hearing this idea, would challenge me to explain the four rivers![3] That is a tough one. We already know the Jordan River flows into the Dead Sea, the lowest point on earth, which is right over the middle of the massive East African Rift. The Tigris, Euphrates, and the Blue Nile are all spring fed rivers rising from that same rift. So my answer is: the *one* river flows into the *four* rivers *underground*![4]

Basket #2. Uncut Stones?

Have you ever noticed that after the Ten Commandments, the first command God gives is to make an altar?[5] Moreover, Moses is told in those same verses to make sure that the altar is built with *uncut stones* and that no tool is to be used on them. You can see uncut stones being used to build Joshua's altar below. Why does God command this? The answer: God's amazing respect for *people*. The uncut stones are a symbol of *us* being fitted into God's plans. Just like the workmen who would build Joshua's altar and the workmen who would later build the Temple, God is willing to work very, very long and hard to position *people* to be used for His purposes. He will use us just as we are — uncut! Will He prune us? Yes! But will

---

[2] Gidon says that it may well have been passed down generationally through Noah to Abraham, and to the tribes of Israel.

[3] The one river that becomes four rivers is indeed a bit of a mystery. Most people place the Garden near the source of the Tigris and Euphrates, which explains all the Iraq/Turkey theories.

[4] Bruce Paul was the first to propose this brilliant idea, as far as I am aware, in his book *The Living Waters of Eden*: https://amzn.to/2XzFIlf

[5] Exodus 20:23-26

Joshua's Altar. Original uncut stones are seen below the black line.

He cut off whole pieces from us? No! We must bow down and worship our God who shows amazing respect and patience with us! May His great name be praised in all the Earth!

Basket #3. The Path of Least Embarrassment?

Our social-media-fueled culture has turned *embarrassing others* into a grotesque carnival freak show. When I first read the five books of the Torah with the Jewish commentaries provided by ArtScroll, I read the commentary on the last two verses just mentioned in Basket #2.[6] Here I saw the words from the most often read Jewish commentator, Rabbi Shlomo Yitzchaki (Rashi) of the 11th century: "*If the Torah commands us to refrain from "shaming" [stones], surely a person should be eternally vigilant never to cause shame or embarrassment to living, breathing human beings.*" These words stopped me in my tracks and had an immense effect on me. Then, as I continued to read the Torah that year, I began to notice place after place where God goes *out of His way* to minimize the embarrassment of Moses, Aaron, and many others.[7] But there are also two great exceptions to this in the Torah: Miriam's leprosy for her speaking against Moses, and Korah's fall into the earth for his rebellion and public denouncement of brothers Moses and Aaron. The sins of Miriam and Korah share a common thread: they were both openly embarrassing

---

6 Exodus 20:25-26 in English Bibles, or Exodus 20:22-23 in Hebrew Bibles.
7 The ArtScroll commentary points out numerous such places.

others. I don't know about you, but I'd rather not be embarrassed by God! I have weaknesses. I've done things, and I've been forgiven for things that I'd rather not broadcast to the world. My solution? My comfort? I will endeavor to care about the feelings of others, and in whatever needs to be done that involves others, I will try to accomplish it in *the path of least embarrassment.*

Basket #4. How many meanings has a verse?

I grew up hearing that each verse in the Bible has one meaning. Even at the time, that seemed boring. Now it seems silly! Is God that simple? Then I learned from the Messianic movement about P(a)RD(e)S which is the word for *paradise* in Hebrew. It describes four levels of meaning in the Bible: Pashat, the simple meaning, Ramez the hint, Drash, the search, and Sod, the hidden meaning. Later I learned from the Orthodox about the seventy facets of Torah, that everything can be viewed in seventy different ways, the number of the nations of the Earth! But I think the real answer for the levels of meaning is *infinite*. God is infinite, and so if the Bible is His Word it must have an infinite amount of self-consistent truth embedded in it. I recall someone saying once: "If God's word is paint, it's always still drying." May that person and all of us enjoy God's Word forever!

Painting by the Edge of a Wood by Claude Monet. Which paint is still drying?

Basket #5. Reconcile what?

The Word of God is so amazing and powerful. The greatest challenge we ever face is to truly believe it — the full extent of what it says. This challenge reminds me of a blog post I once read by Ed Boring. Deceptively simple, he simply listed every verse in the New Testament that speaks of "all things." The reader is simply asked to read these verses in succession. The blog post may be found at this short link: https://bit.ly/Boring-things. Of those verses, some of my favorites are: JOHN 14:26, ACTS 3:19-21, and COLOSSIANS 1:16-17, 20. That very last verse in Colossians says that God plans to reconcile "all things" to Himself. Do we really believe this? Does anybody truly believe this without changing the meaning of the word *all?* But, if you make an attempt to believe that, then it starts to make sense why an altar is made with uncut stones! He wants to reconcile all things (about us) to Himself! Yes, something very big is going on behind the scenes in the mind and heart of God. We will probably spend eternity exploring the rooms of the castle of God's heart, never reaching the end. It sounds perfectly glorious!

Basket #6. Where did I last put down that book?

Some of the most aggravating verses in the Bible, at least for me, are those verses that mention books that have been lost to history. Here are just two examples. JOSHUA 10:13 asks "Is it not written in *the book of Jasher?*"[8] NUMBERS 21:14 actually quotes two lines from *the book of the Wars of the Lord.*[9] Don't worry, I'm not asserting that these two lost books should be considered infallible, but if they are *mentioned* in the Bible, why is everyone so resolved that they are *lost* to history? Now, having just read Basket #5 about God reconciling all things to Himself, where do you stand on the word *all?* How big is your *all?* Then please answer me this: exactly how is "all things" going to happen if those two books aren't found? Therefore, would anybody like to join me in praying that God will reconcile these two books to Himself, by allowing them to be recovered? Never thought of such a prayer? Neither had I. But imagine for a moment, being alive during World War II, and praying that "many more ancient biblical manuscripts would be found." Your prayer would have been answered in less than five years: they're called the *Dead Sea Scrolls.* Let's pray!

---

[8] The book that was first published in 1625 under the same name, *The Book of Jasher*, is unfortunately, not the original book recovered, but a modern book. Nehemia Gordon's podcast Hebrew Voices is the best podcast on ancient Hebrew manuscripts that explains the story quite thoroughly. https://www. nehemiaswall.com/lost-book-of-jasher Nehemia notably says that if the original book of Jasher were found, it would be even more important than the discovery of the Dead Sea Scrolls.

[9] *Therefore it is said in the Book of the Wars of the* LORD, *"Waheb in Suphah, And the wadis of the Arnon, And the slope of the wadis That extends to the site of Ar, And leans to the border of Moab."* Numbers 21:14-15. https:// www.jewishvirtuallibrary.org/book-of-the-wars-of-the-lord

Basket #7. Our streets are paved with what?

Speaking of amazing discoveries, a medical doctor named David Pitcher found something in 2015, and it's hidden in plain sight. Perhaps the early churches never knew it, or perhaps what they knew became lost to history. But Paul knew it. David's discovery? At least **six of the Apostle Paul's letters match up perfectly with the books of the Tanakh**. Match up? For instance, the sequential verses in Paul's letter to Titus can be lined up — paired with or connected to — sequential passages in the book of Joshua. That is, the first verses of Titus can be paired up with the first verses of Joshua, and the last verses of Titus can be paired up with the last verses of Joshua, etc. The same thing holds for the book of Galatians, which pairs up with the book of Exodus. For example, GALATIANS 3:17 pairs with EXODUS 12:40, where both mention "430 years." David Pitcher believes that Paul is writing a midrash on the Torah. I see it differently: I say that Paul is sequentially reading the Torah/Tanakh for spiritual inspiration, and to sequence his thoughts. The pairings of books don't change theology,[10] but they shed bright light on what Paul was thinking, his thought organization, and his inspiration for many amazing and surprising statements. For an introduction see: https://youtu.be/Qmd8ydACDds. David's discovery is going to unlock more understanding of the Bible than any Christian book we've read in hundreds of years. It brings the Old and New Testaments together in a beautiful harmony. Our streets are paved with gold.

Basket #8. Why didn't you talk much about the ultra-Orthodox?

The Orthodox Jews mentioned in this book mostly identify as members of the Religious Zionist movement. If they lived in the USA, we would call them modern Orthodox. The Jews who wear black hats and long black coats are most commonly called ultra-Orthodox.[11] They tend to keep to themselves, and live in their own neighborhoods like Meah Shearim in Jerusalem. The ultra-Orthodox are *Ashkenazi Jews* who immigrated from central and eastern Europe, as compared to the *Sephardic Jews* who immigrated from around the Mediterranean. If you go far back enough in both Ashkenazi and Sephardic lineage, their forefathers became the same Jewish forefathers who had left Israel originally in the Babylonian (first) exile or the Roman (second) exile. Ashkenazi and Sephardim are not different ethnically, but simply drifted apart culturally. But not much. The text of the prayer books they use are almost identical and their synagogue services are very, very similar. The term *Haredi* is pretty much a synonym for *Ultra-orthodox Jews*. They

---

[10] Unless you believe the New Testament is not built on the foundation of the Old Testament, or that all inspiration of the New Testament writers came directly and solely from the Spirit of God.

[11] They don't call themselves ultra-Orthodox. Ultra-Orthodox is an "outsider's label."

value strict observance of the commandments, as in "take it up a notch, or two or three." The term *Hasidic* (In Hebrew *chesed*, meaning *lovingkindness*) refers to a large group of Jews who branched out of, but mostly stayed within the Haredi movement, to follow in the footsteps of one of the major Haredi influencers named the Baal Shem Tov, (literally: *master of the good name.*) *Hasidic Jews* tend to appreciate a more spiritual approach to Judaism. It would be wonderful if someone could write a book called "Five Years with Ultra-Orthodox Jews," but, the chances of that happening very soon seem remote. Religious Zionists such as Gidon Ariel go to the army, work in many sectors, and are more open to interaction with outsiders like me.

Basket #9. Let there be language?

The first words ever spoken were spoken by God. The first day began with God's words, "Let there be light."[12] Rabbi Elan Adler explains that in Jewish tradition the first act of creation must have therefore been the creation of *language*. God had to decide what sounds would be associated with what words on that first day. The Jews go further to suggest another logical idea. Since the book of Genesis is written in Hebrew, and since the words "Let there be light" are writing down what was *spoken*, then wouldn't God's first words *actually be spoken in Hebrew*? The Bible is clear that the world spoke one language before the Tower of Babel. Why couldn't that one language be Hebrew? That means that the creation account we read is *not a translation* of what God said in the days of creation, *but an exact account of what God said, down to the very sounds*! This would also imply that the words of Adam, Eve, the serpent, Cain and so on were exact as well. Why would God speak in one language and then translate it? No, the first language *must* have been Hebrew.[13]

Basket #10. Miracles! Naturally?

In prophetic circles there has been much teaching about land: how it can be blessed, how it can be defiled by sin, and how it can be cleansed. That teaching is fine, but I think something is lacking — the study of the land of Israel: the spiritual characteristics and implications of that physical land. God says that His eyes are always on the land of Israel continually.[14] So whatever is true about land

---

[12] Genesis 1:3

[13] In Jewish tradition, the first language was Hebrew. In addition, I have heard a number of Orthodox Jews interpret *pure speech* in Zephaniah 3:9 as meaning the whole world will return to speaking Hebrew eventually. *"For then I will make the peoples pure of speech, So that they all invoke Hashem by name And serve Him with one accord."* Zephaniah 3:9 (TIB). This fascinating idea does for *language*, what Basket #1 proposed for *location*, restoring everything that was previously lost.

[14] Deuteronomy 11:12

somewhere else, whatever is noticed somewhere else, is more true and more noticeable in the land of Israel. Spiritual revelation comes easier in Israel too. The air in Israel is spiritually supercharged, even more so in Jerusalem. One of my Hasidic friends, musician Yehudah Katz writes a weekly column for Root Source. He notes that miracles become more and more pronounced *the closer you get to Jerusalem*.[15] He also says that "miracles" happen more *naturally* in Israel.[16] Upon my asking, he gave an example. School kids often write letters to the IDF soldiers during conflicts. One Israeli officer got a letter from a little girl with a piece of candy included in its envelope. After mentioning the enclosed candy, she made the suggestion that the soldier say the traditional Jewish blessing before he ate it. Since the man was not religious and her handwriting wasn't perfectly legible, he got up and walked to the other side of the room to ask an Orthodox Jew how to say this blessing. At that very moment a rocket came through the roof and exploded at his desk. That's what Yehudah means when he says "miracles occur *naturally* in Israel."

Basket #11. An Even Newer Testament?

The Jewish people are very satisfied with their canon of **thirty-nine** books of the Tanakh.[17] We Christians are the ones who see Scripture as having been *extended* by the New Testament's **twenty-seven** books. Extended here does not mean superseded or changed; but rather "there is now more of it to help us understand the rest of it." But have evangelical Christians ever considered whether this extension could happen again? Could still more Scripture be written upon the Messiah's arrival/return? My first thought when composing this Basket #11 was that in the Millennium, there should be **thirty-four more books** added, bringing the total number of books to one hundred. But on further reflection, I'm going to go way, way out on a limb and propose that in the Millennium **934 more books will be added**, bringing the total to 1,000!! Some books will document the new activities and sayings of the Messiah when he comes,[18] but most of the others will expound on the Tanakh in new and helpful ways — ways that are going to be much needed in the Millennium! Yet, God will *never* take away our free will. Therefore, I also predict that somewhere in the world, even when Isaiah 11:9 is fulfilled that: *"the earth will be filled with the knowledge of the Lord as the waters cover the sea,"* there will still be a small group of people who will

---

[15] The following video will not only introduce Yehudah to you, but will introduce his music. https://bit.ly/Katz-Maagal

[16] David Ben-Gurion, the first Prime Minister of Israel, famously said in an interview in 1956, *"In Israel, in order to be a realist you must believe in miracles."*

[17] Actually, the original Hebrew canon counts them as twenty-four books, while the translations divide essentially the same material into thirty-nine books in the Protestant Bible.

[18] John 21:25 says that a world full of books could have been written at His first coming. If that is so, then would not even *more* books have the potential to be written at His second coming? In this sense, even my proposed 1,000 seems minuscule!

inform everyone else that we should just be reading **twenty-seven** of them! "Is there anything new under the sun?"[19]

Basket #12. The Twelves?

The most mysterious word that I ever received directly from God, happened when I was travelling to London on a high-speed train. Almost ten years before I started working with Orthodox Jews, God said, "**Compare the times that God spoke to Abraham, to the miracles of Jesus in MATTHEW 8 and 9.**" The resulting study took months, even years, but ended up revealing insights into the ways that "a life well lived" progresses in twelve stages under the covenantal love of God. I call it *The Twelves.* The applications of this idea are enormous, but even so, I've been wrestling with *The Twelves* since 2005, and have been praying for years that God would ripen that teaching so that it will bear fruit. I have no idea where this will lead, but I have to say that God is so cool! (And not just to me, but to everyone!) And so I conclude this *Twelve Baskets Full,* with a disclosure of *The Twelves.* Nothing new ever comes without its connection to the past. The title of this appendix, *Twelve Baskets Full,* is a tip of the hat to a book by Watchman Nee of the same name.[20] And mentioning *The Twelves* is also a tip of the hat to Arthur Burk's teaching on the seven redemptive gifts,[21] without which I would have had no biblical model for how I might begin approaching *The Twelves.* I have always loved the number *twelve.* It reminds me of God Himself, Israel, its tribes, the disciples, and so many wonderful things yet to come.

Amen.

---

[19] A few readers might smile to know that this basket was composed on Shavuot.
[20] In three volumes: https://amzn.to/3gPkb0k
[21] Available at this short link to the Sapphire Leadership Group: https://bit.ly/Burk-gifts

APPENDIX B:

A New Beginning

E very good story, even the Bible, ends with a new beginning. One big, new beginning underway right now was glossed over so quickly by us in this book, you probably didn't even notice it.

The Jubilee.

A Missed Commandment

It started with an observation made by Gidon when we were working on our first book together, *Israel FIRST!*[1] Gidon said that the laws of the Jubilee (*Yovel* in Hebrew)[2] seem to have never been fulfilled (obeyed) by Israel in its entire history. Indeed, the Jubilee may have been the most difficult commandment of all to fulfill because it required the entire people of Israel to come together in advance and agree to many things at the start of a jubilee period. They must agree in advance about how land rights and purchases would all be synchronized and pro-rated towards a future jubilee year, and then obligate their children and grandchildren to remain consistent and true to fulfill all those promises a full fifty years later, when those who made the original promises may be long gone.

It was mentioned in chapter 39 that many commandments cannot be carried out today because the Temple has not yet been rebuilt. But if circumstances were right, the Temple could be rebuilt in about a decade.[3] The Jubilee takes at least fifty years

---

[1] The full title is: ***Israel FIRST! The Key to Understanding the Blood Moons, Shemitah, Promises to Israel, and the Jubilee***. In it we laid out the idea that Israel is a "light tower" for God's plans, that whatever God plans to do in the rest of the world, He does in Israel first. More on that at www.IsraelFirstBook.com.
[2] Leviticus 25
[3] Solomon's Temple was built in about seven years as stated in 1 Kings 6:37-38, which is generally considered to not include the time needed to prepare for and dedicate the Temple after construction stopped. The Second Temple took more than twenty years to build due to delays caused by challenges to those opposed to it. Speaking in Arkansas in 2018, Rabbi Chaim Richman, International Director of

to carry out, and practically speaking, in the democracy of Israel, would take much more legal and legislative preparation in advance of that fifty-year period.

While many prophetically-minded Christians are looking for the Temple to be rebuilt as a precondition for the return of Christ,[4] why would anyone consider the Jubilee as a precondition as well? I believe it hinges on how you read DEUTERONOMY 30:1-14.

*1 "So it shall be when all of these things have come upon you, the blessing and the curse which I have set before you, and you call them to mind in all nations where the LORD your God has banished you, 2 **and you return to the LORD your God and obey Him with all your heart and soul according to all that I command you today, you and your sons,** 3 then the LORD your God will restore you from captivity, and have compassion on you, and will gather you again from all the peoples where the LORD your God has scattered you. 4 "If your outcasts are at the ends of the earth, from there the LORD your God will gather you, and from there He will bring you back. 5 "The LORD your God will bring you into the land which your fathers possessed, and you shall possess it; and He will prosper you and multiply you more than your fathers.*

*6 "Moreover the LORD your God will circumcise your heart and the heart of your descendants, to love the LORD your God with all your heart and with all your soul, so that you may live. 7 "The LORD your God will inflict all these curses on your enemies and on those who hate you, who persecuted you. 8 **"And you shall again obey the LORD, and observe all His commandments which I command you today.** 9 "Then the LORD your God will prosper you abundantly in all the work of your hand, in the offspring of your body and in the offspring of your cattle and in the produce of your ground, for the LORD will again rejoice over you for good, just as He rejoiced over your fathers; 10 **if you obey the LORD your God to keep His commandments and His statutes which are written in this book of the law, if you turn to the LORD your God with all your heart and soul**.*

*11 **"For this commandment which I command you today is not too difficult for you, nor is it out of reach.** 12 "It is not in heaven, that you should say, 'Who will go up to heaven for us to get it for us and make us hear it, that we may observe it?' 13 "Nor is it beyond the sea, that you should say, 'Who will cross the sea for us to get it for us and make us hear it, that we may observe it?' 14 **"But the word***

---

the Temple Institute of Jerusalem, said that he didn't see that construction would take more than a year: https://youtu.be/VTNRQ-ulUFA (at the 44:25 mark). I personally estimate that even a full decade is probably on the lower end of the range, as this project might be the most opposed building project in the history of the world.

[4] 2 Thessalonians 2:4 speaks of a man of lawlessness who enters the "Temple of God" and demands to be worshipped. This Greek phrase is incorrectly interpreted by some to be the "temple of the antichrist." Yet, it is clearly stated to be the "Temple of God," and it must be holy first in order to be defiled as described.

is very near you, in your mouth and in your heart, that you may observe it. (emphases mine)

It seems as if Moses is prophesying a massive new beginning for the Jewish people, where they return from being scattered and **obey all** the commandments of the Torah. Now for sure the Messiah need not wait for all this to be accomplished before He can arrive. But I am amazed at how few people are noticing this passage and raising the obvious question:

Does God want the people of Israel to implement the full Torah before the Messiah comes?

If so, then not only must the Temple be rebuilt, but the Jubilee is incredibly important as well, because this command takes so long to obey! But more than just being a theoretical question, the topic of the Jubilee is an empirical question as well, because God may well be raising our awareness of this topic through world events. This brings us to the aforementioned book which we are excited to describe briefly below.

Jubilee NOW!

Jubilee NOW! Final Edition[5] is a joint effort between Gidon and myself, that came out after our first book together, *Israel FIRST!*

The year 1967 was such a pivotal year in the history of Israel, that many have proposed that in the eyes of God, it was a Jubilee Year, a grand *new beginning* of history when the Jewish people regained possession of Jerusalem.[6] But if that was truly the case in 1967, then that pivotal year should not stand alone. Something important should happen again fifty years later, right?

The book *Jubilee NOW! Final Edition* is a journey of discovery, each chapter bringing you one step closer to solving the ancient mystery, rediscovering God's plans and purposes to reintroduce the concept of jubilee to the world. With many twists and turns, YOU and we will together examine modern history as it unfolds between late 2015 and early 2018, to be inspired, surprised, and amazed to learn that what God sees in the Jubilee is bigger than any of us ever imagined.

This book is written to take you back in time, first learning what to look for in "a jubilee," and then when armed, to watch as the facts and events take place over

---

[5] http://jubilee-now-book.com/
[6] The year 1948 was critical too, and 1948 and its differences from 1967 are discussed in the book as well.

that period, bringing you right into the mystery yourself.

The fact that you already lived through those years, does not spoil the mystery! You must still examine the facts of *what exactly happened*. With the key facts in front of you, will you decide to come to the same conclusion we did, or will you reach another one?

In retrospect, most of us can agree that the journey is usually *its own reward*. Be blessed in your travels, wherever God may take you.

Amen.

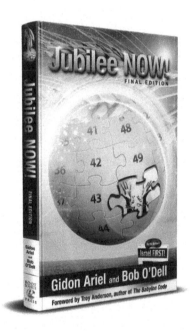

In *Jubilee NOW!*, a Jew and a Christian work together to solve the mystery
of the lost Jubilee, using insights from secular history, Christian history,
Jewish history, the Torah, and our investigative journalism.
Join them and solve the mystery for yourself.

Available on Amazon and at <u>JubileeNowBook.com</u>.

ACKNOWLEDGMENTS

I would like to acknowledge the help of those who would not otherwise be mentioned in this book. My mother always taught me to "respect Israel and the Jews" even though we didn't know any personally in my early years. I had a sense when I began this journey to Israel in 2014 that I was somehow doing this *for her.* Dad lived eleven years after she passed, and was my strongest male encourager during those five years with Orthodox Jews, God having granted him to be of quick wit and sharp mind all the way to his passing. The last time I saw him was to give him the very first printed manuscript of this book. He found his name written in chapter 4 before passing in his sleep. On the female side, and closer to home, I certainly could not have written this book without the support, encouragement and prayers of my PROVERBS 31 wife, Marisa.

My copy editor on this project was Ray Montgomery, who was co-author — actually the primary author — of our book *The LIST.* He suggested and drafted a full half of the footnotes of this volume, and his internet research, precision, and relentless pursuit of clear speech was exactly what I needed. I must cite his patience in correcting my verb tenses. I appreciate the eye of Arnulfo Aquino for the book's interior design and and that of Alexander von Ness for the cover.

Some of the names mentioned in this book, both Christian and Jew, provided very helpful comments during the review period. Because of that review, some material was cut, and five new chapters added, all of them including a more personal approach, rather than teaching moments.

In addition to those names already mentioned in this volume, I would personally like to add: Linda Chandler, John Conrad, Revis Daggett, Richard Davis, Sydney Hewitt, Sister Georjean, Donna Matts, Al McCarn, Dennis Northington, Avraham Norin, Chris Romano, Candi Runyon, Aryeh Schienberg, David Swaggerty, Abe Truitt, Benjamin Wearp, Barb Wilkins. Thank you one and all for your prayers, your comments and encouragement along the way.

In addition, I would like to thank Jim O'Dell, Laurie Sliz, Kevin Barr, Rose Watson, John and Cindy Bibee, Martha Rasco, Donna Lyons, Sandi Pedrotti, Martha Boston, Thomas and Amy Cogdell, Cotton Hance, Sister Joela, Father Peter Hocken, Bill and Deborah Owens, Joseph Parker, Dave and Kathy Sharett, Asaf Matan, Moshe Ganuz, Yehuda Shvager, Alberto Haldeff, Devra Ariel, Ellie

Ariel, Bernie Groveman, Jay Rubin, David Finkel, Steve Gerson, Rachel Lipkin, Eti Lipkin, Dave and Iry Ricci, Larry Samberg, Amos and Yair Mazur, Fabian Trumper, Yoram Yeivin, Stuart Dauermann, Jonathan Kaplan, Joe Krystofik, Brad Blessing, Ray Sanders, Steve and Barb Hawthorne, Geno Hildebrant, Dan Davis, Ron Parish, Matt Ryniker, Jack and Deb Dorman, Bill Taylor, David Taylor, Bill Sellstrom, Binyam Gebrehanna, David Inouye, Marcelo and Mari Franco, Jim Innes, Michael Flute, Troy Anderson, Doris Wearp, Sherri Waller, Galen Walters, Jay Gerrie, Jim Stafford, George Duff, Clif Sullivan, David and Nancy Mossman, Tim Mossman, Darlene Sugarek, Steve Rekedal, Bill McCharen, Felipe Adams, Rita Adams, Gerry and Nancy Gardner, Ron and Sherry Torbert, Mark and Ceci Proger, Jerry Fryer, Thomas Umstattd, Jr., Ken and Marty St. Onge, Richard Short, Barb Bucklin, Dai Sup Han, Allan Parker, Patrick and Helen Lineen, Nancy Crowell, Laurie Chalifoux, Barbara Dingle, Tony Stone, Tudor and Mirela Petan, Gary Chandler, Ann Stacy, Paul and Victoria Sarvadi, Brent Adams, Lori Hinze, Kevin and Leslie Vandivier, John and Vicky Porterfield, Ralph Peil, T.J. Voelker, David Lundy, Kyle Rosenblad, Marshall and Laverne Johnston, Ron Winn, Larry Rueff, and Jeff and Lallie Greinert for their prayers and friendship.

INDEX OF BIBLICAL TEXTS

INDEX OF TOPICS

Index of Hebrew & Greek Words

Note: Bold/italic page numbers indicate where the word is explained or defined.
Italics = song title

IMAGE ATTRIBUTIONS

Preface

Bob O'Dell and Gidon Ariel by the walls of Jerusalem. Photo by Bob O'Dell.

Chapter 1

The Fourth Blood Moon. Photo by Sherwood Burton. Copyright by Root Source Ltd. Image printed in B&W and enhanced for contrast.

Chapter 3

Eve Picks the apple from the tree as the serpent emerges. J.E. Ridinger Etching, *c.* 1750. This file comes from Wellcome Images, a website operated by Wellcome Trust, a global charitable foundation based in the United Kingdom. Refer to Wellcome blog post at: https://wellcome.ac.uk/press-release/thousands-years-visual-culture-made-free-through-wellcome-images Archived at: https://web.archive.org/web/20150815054440/http://www.wellcome.ac.uk/News/Media-office/Press-releases/2014/WTP055466.htm

Copyrighted work available under Creative Commons Attribution only licence CC BY 4.0. Downloaded from Wikicommons. Image cropped, printed in B&W with enhanced contrast.

Chapter 4

Wartime Poster by J. Howard Miller from 1943. Public Domain. Original poster was printed in color.

Chapter 5

The Ten Commandments as displayed in Corpus Christi, Texas. Uploaded by user Jesseruiz498. This file is licensed under the Creative Commons Attribution-Share Alike 4.0 International license. Downloaded from Wikicommons. Image cropped, printed in B&W with enhanced contrast.

Chapter 6

Azusa Street Revival Building. Public Domain. Contrast enhanced.

Azusa Street Group Photo. Public Domain. Contrast enhanced.

Chapter 7

Possible site of Pni'el surrounded by the ancient Jabbok River in Jordan. From Google Maps. Printed in B&W with enhanced contrast.

Chapter 8

Mosque on the left and Crusader period Church on the Right. Photo by Bob O'Dell, is released under the CC0 1.0 Public Domain Dedication.

Place where Jacob probably slept. Photo by Bob O'Dell, is released under the CC0 1.0 Public Domain Dedication.

Looking south from Bethel. Photo by Bob O'Dell, is released under the CC0 1.0 Public Domain Dedication.

Raised Mound used for the Golden Calf. Photo by Bob O'Dell, is released under the CC0 1.0 Public Domain Dedication.

Chapter 9

The Young Generation. Photo: Young Generation.

Bob gets ready to play for the camera. Photo: Young Generation.

Chapter 11

St. Paul in Prison. By Rembrandt. Public Domain. Printed in B&W with enhanced contrast.

Chapter 12

ArtScroll Chumash. Photo by Bob O'Dell. Printed in B&W.

Shabbat Shalom, by Sondra Oster Baras. Image of book cover. Printed in B&W.

Light from Zion, edited by Britt Lode. Photo by Bob O'Dell. Printed in B&W.

Reading of the Torah, Aish Synagogue, Tel Aviv, Israel. Photo by Roy Lindman. This file is licensed under the Creative Commons Attribution-Share Alike 3.0 license. Downloaded from Wikicommons. Image printed in B&W.

Chapter 13

Bible Gems from Jerusalem. Photo by Bob O'Dell.

Chapter 14

Elephant in the Room. Coloured etching by S. Milne after Captain T. Brown and E. Marechal. This file comes from Wellcome Images, a website operated by Wellcome Trust, a global charitable foundation based in the United Kingdom. This file is licensed under the Creative Commons Attribution-Share Alike 4.0 international license. Gallery may be found at: https://wellcomeimages.org/indexplus/image/V0020918ER.html. Printed in B&W. Labels "Scribes" and "Pharisees" were added by Bob O'Dell.

Chapter 15

Route from Aliyah Return Center to Jeruslaem. From Google Maps. Printed in B&W with enhanced contrast.

Sixty-four scriptures on aliyah. Reprinted by permission of The Galilee Calendar Company. Photo by Bob O'Dell. Original document may be accessed here: https://bit.ly/aliyah-64

Chess Board. Graphic is a derivative work by Beao. SVG, Chessboard and chess pieces; Schachbrett und Schachfiguren; sources: Chessboard based on Image:Chess Board.svg by User:Nevit, Chess pieces based on images Image:Chess blt45.svg. This file is licensed under the Creative Commons Attribution-Share Alike 3.0 Unported License. Downloaded from Wikicommons. Image printed in B&W.

Chapter 16

Isa Dreams Conference. Source: IsaDreams.org website.

Indonesia Sunda Straits. Photo by flydime. Licensed under the Creative Commons Attribution 2.0 Generic license. Downloaded from Wikicommons. Cropped and printed in B&W with enhanced contrast.

Chapter 18

Unoffendable, by Brant Hansen. Image of book cover. Printed in B&W.

Chapter 19

Hinnom Valley. Photo by Bob O'Dell, is released under the CC0 1.0 Public Domain Dedication. Printed in B&W.

Chapter 21

Total Lunar Eclipse of January 2018. Photo by Bob O'Dell, is released under the CC0 1.0 Public Domain Dedication. Printed in B&W.

The dates of the Four Blood Moons in 2014/15. Chart by Root Source, Ltd. Printed in B&W.

Chapter 22

Earth from the Moon. Photo by NASA. Public Domain.

Four Wine Cups at Seder Dinner. Copyright by Creative Market. Used under license.

Chapter 23

Revelation at Mount Sinai. Providence Lithograph Company, 1907. Public Domain. Printed in B&W with enhanced contrast.

Chapter 29

First Light in Austin, Texas. Photo by Bob O'Dell, is released under the CC0 1.0 Public Domain Dedication. Printed in B&W.

Chapter 30

Satellite image of probable overlook locations near Hebron. Image by GoogleEarth. Labels by Bob O'Dell.

Ma'ale Hever, the community in the Judean Desert where Gidon Ariel lives. Photo by Gidon Ariel. Printed in B&W with enhanced contrast.

Gidon shares his new Idea. Photo by Bob O'Dell. Printed in B&W. Very small modifications were made to darken the sky for the B&W printing. All rights reserved.

Battle in the Heavens directly overhead. Very small modifications were made to darken the sky for the B&W printing. Photo by Bob O'Dell, is released under the CC0 1.0 Public Domain Dedication.

Looking back at the sun, hidden behind the tower. Very small modifications were made to darken the sky for the B&W printing. Photo by Bob O'Dell, is released under the CC0 1.0 Public Domain Dedication.

Chapter 32

The keyboard of a Steinway Grand Piano. Source image from flickr.com/photos/lecates/438919834 photographed by flickr.com/people/23688516@N00. Licensed under the Creative Commons

Attribution 2.0 Generic license. Downloaded from Wikicommons. Image cropped, flipped and printed in B&W with enhanced contrast.

Chapter 35

J.J. Seabrook Bridge. From Google Maps. Printed in B&W with enhanced contrast.

Diagram of the Altar from the Second Temple Period. Photo by Bob O'Dell of the diagram as printed in *A Nation Born* by Adam Zertal. Reprinted with permission of Mishnayot Kehati.

Joshua's Altar reconstruction similar to the diagram Adam Zertal had held in his hands. Reconstruction diagram by Yehudit Dekel. Photo by Bob O'Dell of the diagram as printed in *A Nation Born* by Adam Zertal. Reprinted with permission of Yehudit Dekel.

Joshua's Altar today, being visited by a tour group. Photo by Bob O'Dell, is released under the CC0 1.0 Public Domain Dedication. Printed in B&W.

Giant Footprint on the side of Mount Ebal with Joshua's Altar inside. Photo by Aaron Lipkin. Printed in B&W with enhanced contrast.

Argaman Footprint. Also a right-foot footprint in the shape of a sandal. Photo by Aaron Lipkin. Printed in B&W with enhanced contrast.

Argaman footprint with amphitheater viewing area behind. Photo by Aaron Lipkin. Printed in B&W with enhanced contrast.

Chapter 36

Argaman Footprint. The Sandal is pointing to the upper right. From Google Maps. Label added by Bob O'Dell. Printed in B&W with enhanced contrast.

Argaman Eagle. Tailfeathers to the left, wing at the top, head to the right. From Google Maps. Label added by Bob O'Dell. Printed in B&W with enhanced contrast.

View from behind the eagle shows four unusual rocks in a line, equally spaced. Photo by Bob O'Dell with labels added. Printed in B&W with enhanced contrast. Photo is released under the CC0 1.0 Public Domain Dedication.

Stone Circles were found all over the valley, going all the way back to the peak shown to the south, and to an area almost that wide as well. Photo by Bob O'Dell, is released under the CC0 1.0 Public Domain Dedication. Printed in B&W with enhanced contrast.

Argaman Theme Park Site Map. Photo by Aaron Lipkin. Labels added by Bob O'Dell. Printed in B&W with enhanced contrast.

The Marah Rock? Photo by Bob O'Dell, is released under the CC0 1.0 Public Domain Dedication. Printed in B&W.

The Manna Rock? This boulder might have been the stop where they discussed the manna in the wilderness. Photo by Bob O'Dell, is released under the CC0 1.0 Public Domain Dedication. Printed in B&W.

The Fourth Rock at Argaman. The tour grand finale. Photo by Bob O'Dell, is released under the CC0 1.0 Public Domain Dedication. Printed in B&W.

Comparison of Argaman Split Rock, and Saudi Arabian Split Rock. Left photo by Bob O'Dell. Right photo by Joel Richardson. Used by permission. Cropped and printed in B&W.

The Eagle from above. Photo by Aaron Lipkin. Labels and eagle insert added by Bob O'Dell. Printed in B&W with enhanced contrast.

Appendix A

Joshua's Altar. Original uncut stones are seen below the black line. Photo by Bob O'Dell, is released under the CC0 1.0 Public Domain Dedication. Printed in B&W.

Painting by the Edge of a Wood by Claude Monet. Which paint is still drying? Photograph by Tate Britain. http://www.tate.org.uk/ Work is in the Public Domain. Downloaded from Wikicommons. Printed in B&W.

Appendix B

Jubilee NOW! Final Edition by Gidon Ariel and Bob O'Dell. Image of book cover. Printed in B&W.